The Complete Book of

Watercolour

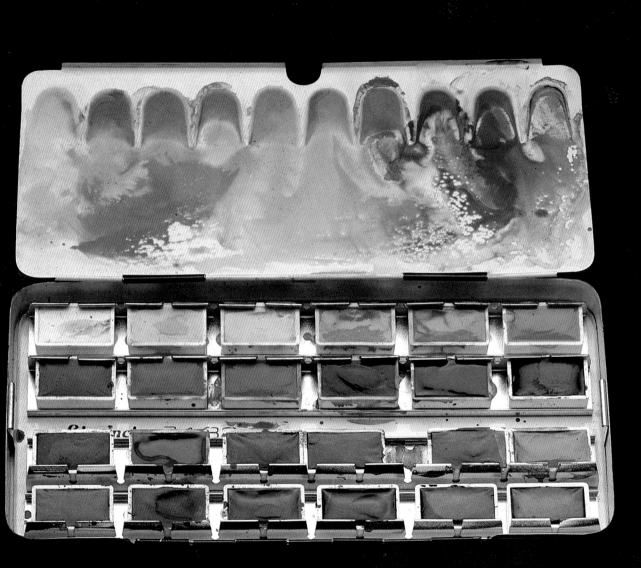

The Complete Book of

Watercolour

The history, materials, techniques, theory and
practice of watercolour

José M. Parramón

Phaidon Press Ltd
140 Kensington Church Street
London W8 4BN

Copyright © 1985 José M. Parramón Vilasaló
Copyright © Parramón Ediciones, S.A.

Cover design © copyright 1993 Phaidon Press Limited

First published in Great Britain 1993

ISBN 0 7148 2827 0

A CIP catalogue record for this book is available from
the British Library.

Printed in Spain

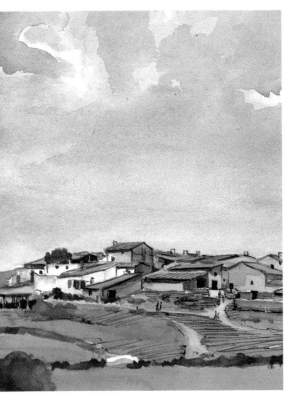

José M.ª Parramón, *Villar del Saz (Cuenca)*, private collection.

Contents

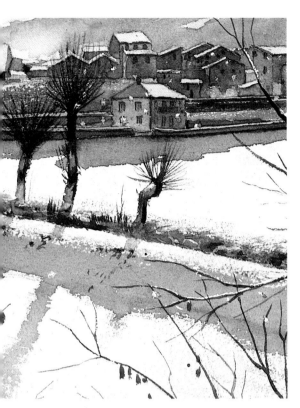

José M.ª Parramón, *A snowy landscape*, private collection.

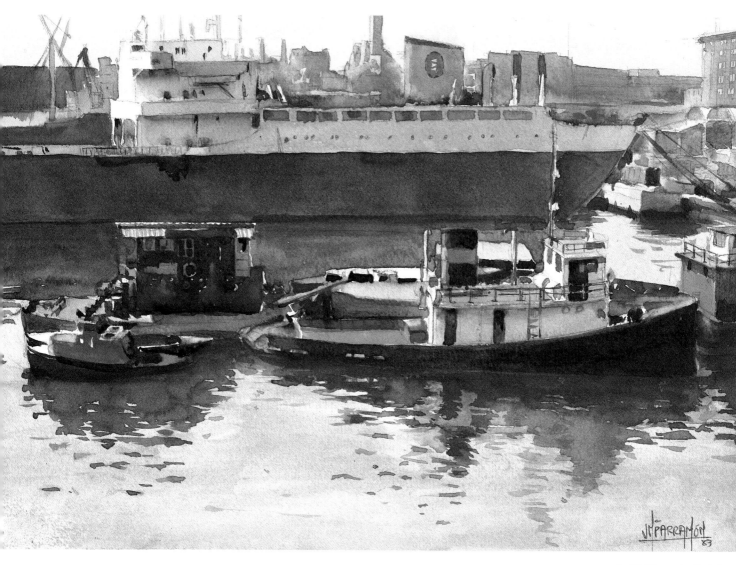

José M.ª Parramón, *Port of Genoa,* **private collection.**

Introduction

Painting as a hobby, only a hobby...? It sounds fine. But there are hobbies that never take off, they never quite crystallize, because they are not taken seriously. Can you imagine someone who plays the piano for a hobby but only sits down to practise once a month?

Painting is like the piano: one must play it often. It has its technique, its mechanics, its skills. Likewise one must paint often, even more so in watercolours.

It is a process, as you well know, which requires assiduous practice; the more one paints, the better. Van Gogh, who was an indefatigable worker – close to 850 paintings and more than 1,000 drawings in the last year of his life! – was pleased to quote a remark on watercolours made by the Impressionist, Whistler: 'Yes, I painted it in two hours, but I worked for years in order to be able to do it in two hours.'

Painting in watercolours is most certainly an art for amateurs with the will and capacity for work:

An art which must be learned and practised.
In this book, I have tried to bring together the knowledge necessary to learn to paint in watercolours. I have researched and written, first, about the history of watercolours, so that you may know when, who, why, and how the first watercolour painters painted, and along the way I discovered some early figures – such as Dr Monro and his academy, in London – which filled me with surprise. I have brought together all manner of information and pictures, by and about everybody in order to inform you with regard to furniture, materials, and tools for watercolour painting; I comment on the different types and qualities available, and give my opinion of different brushes, colours, papers, etc. I have dedicated an important part of this book to explaining, by means of pictures and practical examples, the habits and techniques of professional artists, from the different systems for absorbing and reducing colours, to the different procedures for 'opening up' white spaces before or after painting, wet or dry. I have painted wet in wet, and I have brought colour theories into practical use by proposing a series of practical exercises beginning with painting with only three colours, which tests and proves that all of the colours found in Nature may be made with only the three primary colours.

I have applied to painting in watercolours all of the laws, rules, experiences, and findings which I know after many years of teaching art, in the areas of drawing, colour, mixing colours, composition, interpretation, and blending. And finally, I have carried out a series of demonstrations – some with the cooperation of my friends, leading names in Spanish watercolour painting – in which I explain step by step and in a practical manner the lessons contained in this book.

It is a book illustrated with active and instructive illustrations – 450 in all – and it is a book to take part in, with practical exercises you can carry out in colour mixing, perspective, composition, and other technical lessons.

Ah, but we must play our whole hand! I have done all I can and all I know how to do. Now it is your turn. It's not enough to say that you haven't the time or that you don't feel inspired. 'Waiting for inspiration is a vain act,' said Balzac, 'one must begin, take up the material and get one's hands dirty.'

Introduction

Beginning to paint, like any intellectual process, always requires effort: 'We try to put it off with all type of excuses, the pencil is dull, the palette is dirty...' Yes, but it is also almost always true that, no sooner do we start than we feel an uncontainable passion to continue to work. When this passion is cultivated it becomes a habit: the habit of working.

Van Gogh acquired this habit of working from the first day, with all the passion which is reflected in his paintings:

'From the time I bought my first colours and painting tools, I have been coming and going, painting all day and finishing exhausted. I haven't been able to contain myself, I haven't been able to hold myself back nor stop working.'

I hope this book will help you to begin to feel a passion watercolours.

José M. Parramón

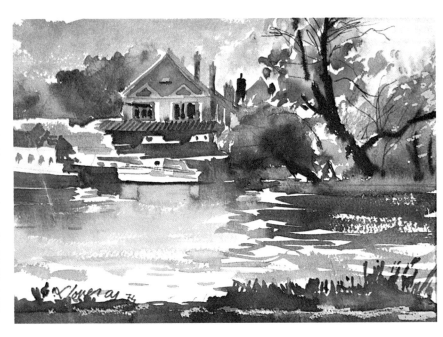

Federico Lloveras, *Embarcadero,* private collection.

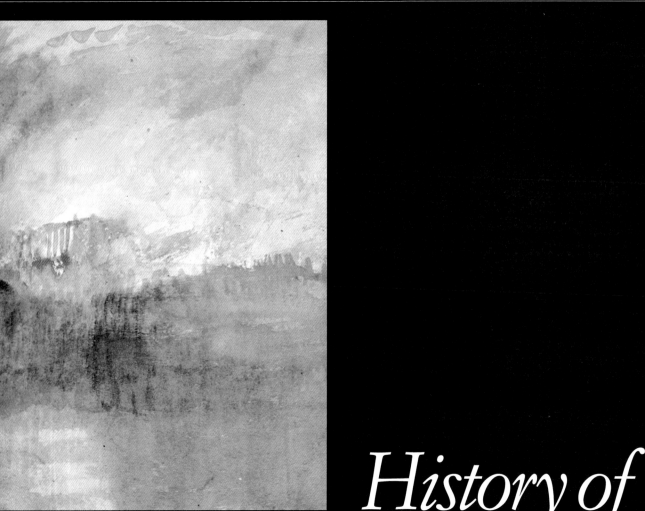

History of

Origins

Man has been writing and illustrating books for 3,500 years.

It was originally on the banks of the Nile in Egypt that a fibrous plant named *cyperus papyrus* was discovered whose bark, cut into strips, could be rolled into a scroll. These rolls of papyrus were used to write and illustrate accounts dealing with science, history, magic, and religion. Another important use was that of burying the scrolls with the dead as an aid in their journey to the other world. The writings were to help them explain their deeds to Osiris, judge of the dead. The images in these scrolls, known since then as miniatures, were painted with transparent colours. The pigments used for ochres and siennas came from the earth; red came from minerals such as cinnabar; azurite was used to obtain blue; malachite for green; cropiment for yellow, and rexalgar for orange. Black was made from burnt willow wood; chalk produced white. These pigments were blended with gum arabic and egg white and were applied diluted in water. In short, they were watercolours.

One thousand years later, around 170 B.C., parchment was used for the first time by Eumenes II, king of Pergamum. This new writing surface was obtained from sheep or goat skin treated with lime and sheared then softened with a pumice stone. These parchment sheets were joined into small notebooks known as codices which were in turn joined to form a book called a codex. Parchment has been used ever since to make manuscripts.

Until the 9th century most miniatures, whether in Greece, Rome, Syria, or Byzantium, were painted from a mixture of watercolour and lead white, producing an opaque watercolour. The 9th century marked the beginning of the reign of Charlemagne, emperor of the Franks.

Charlemagne placed great importance on the creation of manuscripts; he found great artists who alternated in the use of both opaque and transparent watercolours. This mixture was used during the late Middle Ages and even reached the Renaissance when the use of watercolours in miniature paintings become common.

These are the origins of watercolour painting.

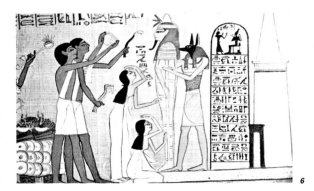

Fig. 6 *Opening of the Mouth*, Hunefer mummy from the book of the dead of the same person, papyrus from the 13th century B.C., British Museum, London.

Fig. 7 (Below) *Adam and Eve*, page from a Bible manuscript by Alcuin or Moutier Grandval, from the Carolingian period, A.D. 834-43, watercolour on parchment, British Museum, London.

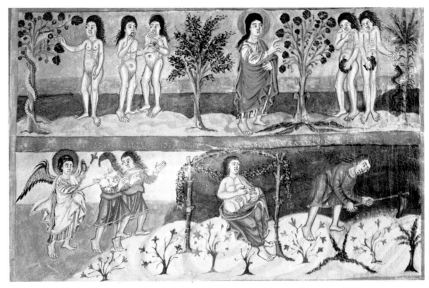

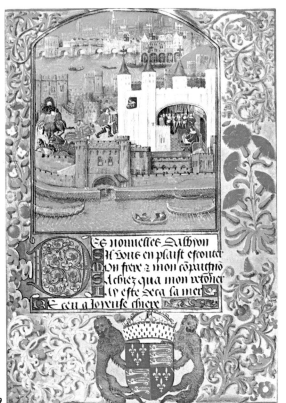

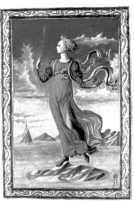

Fig. 8 (Above) Francesco Pesellino, *Allegory of Rome*, miniature, gouache on parchment; borders of the frame painted in watercolour. From the manuscript *De Secundo Bello Punico Poema*, 1447-55, Hermitage Museum, Leningrad.

Fig. 9 Page from the manuscript of the *Poems* of Charles d'Orléans (imprisoned in the Tower of London around 1500), watercolour and gouache on parchment, British Museum, London.

Dürer: the first 'watercolourist'

Albrecht Dürer from Nuremberg, who was described as 'ardent and austere' by the painter Cornelius, was the greatest German painter and engraver of the 16th century. During his lifetime (1471-1528) he wrote three books, executed over 1,000 drawings, almost 250 woodcuts, 100 copper engravings, and painted a grand total of 188 canvases, of which 86 were watercolours. Dürer's first known painting is a watercolour landscape which he painted at the age of eighteen. All this is quite amazing. Very few people know that Dürer alternated between oil and watercolour painting. Although his oil paintings, such as *Adam and Eve* and *Self-Portrait with Gloves*, both in the Prado in Madrid, are well known, few people are aware that he did watercolour paintings as good as the landscape shown here. Why is it that watercolours are not considered on a level with oil paintings? As we shall learn later on, the use of watercolour for its own sake did not gain recognition until the latter part of the 18th century. During Dürer's time watercolours were said to serve a

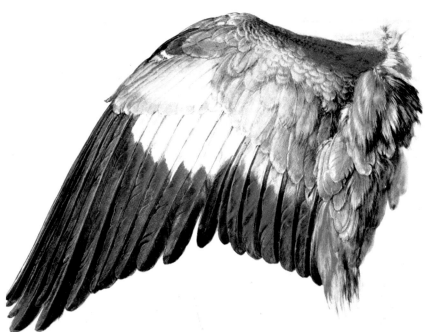

Fig. 10 Albrecht Dürer, *Wing of a Small Blue Bird*, watercolour on parchment, Albertina, Vienna.

Fig. 11 Albrecht Dürer, *View of Kalchreuth*, watercolour on paper, previously in Kunsthalle, Bremen.

10

11

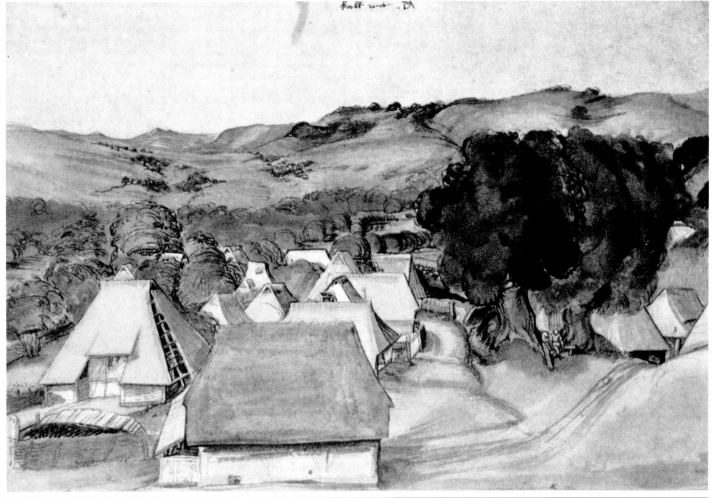

Dürer: the first 'watercolourist'

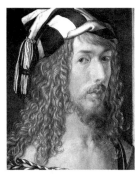

12

Fig. 12 Albrecht Dürer, *Self-Portrait with Gloves* (detail), Prado, Madrid. On this painting there is an inscription in German that reads: 'I have painted this portrait according to my features at the age of twenty-six.' This self-portrait in oils was painted the same year (1498) that Dürer did the series of engravings of the Apocalypse that brought him international fame. Dürer is said to have wanted to emphasize his mastery and merit as an artist and man of letters in this self-portrait.

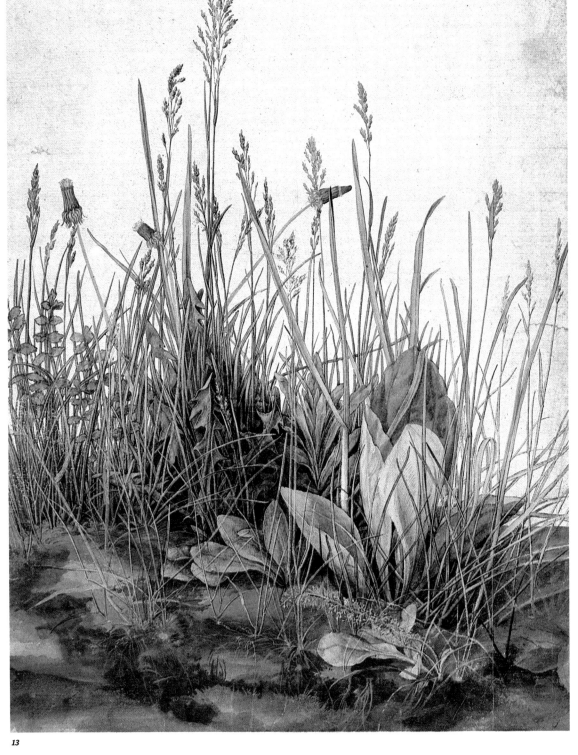

Fig. 13 Albrecht Dürer, *The Piece of Turf*, watercolour on paper, Albertina, Vienna. In contrast with the landscape on the previous page - loose, carefree, with a style and brushstroke comparable to those of a modern artist - Dürer offers us here a detailed, hyper-realist finish, in which opaque watercolour is used with sureness. The work, 41 cm x 31.5 cm (16" x 12.5"), was painted from nature, as was customary with Dürer who, according to his biographers, felt a true passion for animals and nature.

13

documentary function. They were the first draft of a future oil painting. This underestimation of watercolour was still evident in the early part of the 20th century. During the 1930s the Tietze brothers, who wrote the most complete catalogue of Dürer's work, did not add a separate chapter for his watercolours, but instead meshed them with the sketches. Other authors who have written about Dürer, such as Lippman, Winkler, and Panofsky, have followed their classification.

Albrecht Dürer was undoubtedly one of the

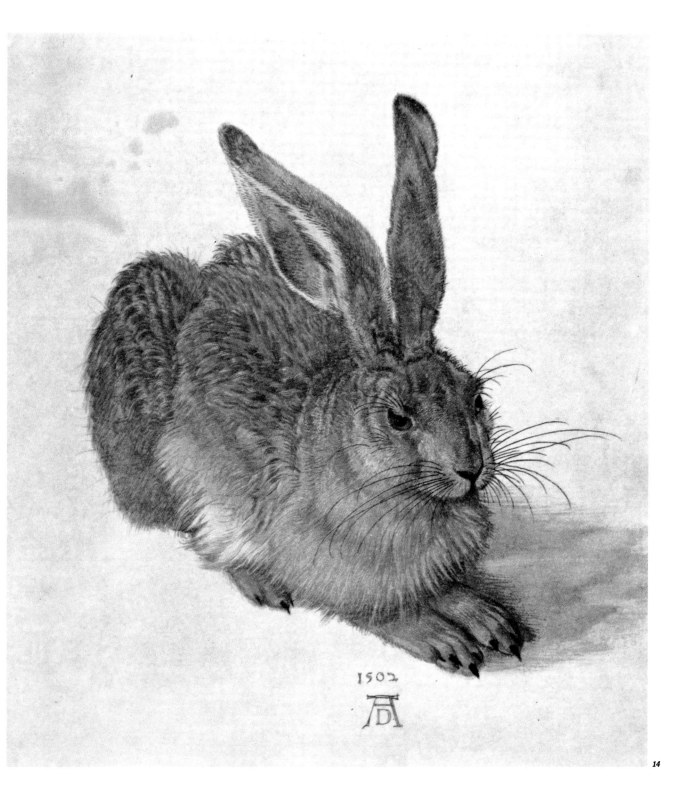

1502

14

first masters of watercolour. His example, however, was not followed by artists after him. For close to 300 years watercolour remained a step in the process of oil painting.

Fig. 14 Albrecht Dürer, *A Young Hare*, watercolour on paper, Albertina, Vienna. In the course of his life as an artist, Dürer painted various animals: horses, lions, a crab, a parrot, squirrels, a lobster, and even a sea lion, always with the meticulousness of this hare, always in watercolour, although, as with this model, he sometimes used opaque watercolours to outline, for example, light fur on a dark background. Dürer always painted from nature: critics and students assure us that this hare was caught alive and shut in a room where the artist painted it. To prove this assertion they say that a window is reflected in the animal's eye and that its shadow falls on a smooth floor. If so, Dürer painted from nature, with the model in front of him, but he also painted from memory, using the model as a live reference that he consulted as it moved.

Watercolour as an aid: 16th and 17th centuries

Dürer was an exception. Fifty years before him, Jacopo Bellini had painted some watercolours as preliminary sketches, which served as inspiration for the paintings and murals of his sons, Gentile and Giovanni, and his son-in-law Mantegna. Bellini, however, never really painted with watercolour.

Watercolour for its own sake disappeared after Dürer. However, it was frequently used as an aid for oil painting. This technique is most common among the Flemish artists, specifically Rubens.

Peter Paul Rubens painted close to 1,000 paintings (to be exact, Bodart's catalogue names 993). A great part of his work consisted of large paintings used to decorate churches and palaces. His famous cycle of 24 paintings on the life of Marie de Medici, now in the Louvre, is made up of panels that measure 3.94 x 2.95 m. Its central work, *Henry IV*, measures 3.94 x 7.27 m. Rubens organized his workshop in a way that facilitated the creation of many paintings of large proportions. His young assistants, such as van Dyck, Jordaens, and Snyders, later achieved independent recognition. Rubens would first draw a preliminary sketch and then paint a watercolour. From this watercolour draft he painted a scaled-down preliminary work. Then his assistants were given all the sketches and they painted the original almost to completion, leaving Rubens the job of applying the final touches.

When Anthony van Dyck left Rubens's workshop, he travelled to England. He painted some watercolour landscapes which he would later use as backdrops to his oil portraits. Jacob Jordaens used watercolours as a young man in cartoons for tapestries. He stayed with Rubens until the latter's death. Jordaens tried to follow in his master's footsteps by continuing Rubens's technique of using small watercolour sketches.

This use of watercolour is seen throughout Europe during the 16th and 17th centuries. The only exception is Holland where Avercamp, van Everdingen and the van Ostade brothers, among others, painted sketches and first drafts which they would sell to craftsmen and the petit bourgeoisie of Amsterdam.

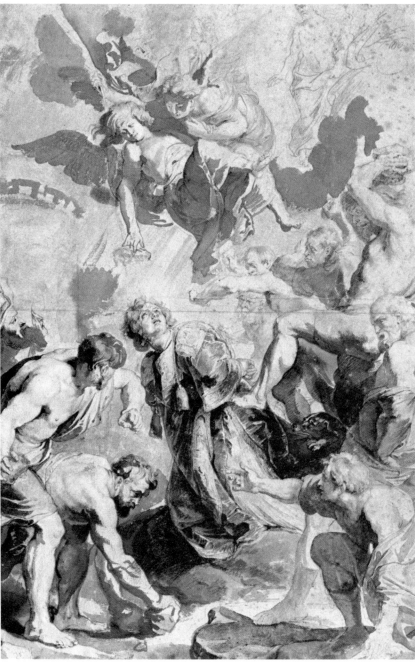

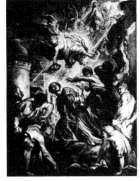
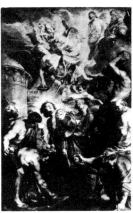

Figs. 15, 16, 17 (Above) Rubens, *The Stoning of St Stephen*, watercolour sketch, Hermitage Museum, Leningrad. (Right, fig. 16.) Sketch in oil, Royal Palace, Brussels. (Right, fig. 17.) Final rendering of *The Stoning of St Stephen*, Museum of Fine Arts, Valenciennes.

16

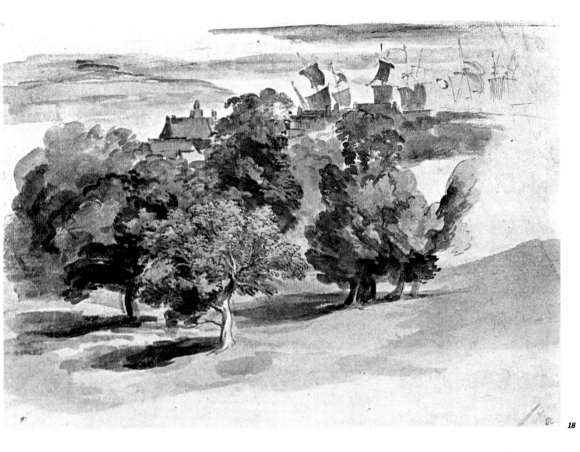

18

Fig. 18 Anthony van Dyck, *Landscape at Birmingham Port*, Barbierov Institute of Fine Arts, Moscow. It is believed that during his second stay in England, from 1632 until his death in 1641, van Dyck painted several landscapes in watercolour that served as studies and models for oil paintings and as backgrounds for some of his portraits.

20

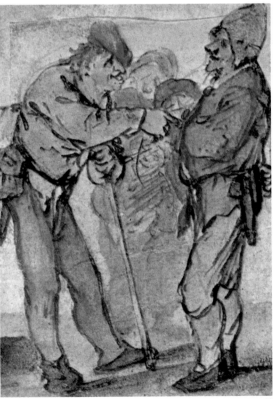

19

Fig. 19 Adriaen van Ostade, *Peasants*, Hermitage Museum, Leningrad. In the 17th century, when watercolour painting was an aid to oil painting, some Dutch artists painted small watercolours on popular themes, which were sold to craftsmen and the petit bourgeoisie of Amsterdam.

Fig. 20 Jacob Jordaens, *The Arrival*, British Museum, London. When Rubens died, Jordaens tried to continue his master's work and he even finished the uncompleted paintings that Spain had commissioned Rubens to do. He followed Rubens's work methods very closely, studying watercolour sketches prior to completing his works in oil.

Monochromatic watercolour

According to Cennino Cennini, an Italian artist and educator, during medieval times and the Renaissance, all artists used watercolour... with only one colour. In his book *Il Libro dell'Arte* (about 1400) he says: 'After accentuating the design you will give shading to the shapes by using ink washes. It is necessary to use the amount of water that fits in a nutshell with two ink drops. The shading must be done with a brush made of hair from a sable's tail. When the washes must be darker the same technique should be applied but more ink drops should be used.'

Cennini's book merely explains artistic procedures that were already in use during the 14th century. Thus, from Giotto to the mid-18th century, 400 years later, when watercolour paint began to be used for finished works, artists in general continued to paint according to Cennini's formula.

An example are Raphael's frescoes in the Stanza della Segnatura. Raphael was commissioned by Pope Julius II between 1509 and 1511 to paint some murals for the Pope's new rooms in the Vatican palace. Different museums now house the preliminary sketches and studies of figures and parts of the body in foreshortened perspectives, as well as the final cartoon, a monochrome watercolour painted with two sepia colours (fig. 21, mural project *The School of Athens* from the Stanza della Segnatura). This work method was followed by Raphael, Leonardo, and Michelangelo whenever they had to paint an important mural or painting.

Monochromatic watercolour was also the medium used when sketching outdoors. On these occasions the paper used was grey or was painted previously with a yellow or ochre background. This was then painted with sepia and water according to Cennini's formula. These sketches were used only as notes and as an aid when doing an oil painting.

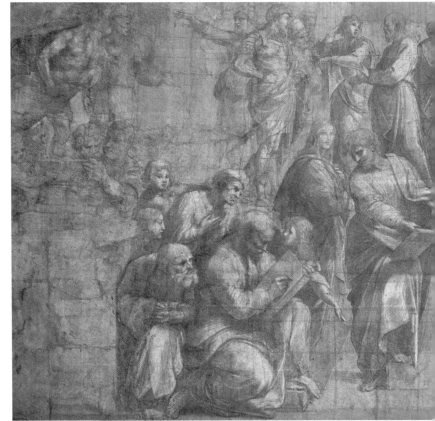

21

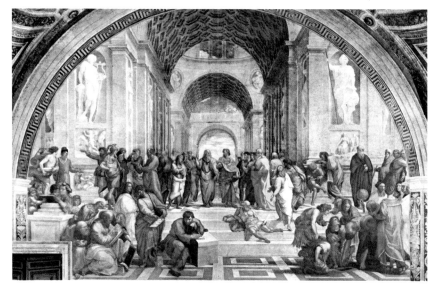

22

Fig. 21 Raphael, *The School of Athens*, project painted in watercolour, Ambrosiana, Milan.

Fig. 22 Raphael, *The School of Athens*, fresco in the Stanza della Segnatura, Vatican, Rome. Observe the differences between the final painting and the project painted in wash in shades of sepia. Several figures were added for the final picture, but the projection shows the exact character of the figures, their form, expression, position, light and shadow, etc., enabling Raphael's assistants to work more easily when doing the actual fresco.

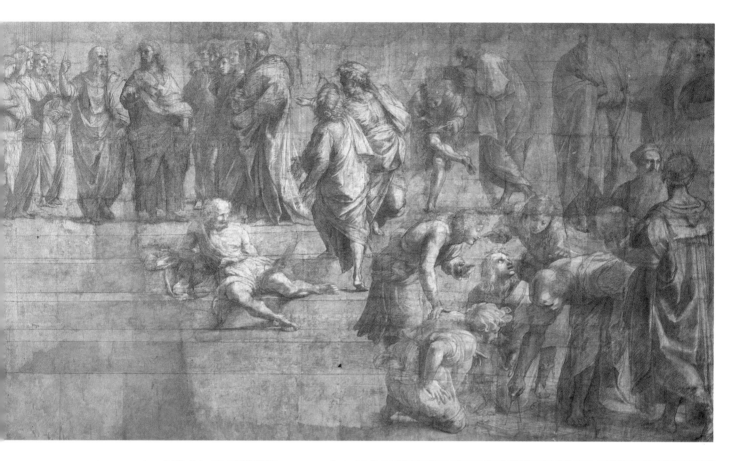

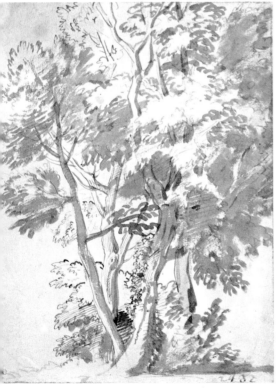

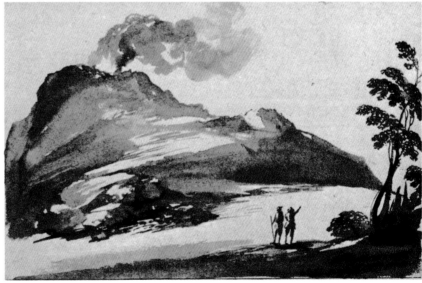

23

24

Fig. 23 Salvator Rosa, *Study of Trees*, wash, Hermitage Museum, Leningrad. The dexterity, sureness, and skill with which this study of trees was done is of a quality comparable to the resolution of a professional watercolour artist of today.

Fig. 24 Guercino, *Landscape with a Volcano*, British Museum, London. This is an example of the use of sepia wash on grey paper. In this wash we can see the artist's skill and knowledge of the medium in the way in which he indicates the model's position and the effects of light and shadow. He even adds a few figures to help the viewer understand distances and proportions, all with just a few brushstrokes.

Wash: forerunner of watercolour

In the historical evolution of watercolour we must also mention Rembrandt. For although Rembrandt never painted watercolours, he made hundreds of sketches in brown bistre or sepia wash (the latter made from the 'ink' of the cuttlefish) with such skill and practice he was able to successfully reflect volume, shadow, darkness and ... such colour: these sketches were Rembrandt's colour notes.

While Rembrandt worked in Amsterdam, Claude Lorraine was busy painting landscapes in Rome. His landscapes were of enormous proportions and were commissioned by clergymen and kings such as Urban VIII and Philip IV of Spain. Constable, the well-known British landscape artist, said the following in one communication to the Royal Academy of London: 'It has been said that Lorraine is the best landscape artist in the world and this is well-deserved praise. His main attribute is a mixture of splendour with quietude, colour with freshness, shadow and light.' Lorraine would first make a preliminary wash sketch of his idea and would then return to the countryside and continue the process out of doors. He used two or three colours in the same range: sienna, sepia, umber. His landscapes in oils, which often measured up to 2.5 x 2 m, would require at least eight wash drawings as well as some pencil or charcoal sketches before completion. It took him two months to complete a painting.

The same can be said of Frenchman Nicolas Poussin who, together with Claude Lorraine, is considered a precursor of the English landscape school. These two artists were undoubtedly a great influence on the group of English artists who used watercolour from the 18th century on. Nicolas Poussin alternated religious or mythological figure paintings with landscapes in which mythological figures also appeared. Poussin worked, as did Lorraine, from a series of preliminary wash sketches drawn from nature. In some of his sketches made with just two colours and occasionally black, the richness of tones and range of light are so marvellous that they seem to be actual colour notes.

Like many 17th-century artists, Rembrandt, Lorraine, and Poussin did not yet use watercolour. However, they gave wash, which was a procedure which required techniques similar to those of watercolour, its own place as something more than just an aid in oil painting. At this point all that was needed was one factor that would give watercolour the necessary push. This happened with the 'Grand Tour'.

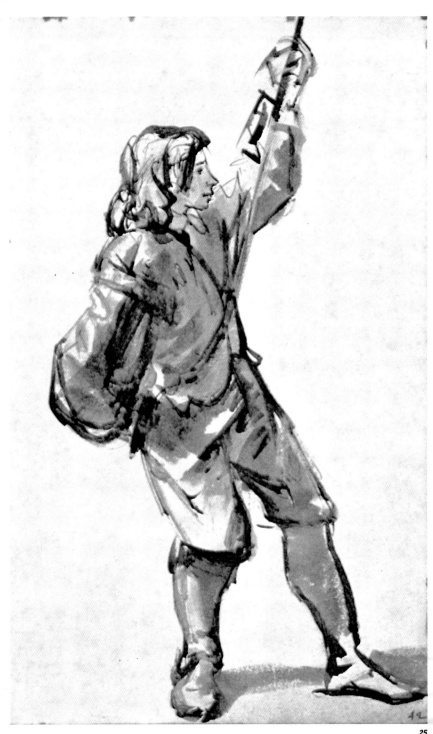

25

Fig. 25 Rembrandt, *Figure Study*, Rijksmuseum, Amsterdam. As this sketch shows, Rembrandt's mastery of wash was incredible. This mastery derives from an absolute sureness in constructing and drawing.

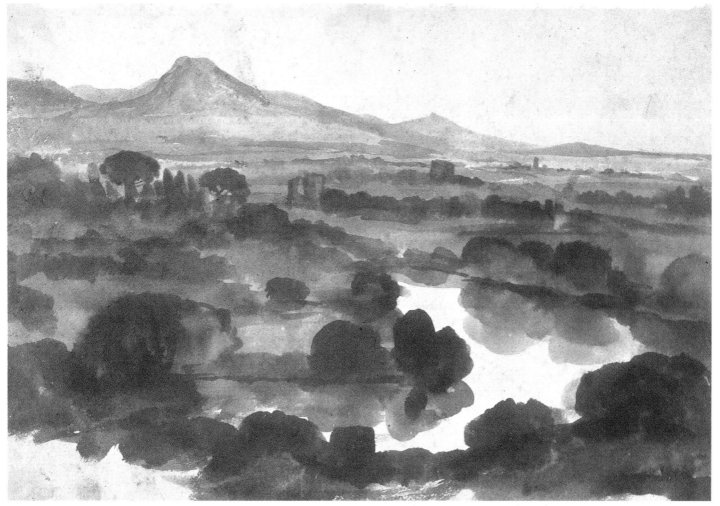

26

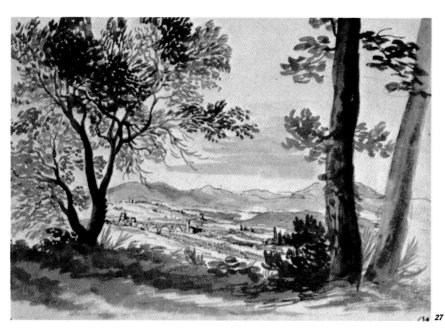

27

Fig. 26 Claude Lorraine,
*Landscape with River, View of
the Tiber from Monte Mario,
Rome*, British Museum,
London.

Fig. 27 Nicolas Poussin, *The
Moller Bridge Near Rome*,
Albertina, Vienna.

The 18th century: the English discover Rome

The English 'discovered' Rome toward the middle of the 18th century. At this time King George II was determinedly trying to transform England from an agricultural country into an industrial and commercial nation. Small cottage industries were being replaced by factories, and commerce was looking to broaden its horizons overseas and in the colonies. Hundreds of businessmen, industrialists, intellectuals, artists, and aristocrats travelled frequently between England and the Continent. Travelling was fashionable. It was the century of the 'Grand Tour'.

The popular itinerary was France, Switzerland, and Italy, with Rome as the final destination. Once there, it was a must to visit the Colosseum, the Arch of Titus, the public baths of Caracalla. Ruins were also in fashion. The century of the Grand Tour was also the period of Neoclassical art.

Touring and the 'discovery' of Rome had a great influence on English taste in art. The first stop in Paris led the English tourists to the Louvre where they could admire the great paintings of Poussin and Lorraine. These two pioneers of the Neoclassical style painted classical figures and ruins into their wonderful romantic landscapes. During their stay in Switzerland, the English were able to cross the Alps and live in close contact with 'Nature', the subject of an almost religious cult at the time. Finally, they would reach Italy and admire the classical beauty of ancient Rome. Every experience and sensation made the tourists anxious to return to London with some pictorial souvenir of their trip to the 'Eternal City'.

These pictorial souvenirs were etchings printed in black or sepia. They could already be bought in Rome and Venice in the early 18th century. By 1703 Lucas Carlevari had already published 103 of his engraved views of Venice. Giovanni Antonio Canaletto, famous for his *vedutas* (views) of Venice and Rome, signed a contract in 1730 with Joseph Smith, later the British consul, for the sale and distribution of over 140 etchings in Britain. In 1745 Piranesi published 135 *vedutas* of ancient Rome. Thousands of copies of these were printed.

The production of *vedutas* was constantly being expanded upon by the many European artists who began to do this type of work. These include the Italians Ricci, Panini, and Guardi, and the English Pars, Grimm, Rooker, and Cozens, to name a few. By this time, also, the English were printing a large number of illustrations from copper etchings or

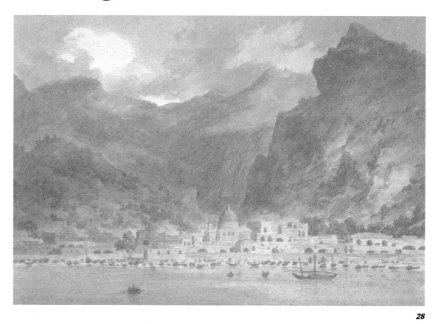

Fig. 28 John Robert Cozens, *Cetara, a Fishermen's Village in the Gulf of Salerno*, Mrs Cecil Keith Collection, England. It was J. R. Cozens who broke with the English tradition of 'illuminated drawings' and began to paint and delineate forms with colour and tone, instead of line.

engravings in black and sepia which portrayed landscapes, cityscapes, monuments, flowers, still lifes, horses, and dogs, among other things. These drawings, made by artists called 'topographers', served as decoration for the walls of private homes. It occurred to someone, inspired by Italian *vedutas*, that the etchings would be enhanced if they were coloured with transparent watercolours. Shortly thereafter the colour became more and more important until finally the drawings appeared to be painted rather than etched.

Paul Sandby, known as the 'father of English watercolour', was one of the artists involved in the transformation of drawings into paintings. Although he did not travel to Italy, he followed the 'Grand Tour' phenomenon closely. He sketched and etched many ruins which he would then illuminate with watercolour. His desire to make each watercolour a unique work of art rather than a means to an end allowed him to study and experiment with different formulas.

Paul Sandby and his brother Thomas – also a watercolour painter and topographical draughtsman for the government – were founding members of the Royal Academy of London. Paul also painted pictures in watercolour and gouache of urban and rural landscapes. Outstanding among the latter were his renderings, often directly from nature, of the Great Royal Wood, Windsor Park, and of Windsor Castle where Thomas was keeper. Sandby was 27 in 1752 when he started painting these forests. His technique and style were to greatly influence other English watercolour landscape painters including William Pars,

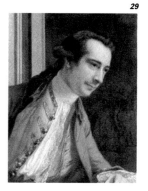

Fig. 29 Francis Cotes, *Portrait of Paul Sandby*, Tate Gallery, London.

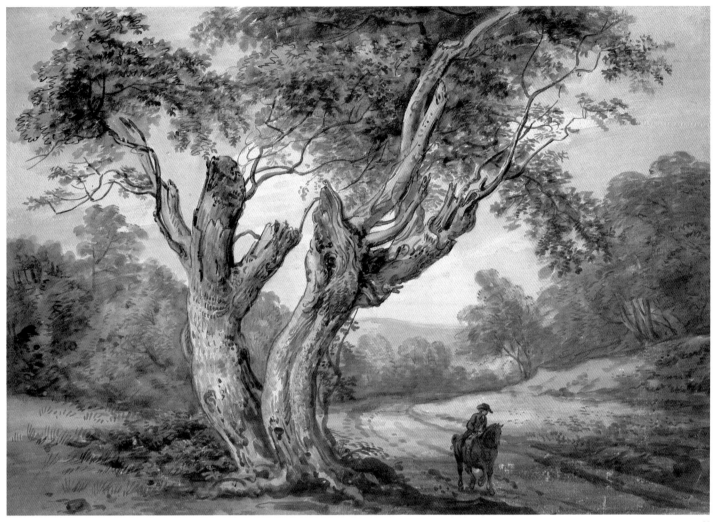

30

Francis Towne, Thomas Rowlandson, Francis Wheatley, and the especially noteworthy John Robert Cozens. William Pars travelled to Greece when he was 22 as the artist for an archaeological dig. He became well known for his drawings of the dig. Some years later he went to Rome, where he lived until his death in 1872. His companions in Rome included Cozens, Jones, and his close friend Towne. William Pars quickly embraced the idea of painting without the sharp outlines made with a pen or pencil. His watercolours of old buildings are truly wonderful works of art.

Francis Towne, on the other hand, used sharp contours and more daring colours to illumi-

Fig. 30 Paul Sandby, *Road through Windsor Forest*, Victoria and Albert Museum, London. Called the 'father of English watercolour', Paul Sandby started out as a topographical draughtsman of landscapes with ruins and classical buildings. He developed techniques for watercolour painting which matured while painting in the forest of Windsor. His concepts were followed for 30 or 40 years by English artists who painted watercolour landscapes.

nate his figures. Rowlandson was a well-known caricaturist, and his personality was apparent in his portraits and landscapes. Wheatley introduced a palette of bright colours with reds, blues, and yellows in his rural landscapes with figures.

John Robert Cozens learned his trade from his father. He was described by Constable as 'a brilliant landscape' artist, all poetry'. Cozens used a limited palette of greens, blues, siennas, and greys but the composition of each painting was studied to such a degree that each of his pictures was really like a poem. He profoundly influenced the Romantic period in England and the artists of the next generation such as Girtin and Turner.

The English national art

In the spring of 1804 the first society of watercolour artists, the Old Water-Colour Society, was founded. One year later, also for the first time in the world, an exhibition of watercolour paintings was held.

In England, of course.
Until then, the members of the Royal Academy of London, which was already thirty years old, had very discriminatory policies towards watercolour artists. Watercolours were only allowed into a show if the artist also had oil paintings. Furthermore, the watercolours were always off to the side, with the most visible and best-lit areas of the salon being reserved for oil paintings. This lack of importance given to their work angered the artists into founding a separate society and organizing their own showing at a different salon – which succeeded in attracting the public and buying customers. By the late 18th century the merit and value of watercolour as a medium in itself was recognized, and it was used as a means of expression by such renowned artists as Hogarth, Reynolds, and Gainsborough.

Artists were no longer limited to landscapes; they now went indoors to paint figures and still-life scenes. In this new area both William Blake and John Henry Fuseli showed extraordinary talent and imaginative power. Fuseli's paintings are characterized by the exaggerated drawing of the movements and gestures of the figures. William Blake wrote poems which he would then illustrate with watercolours and publish. Among the best-known works are the watercolours illustrating the *Book of Job*, Dante's poems, and his critique of the Age of Reason.

By this time, thousands of amateurs were painting watercolours in England. It was already the 'English national art', as it was to be named years later by the journalist Edmond About in his reports on the International Exhibition in Paris.

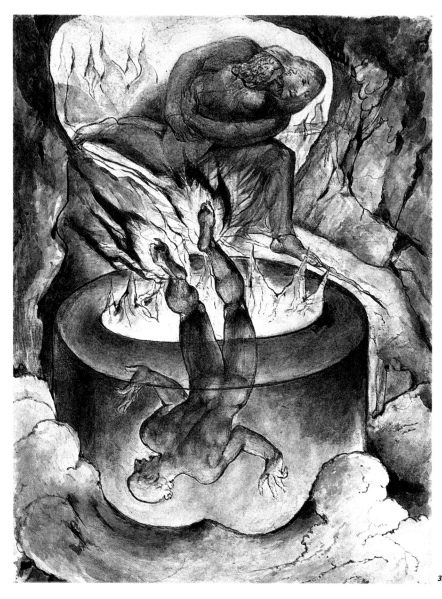
31

Fig. 31 William Blake, *The Simoniac Pope*, Tate Gallery, London. Blake was an inspired and ingenious artist, poet, painter, and engraver, who once wrote and illustrated his own poems on the Bible, Milton, Shakespeare, and Dante, interpreting the texts of these works and authors and demonstrating extraordinary ability and imagination.

Fig. 32 John Henry Fuseli, *Kriemhild in a Dream Sees Siegfried Dead*, Kunsthaus, Zürich. Fuseli was an intellectual of Swiss origin who settled in England and worked as a freelance translator and illustrator. Reynolds encouraged him to paint, and he won fame with paintings and watercolours distinguished by the originality of their themes.

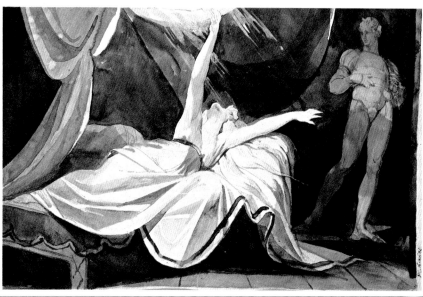
32

Dr Monro and Turner

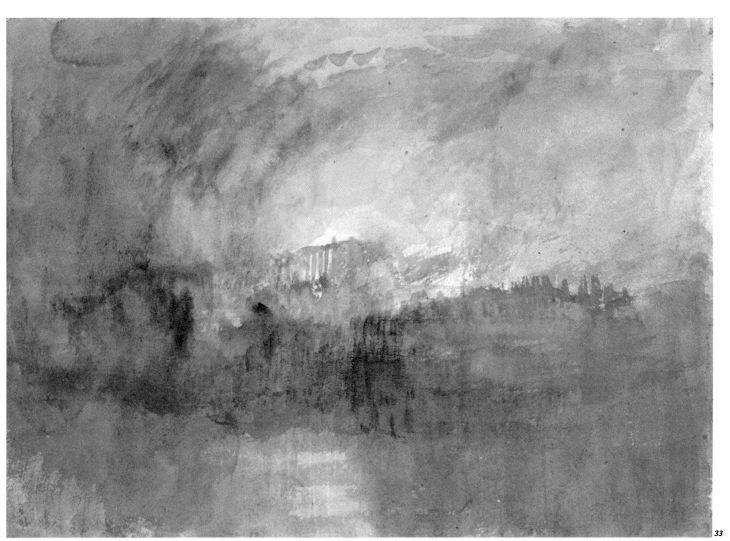

33

Dr Monro's residence on Adelphi Terrace overlooking the Thames played an important role in the history of watercolour in England. Dr Monro's hobby was painting watercolours, and when he was not busy with his career in medicine he collected paintings. He was friendly with many young watercolour artists and would try to help them out by finding buyers for their paintings or buying them himself. His collection included works by Rembrandt, Canaletto, and Lorraine, water-colours by Sandby, and paintings and sketches by Cozens and others. In 1794 he decided to open a school for watercolour artists in his own home. He bought chairs, tables, paints, brushes, and paper, and as word of his intentions quickly spread, several young artists went to him. Dr Monro told them: 'I'll pay you half a crown and give you supper for coming here every night to paint. You will learn by copying some travel notes drawn by Cozens.' Dr Monro promoted the study of Cozens's creative style and technique and

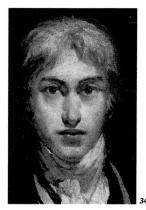

34

Figs. 33, 34 (Above) **Joseph Mallord William Turner,** *The Burning of the Houses of Parliament, on the Night of 16 October 1834*, **Tate Gallery, London. (Below)** *Self-Portrait*, **Tate Gallery, London. Turner is, without a doubt, the best and most famous English watercolour artist.**

kept all the paintings in his possession. A few days after the school opened, Turner, Girtin, Cotman, Cox and de Wint were busy at work. These young men later became the greatest English watercolour artists of the 18th and 19th centuries. The most able and famous of all was Joseph Mallord William Turner, followed by Thomas Girtin. According to Murray, their biographer, when they were both 19 they went to Dr Monro's house where Girtin drew and Turner painted.

Turner's skill as a watercolour artist started early on. At 9 he was colouring prints for a beer merchant; when he was 13 he was apprenticed to Thomas Malton, a topographer who taught him about perspective. The Royal Academy accepted one of his watercolours when he was 15 and six years later they exhibited one of his paintings. At the mere age of 24 he was accepted as a member of the Royal Academy, something that had never happened before to such a young artist.

Turner and Girtin

Figs. 35, 36 (Above) Turner, *Venice: The Grand Canal with San Simeone Piccolo, Dusk.* (Below) Turner, *Venice, San Giorgio Maggiore from the Customs House,* both in the Tate Gallery, London. These are two of the watercolours done by Turner on his last trip to Venice, considered the most creative paintings of all his work because of their effects of light and colour.

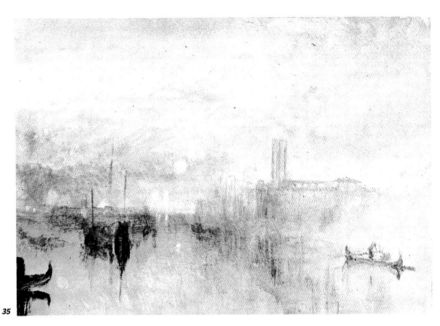

35

36

Thomas Girtin died when he was 27 years old. Together with Turner he was one of the best watercolour artists of the late 18th century. Girtin exercised considerable influence over Turner who imitated his style and use of colour. When Girtin died, Turner said: 'If Tom had lived I would have died of hunger.' After his experience at Monro's school in 1797, Turner began to paint in oils, alternating this medium with watercolour, which he never abandoned. He travelled to Italy four times and painted the watercolours in Venice where

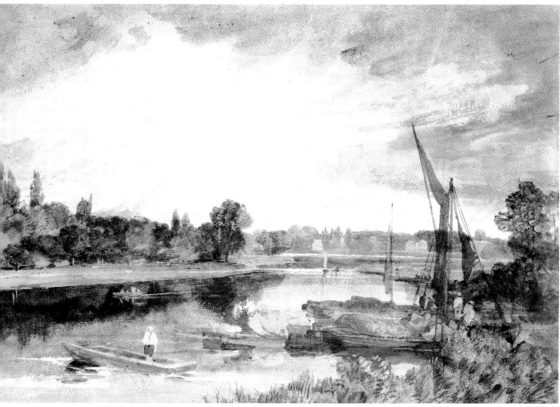

Fig. 37 Turner, *Scene on the Thames with Barges and a Canoe*, Tate Gallery, London. Turner was 33 years old when he painted this watercolour on the banks of the Thames. In it, he shows us his ability as a draughtsman and painter, as well as his mastery over watercolour, either wet or dry. The watercolours of Venice on the previous page were painted 13 years later.

37

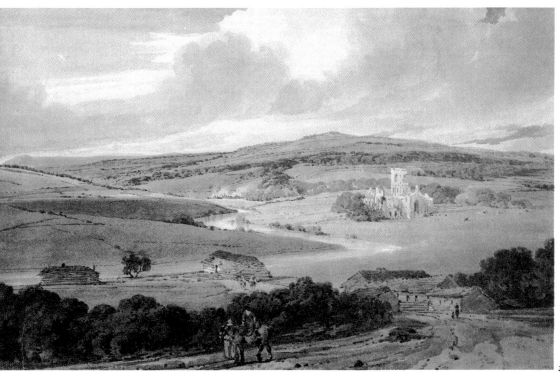

Fig. 38 Thomas Girtin, *Kirkstall Abbey in Yorkshire*, British Museum, London. Born the same year as Turner (1775), and a classmate of his at the Monro Academy, Girtin was a reference and indispensable model for Turner and many other artists of the 18th century, consulted and imitated because of his technical and artistic merit. Thomas Girtin was one of the most important links in the development of watercolour in England.

38

he achieved the most creative play of light and colour of his career. The French Impressionists said: 'We are followers of a great master of the British school, the illustrious Turner.'

Bonington and Cotman

Richard Parkes Bonington was an important artist in the history of English watercolour. When he was 15, he emigrated with his family from Nottingham to Calais, where he studied with Louis Francia, a French watercolour artist who had started out at Dr Monro's school with Turner and Girtin. Bonington then travelled to Paris, where he learned oil painting from one of the great painters of French Romanticism, Antoine-Jean Gros. Another artist who frequented Gros's workshop and greatly admired him was Delacroix. Bonington and Delacroix, three years his senior, became friends; thus the Englishman became known to Paris society of the time.

Jean-Baptiste-Camille Corot, one of the first landscape artists to paint outdoors, was struck with surprise and admiration when he saw one of Bonington's watercolour landscapes. The total range of possibilities that watercolour gave the artist had been unknown to Corot. It is therefore not exaggerating to say that Bonington spread the virtues of the watercolour medium throughout France by way of his fellow artists and their social connections. In 1825 Bonington returned to England, at the same time as Delacroix. Meanwhile back in France, artists like Roqueplan and Isabey had begun to paint with watercolours following his style. The 'Bonington style' outlasted the artist, who died of tuberculosis at the age of 27 in 1828.

John Sell Cotman deserves a special mention as 'one of the best landscape artists of the 19th century in England'. Cotman was also a member of the privileged few at Dr Monro's school during the time Turner and Girtin were there. He began by imitating Girtin's style until he developed and achieved fame with his own style. It is said that Cotman advised his son who also wanted to be a painter to 'draw strictly the truth; if you wish, take away or eliminate certain things, but do not add anything'. Cotman was an expert in drawing and synthesis; he favoured summarizing, harmonizing forms, and enriching colours, paying careful attention to the composition of the picture. He dominated the wet watercolour technique.

Figs. 39, 40 (Right) Richard Parkes Bonington, *St Armand's Abbey in Rouen*, private collection, England. (Below) Bonington, *Venice, The Doges' Palace*, Wallace Collection, London. It is enough just to see these two watercolours to confirm that Bonington was an exceptional artist. Observe, first of all, the composition, following Rembrandt's scheme, on the diagonal; note how depth is achieved by the effect of perspective; observe the idea of atmosphere or interposed space in the painting of Venice below, comparing the foreground with the diffuse and imprecise background; note the change in the colour spectrum (cold spectrum above, warm below) and the inclusion of figures that, besides giving life to the paintings, serve as a reference to give a better idea of sizes and distances.

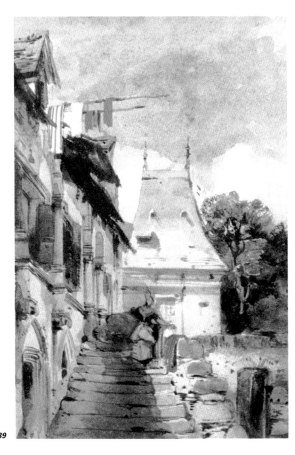

39

40

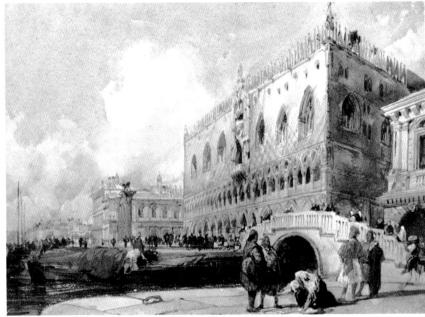

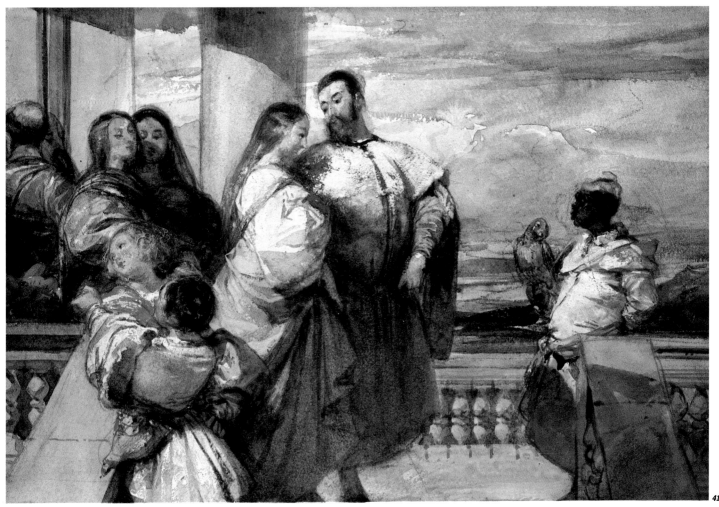

41

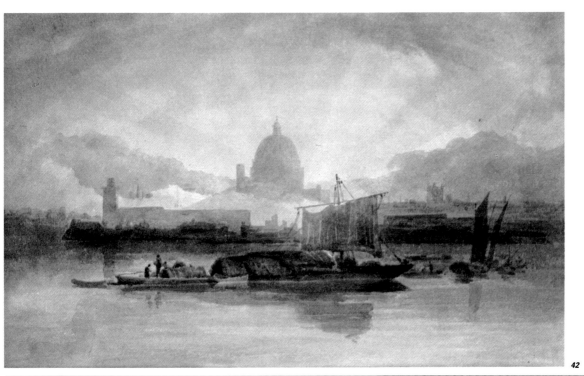

Fig. 41 Richard Parkes Bonington, *Venetian Scene*, Wallace Collection, London. The quality of the watercolours of Bonington, who painted landscapes just as perfectly as figures, was a decisive influence on the diffusion of watercolour painting in France, where Bonington lived for several years, associating with the major artists of the time, including Delacroix, Corot, Gros, and others.

Fig. 42 John Sell Cotman, *St Paul's Cathedral*, British Museum, London. Cotman had an instinctive sense for the art of composition and an extraordinary capacity for creating contrasts and harmonizing the colours of a painting. This, combined with his fortunate choice of subjects, made him one of the best English watercolour landscape painters of the 19th century. Cotman attended Dr Monro's academy for a time and was the most important artist of the 'Norwich School'.

42

Great English masters of the 19th century

John Varley and Joshua Cristall were members of the society of watercolour painters first founded in 1804. Varley was aided by Dr Monro and became an expert in composition and colour harmony. Cristall may have been somewhat more original and was definitely more spontaneous.

A few years later three important artists joined the society. They were Peter de Wint, A.V. Copley Fielding, and David Cox. De Wint had been to Monro's school, where he met Girtin and studied with Varley. He was very successful painting landscapes that pictured his home region, the Lincoln plains. Copley Fielding was a master at capturing the atmosphere of landscapes with lakes and mountains. His watercolours showed some resemblance to those Turner had painted earlier. David Cox was a disciple of Varley, and a very studious one at that. He wrote some books and was always trying to improve his watercolours. He tried using a new coarse-grain paper and was inspired by Turner, on the latter's return from Italy, to use a richer palette.

Constable's story is different, as he usually painted with oils. He was one of Europe's best landscape artists and he experimented with gouache and watercolour.

The list of watercolour artists could be further increased by adding a group of Bonington's followers, among them Thomas Shotter Boys, William Callon, and James Holland. Other artists formed different groups throughout the 19th century. One of these groups was the Sketching Society, and its members, John Linnell, Edward Calvert, George Richmond, and Samuel Palmer, were all followers of William Blake. Of this group, Samuel Palmer was the most famous. He was greatly in awe of some of Blake's work. According to Cotman's son, Palmer went through a visionary period during which he painted in a truly original and fantastic style. Another group, the Pre-Raphaelite Brotherhood, had Millais, Hunt, and the well-known Dante Gabriel Rossetti as members. They used oil paints mainly but also dabbled somewhat in watercolour. The members of the Brotherhood were grouped according to a series of precepts: painting sincerely, symbolizing ideas and subject matter, and studying iconography in depth; using bright colours, paying attention to small details; incorporating painting out of doors; and incorporating watercolour techniques. They painted mediaeval and biblical themes like Rossetti's famous *Ecce Ancilla Domini.*

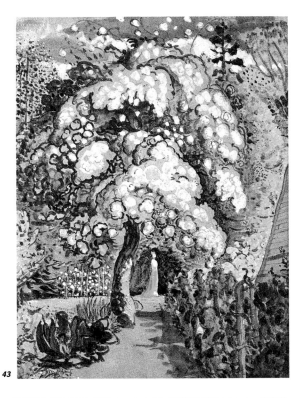

Fig. 43 Samuel Palmer, *In a Shoreham Garden*, Victoria and Albert Museum, London. A few touches of gold and those white circular marks, painted with white gouache, are characteristic of the paintings that Palmer produced during his 'Shoreham' period. He lived in Shoreham for nine years, during which he had the 'dreams and visions' that unleashed his imagination.

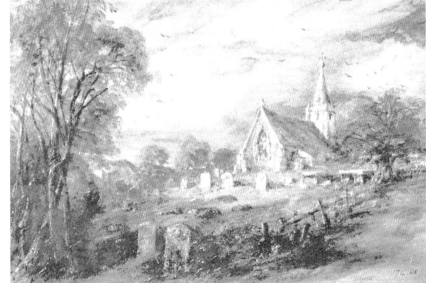

Fig. 44 John Constable, *The Church at Stoke Poges*, Victoria and Albert Museum, London. Constable was basically a painter of oils, recognized as one of the greatest masters of English landscape painting of the 19th century. Nevertheless, he occasionally painted with watercolour, in the characteristic style that can be observed in this work.

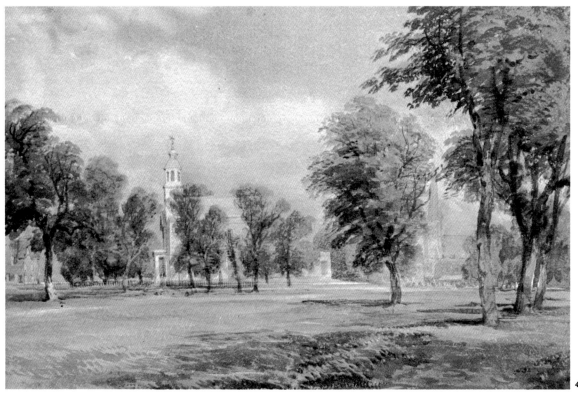

Fig. 45 David Cox (son), *The Old Church and Community of Clapham*, British Museum, London. David Cox's son, also named David, painted watercolours like his father, imitating his expert professional style, with apparent ease of technique and pleasing colours. Father and son both exhibited their works at the annual exhibitions held by the Royal Academy of Watercolour Artists.

45

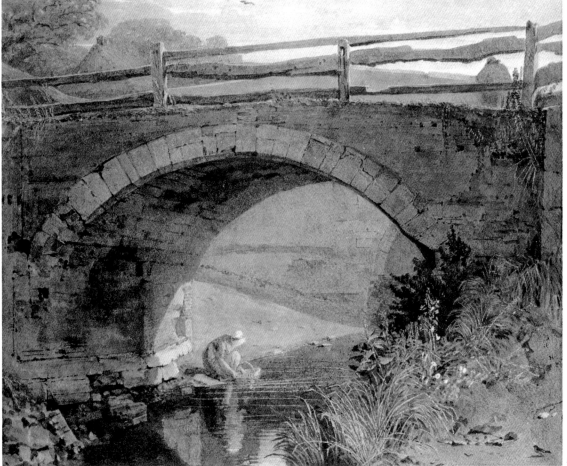

Fig. 46 Peter de Wint, *Bridge Over a Tributary of the Witham River in Lincolnshire*, Tate Gallery, London. De Wint attended Dr Monro's academy, where he met Girtin, whose influence was apparent in all his work. The plains and landscapes of Lincolnshire were his favourite subject. In the fine horizontal lines of the water and the thin blades of grass in the foreground of this watercolour, one can see lines that de Wint probably made with the end of the brush handle, using it to scratch the paint while it was still wet.

46

The success of watercolour painting in England

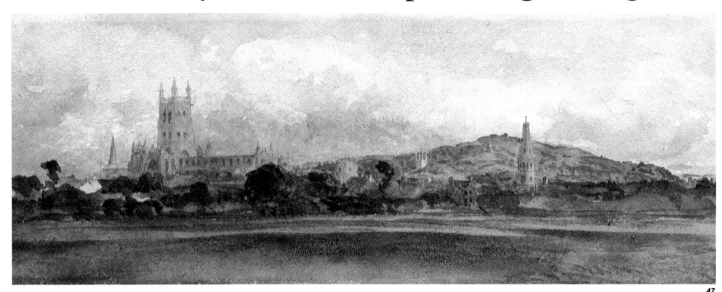

47

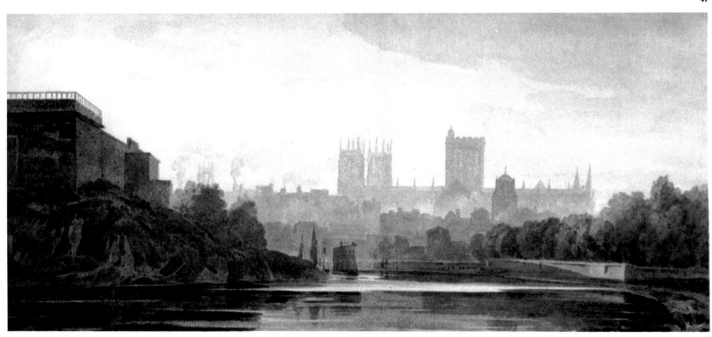

48

The success of watercolour painting can be followed chronologically.

The year 1768 marked the founding of the Royal Academy of Arts in England with Joshua Reynolds as the first president. The founding members included watercolour artists and brothers Paul and Thomas Sandby.

From the first annual exhibition held by the Academy, watercolours were shown. In 1804 watercolour artists, who felt discriminated against by the Academy, which deferred to works in oil paints, founded the Old Water- Colour Society. This new society held its first exhibition in 1805. Although they achieved great success, there was too much competition among members and in 1807 a rival society was founded. This group was called the Society of Painters in Miniature and Water- colours. In 1824 the Society of British Artists had as its members both oil and water- colour painters. In 1855 England sent 114 watercolours to the exhibition at the World's Fair in Paris. Both French critics and the public were amazed at how well this medium

Figs. 47, 48 (Above) Peter de Wint, *Gloucester*. (Below) John Varley, *York*, both in the British Museum, London. Two wonderful watercolours of the 19th century that would be difficult to surpass even today. Peter de Wint showed a special preference for this panoramic format, which was in fashion during the first half of the 1800s. De Wint's watercolour is truly tiny, measuring only 147 x 384 mm (5.8" x 15"). John Varley's, a bit larger, is 219 x 472 mm (8.8" x 18.6").

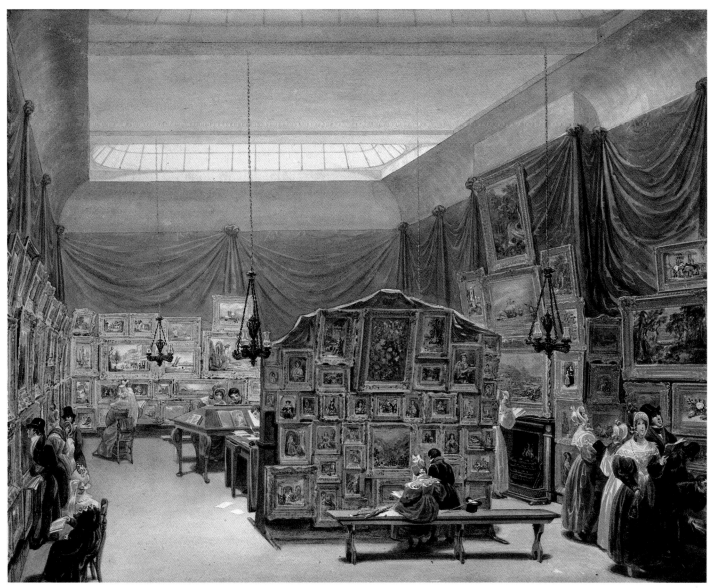

49

had developed in England. In 1881 Queen Victoria decreed that the original (called the 'Old' because it was the first) Water-Colour Society could add the word 'Royal' to its title. When that Society had its first exhibition in 1805, over 12,000 paying visitors went to see it.

Watercolours had achieved a clamorous success in England, a success which spread through Europe and the rest of the world.

Fig. 49 George Scharf, *The Interior of the Exhibition Hall of the New Society of Painters of Watercolours,* Victoria and Albert Museum, London. The precision, fidelity of design, effects of light and shadow, and the feeling of atmosphere – interposed space – that Scharf achieved in this magnificent watercolour are admirable. It is a remarkably faithful reproduction of the building and ambience of this watercolour exhibition mounted by the New Society of Painters of Watercolours. To understand the significance and excellence of Scharf's work, it is enough to recall that this took place in 1808 – it was the second exhibition held in London – and that photography did not yet exist.

Europe: 18th century

Watercolours were not well known in France until the late 18th century. It was only in 1775 that the French word *aquarelle* first became used as a translation of the English 'watercolour'. There was, however, a French artist, Hubert Robert, whose watercolours had been well received by the critics and the public. In 1754, Robert went to Rome and spent 11 years in Italy. He studied with Piranesi and Panini, painting landscapes with ruins. He was accompanied briefly by another French artist, Fragonard, in 1761. Two other Frenchmen, Desprez and Challe, also went to Rome to paint *vedutas*. The activities of these artists helped to promote watercolour painting in France.

Switzerland, land of fascinating landscapes, gave us outstanding artists such as Johann Ludwig Aberli and Abraham Louis Rodolphe Ducros. Aberli was a bucolic artist and a nature lover. Ducros used such powerful contrast and intensity in his watercolours that at first sight they seemed to be painted in oils. He worked with a reduced range of colours, made up mainly of ochres, siennas, and blues. It is possible that during his stay in Rome his style influenced the English watercolour painters.

An interesting theme of 18th-century art is that of botanical paintings. One of the best-known artists was Pierre Joseph Redouté, who was born in the Ardennes. In Holland we can admire Jan van Huysum and his follower Gerard van Spaendock.

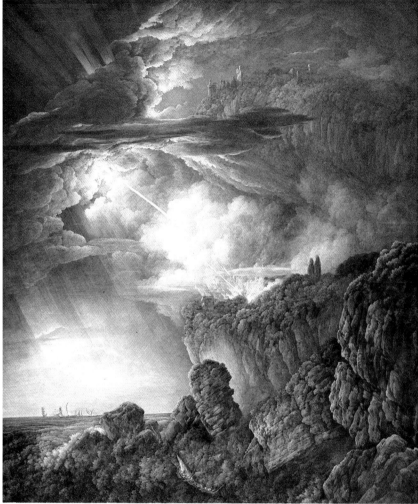

50

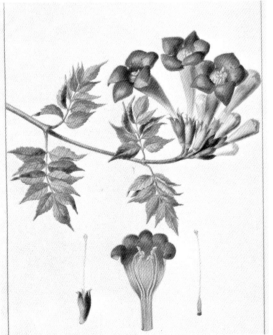

51

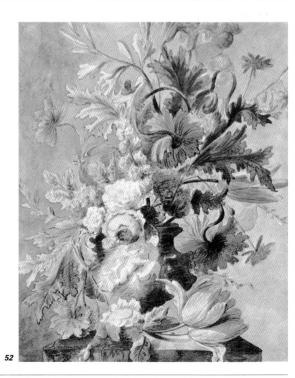

52

Fig. 50 Abraham Louis Rodolphe Ducros, *Night Storm in Cefalou*, Calabria, Cantonal Museum of Fine Arts, Lausanne, Switzerland. With a limited spectrum of colours – ochre, sienna, and blue – Ducros achieved this spectacular richness that even fooled the experts into thinking that this was an oil painting. Ducros also demonstrated a magnificent talent for construction and drawing, enabling the artist to sell his etchings easily while he was in Italy.

Figs. 51, 52 (Left) Gerard van Spaendonck, *Campsis Radicaus*. (Right) Jan Van Huysum, *Study of Flowers in a Vase*, both in the Fitzwilliam Museum, Cambridge.

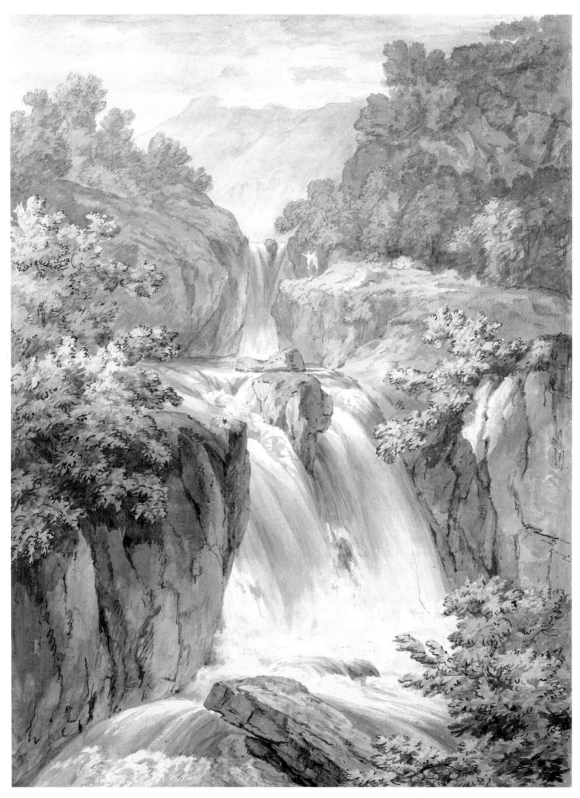

Fig. 53 Johann Ludwig Aberli, *The Waterfall*, Victoria and Albert Museum, London. In this watercolour, painted around 1750, one can still note the style associated with *vedutas* or etchings in the definition of forms by fine penstrokes or intense colour. This formula, which made it possible to 'fill in' etchings done in a series by painting-in, is less obvious here thanks to Aberli's skill. He controlled the contrasts between foreground and background in order to create the so-called 'aerial perspective' or illusion of interposed atmosphere. These same be seen in the reproduction of the watercolour by Paul Sandby in fig. 30.

53

Europe: 19th century

During the early part of the 19th century, Ingres was against Delacroix and vice versa. Jean-Auguste-Dominique Ingres was a staunch believer in Classicism, Raphael, academic painting, and maintaining the status quo in art. On the other hand, Eugène Delacroix was the leader of Romanticism and opened the doors for Realism, Impressionism, and modern art. Delacroix emerged victorious and his success became that of watercolour as well. 19th-century art grew in the direction of greater colour, synthesis, and light, and a brighter palette. In essence, watercolour art is colour, synthesis, and light.

Because of his ideas Ingres painted few watercolours, while Delacroix was an ardent watercolour artist. He was Bonington's friend and visited London, Rome, and North Africa. In the latter he painted numerous watercolours depicting typical scenes and people.

Outstanding in France were Paul Gavarni and Eugène Lami. The latter founded the Société d'Aquarellistes in 1879. Founding members included Gustave Doré, Isabey, and Harpignies. It is well known that Honoré Daumier used watercolour to illuminate his political cartoons. It is surprising to learn that, except for Berthe Morisot and Eugène Boudin, the Impressionists did not use watercolours. (Cézanne is a separate case.) Lastly there is the painter and teacher Gustave Moreau, whose pupils included Roualt, Matisse, and Marquet. The Dutchman Johan Barthold Jongkind painted marvellous watercolours as well as oil paintings. He spent a great part of his life in Paris and, with Boudin, became a prime supporter of the Impressionist movement.

Watercolours became appreciated in Germany during the second half of the 19th century. Among the well-known artists are Johann Lucas von Hildebrandt and Adolf von Menzel. Scotsman David Roberts took watercolour art to Spain where it caught on thanks to the enthusiasm of Perez Villaamil. The pair travelled with the new art throughout the Iberian peninsula. Two excellent watercolour artists, Lucas and Algarra, collaborated with Villaamil. It was Mariano Fortuny, however, who made watercolour better known through Spain. He was one of the best artists of the 18th century and had a great knowledge of the procedures that watercolour involved.

Mariano Fortuny, born in Reus, in the province of Tarragona, but who had his own studio in Barcelona, was, furthermore, the instigator of the first Spanish association of watercolour painters, which was founded in

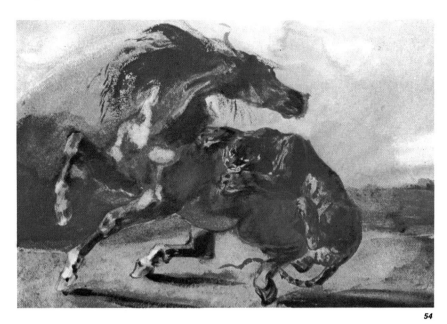

54

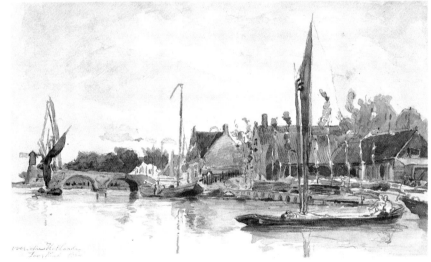

55

Fig. 54 Eugène Delacroix, *Horse Attacked by a Panther*, Louvre, Paris. Quick notes, like sketches, on subjects in his imagination or painted from nature, were a constant occupation and exercise for Delacroix. The thousands of notes that he made during his trips – drawings of animals or subjects in the countries he visited – were almost always done in watercolours.

Fig. 55 Johan Barthold Jongkind, *Dutch Harbour*, Fine Arts Museum, Budapest. Pupil of Isabey and born in Holland, he spent most of his time in Paris, where he studied under Isabey and mixed with the Impressionists. Jongkind worked with oil paint as well as with watercolours, specializing in maritime subjects characterized by their precise drawing.

1864, in Barcelona, under the name of Centre d'Aquarel-listes. From this emerged, first in 1881 the Cercle Artistic and later in 1920, the present Agrupació d'Aquarel-listes de Catalunya. At the national level, the first association known as the Sociedad de Acuarelistas was founded in Madrid in the year 1878.

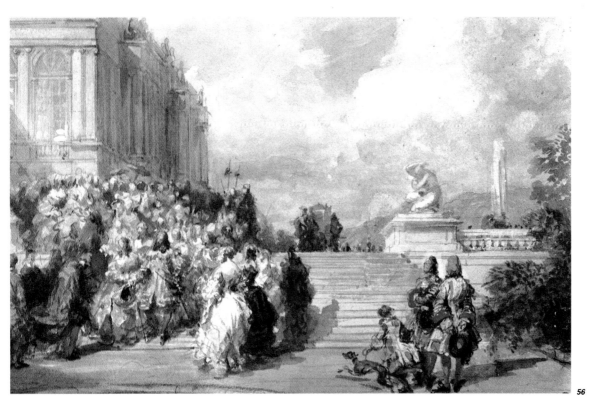

Fig. 56 Eugène-Louis Lami, *Louis XIV in the Gardens of Versailles*, Louvre, Paris. Lami was an expert in watercolour. His good relations with the upper class of the French Second Empire allowed him to join the court and specialize in subjects like this one, inspired by French history.

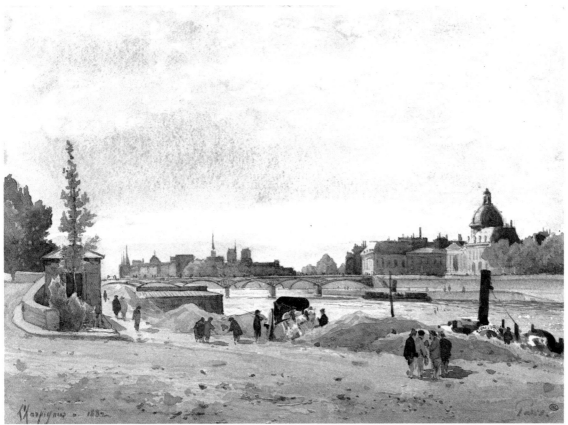

57

Fig. 57 Henri Harpignies, *View of the Seine with the Tuileries*, Louvre, Paris. Contemporary of such illustration and watercolour experts as Ciceri, Lami, Gavarni, Daumier, and Doré, Harpignies is one of the most renowned French watercolour painters of the last century, remarkable for the soberness of his colours and the perfection of his drawing.

Mariano Fortuny

Fig. 58 Mariano Fortuny y Carbo, *Half-naked Man*, Goya Museum, Castres, Spain. Fortuny was an all-round artist. He drew with great ease; he left oil paintings which exhibit a control over the figure that won him the title of 'master', and he used watercolours with truly remarkable craftsmanship. He went to Rome when he was 20. After two years of study he travelled to Morocco where he produced the official commission of ten big paintings about the Spanish-Moroccan war. In Morocco he also made several watercolours, including the one reproduced here. Then came trips to Paris, London, Rome, Granada, Rome again... Unfortunately, Fortuny died at the age of 36, considered among the greatest watercolour artists of the 19th century.

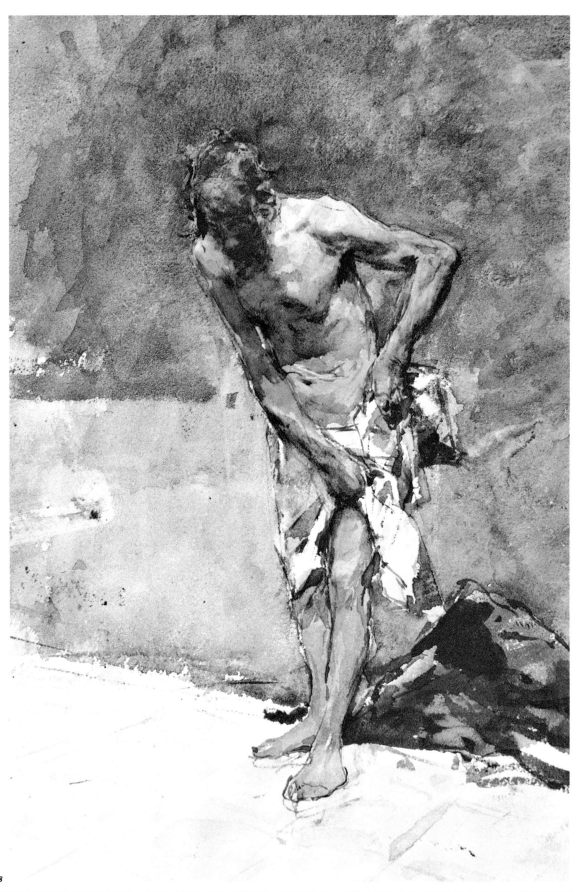

58

Cézanne

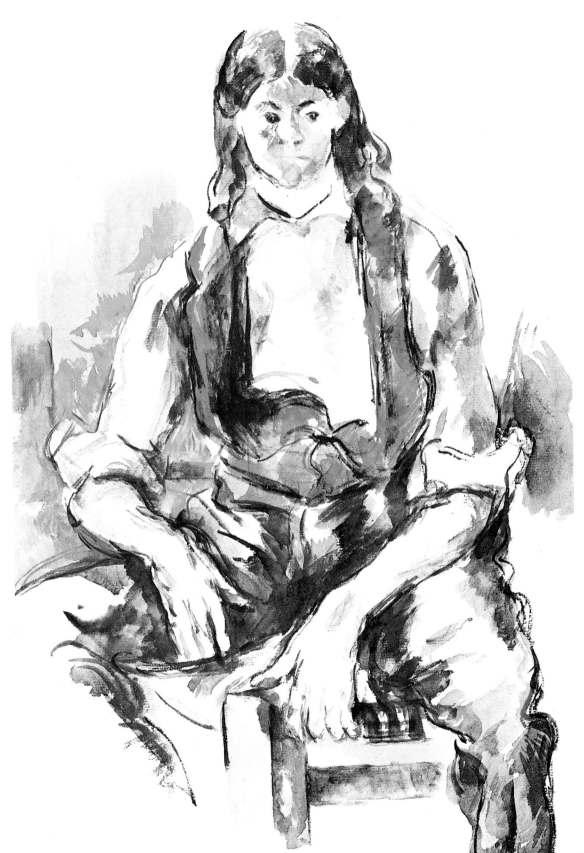

Fig. 59 Paul Cézanne, *Boy with Red Coat*, Walter Filechenfeldt Collection, Zurich. Without doubt, Cézanne is modern, contemporary. Between Mariano Fortuny's painting on the previous page, made around 1862, and Cézanne's work of 1902, some 40 years have passed. What a jump, what a radical change! During those 40 years, Impressionism was born, the palette was purged, shape and colour were resumed, details lost their importance. Cézanne went beyond Impressionism: he embodied Post-Impressionism, and laid the foundations of Cubism. He is credited today as one of the great promoters of modern painting. This watercolour confirms this: it could have been painted in the late 20th century.

59

Europe in the first half of the 20th century

The first abstract painting in the history of art was a watercolour painted in 1910 by Wassily Kandinsky.

However, watercolour artists, with a few exceptions, did not participate in this art form. As a matter of fact they kept their distance from the styles and movements that came in rapid succession during the first half of the 20th century. They did, however, incorporate into their works the light and spontaneity of the Impressionists and use the colours and contrasts and some new schemes of composition from modern art in general.

On the other hand, the great masters of modern art, Picasso, Dali, Miró, Matisse, and Braque, hardly ever used watercolour. In spite of this the quantity and quality of watercolour artists throughout Europe grew to such proportions that it becomes difficult for us to single out any one here. There are, however, certain important innovations that bear mentioning. There was a tendency to use watercolour to imitate oil paint, using greater body and colour and sacrificing transparency. Another innovation was the use of 'tricks' such as using wax or masking fluid to set off open spaces or

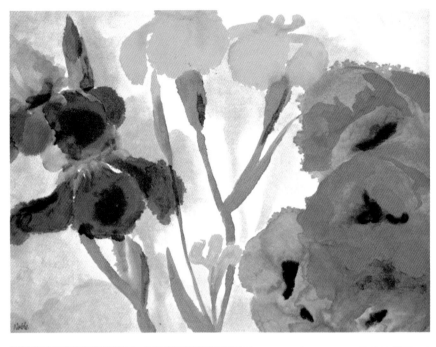

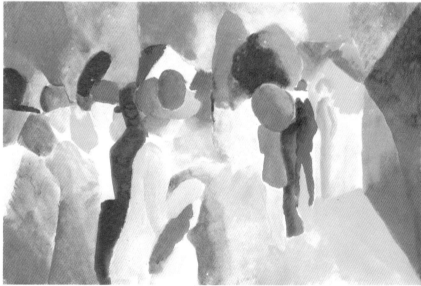

60

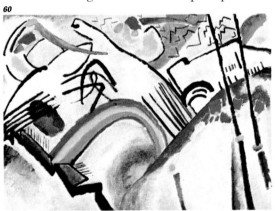

using turpentine, salt, stains, or spray guns to achieve special effects.

On this page you can see some watercolours from the early 20th century. They include works by Wassily Kandinsky, the artist of the first abstract mentioned earlier, Emil Nolde, and August Macke. On the next page we see works by Maurice de Vlaminck, Maurice Utrillo, Juan Gris, and Pablo Picasso. These are all well-known artists who, except for Nolde, did not usually work in watercolours.

Fig. 60 Wassily Kandinsky, *The Cossacks*, Tate Gallery, London. A watercolour similar to this was the first abstract painting, painted in watercolours by Kandinsky in the year 1910.

Fig. 61 Emile Nolde, *Irises and Poppies*, Ada and Emil Nolde Foundation, Seebull. Nolde was a German Expressionist painter who felt a great passion for primitive art and nature.

Fig. 62 August Macke, *Yellow Jake*, Ulmer Museum, Ulm, Germany. In this watercolour, Macke offers us a sample of his Futuristic style and his Post-Impressionist colouring, both factors directly influenced by Delaunay, who with Kandinsky and Macke formed part of the Blaue Reiter (Blue Rider) group.

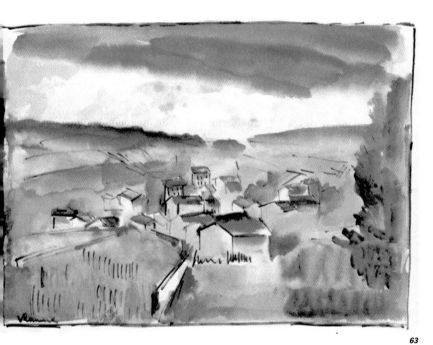

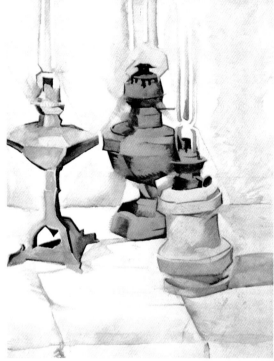

63

65

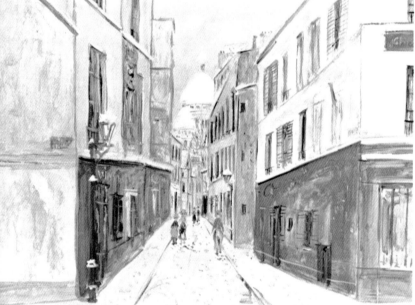

64

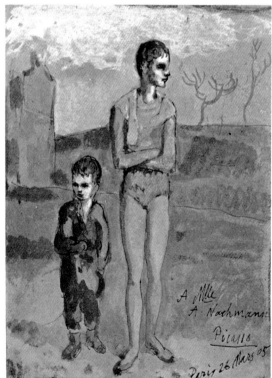

66

Fig. 63 Maurice de Vlaminck, *Landscape*, Staatsgalerie, Stuttgart. Matisse, together with Derain, Vlaminck, and other artists, were the initiators, along with an exhibition held in Paris in 1905, of the tendency or style called Fauvism (*fauve* is French for 'wild beast'). This title, first applied by an art critic, described a way of painting with violent colours and contrasts. However, after two or three years, Vlaminck stopped painting like a Fauve and came closer to the theories and style of Cézanne.

Fig. 64 Maurice Utrillo, *The Rue Sainte-Rustique Covered in Snow*, Paul Petrides Collection, Paris. This watercolour with a mixture of white gouache is typical of Utrillo's style: an innocent, childlike way of drawing and painting, appropriately called 'the difficult innocence'.

Fig. 65 Juan Gris, *Three Lamps*, Museum of Fine Arts, Berne, Switzerland. Between 1909 and 1910 the Spanish painter Juan Gris did some watercolour paintings to practise drawing forms and colour. Apparently, what Gris was trying to determine with these oversized studies – 47.8 x 61.8 cm (19" x 24") – was what direction to follow in the future. In fact, a year later, together with his friends Picasso and Braque, he started on the adventure of Cubism.

Fig. 66 Pablo Picasso, *Young Acrobat and Child*, Guggenheim Museum, New York. This is one of the many sketches that Picasso did for the painting *Trapeze Artists (Family of Saltimbanques)*, just as he was in transition between his blue and pink periods. This is a watercolour with a mixture of gouache.

Watercolour painting today

On this page and the ones that follow you will see some contemporary watercolours whose form and colour reveal a language in harmony with today's art. While some are Impressionist and others Expressionist, they are linked by the constructive base watercolour painters have never abandoned.

Watercolours still depict traditional topics: country landscapes, seascapes, ports, railways, still lifes, portraits and figures, and nature in general. Present-day scenes, such as urban areas and suburban houses and streets, are also represented.

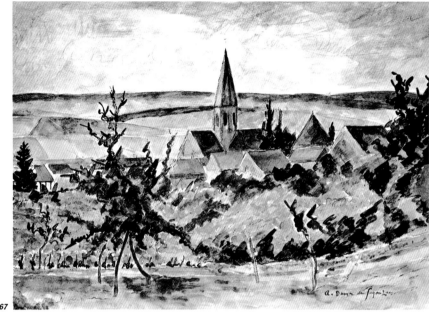

67

Fig. 67 André Dunoyer de Segonzac, *Feucherolles in Autumn*, private collection. Segonzac was primarily an Impressionist, influenced by Cézanne, who also did many etchings – 1,500 of them from 1919 onward – which are today considered his best works.

68

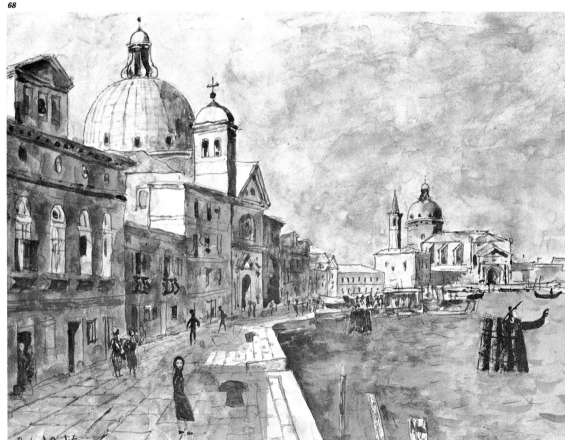

Fig. 68 Roland Oudot, *La Giudecca, Venice*, Albert Balser Collection, Geneva. Roland Oudot's style draws our attention by its emphasis on the drawing, with the forms outlined with a fine line of India ink. The colouring is also characteristic of his style: the shadowed areas where blues, siennas, greys, and reds interact with a vibration that undoubtedly gives quality to the work.

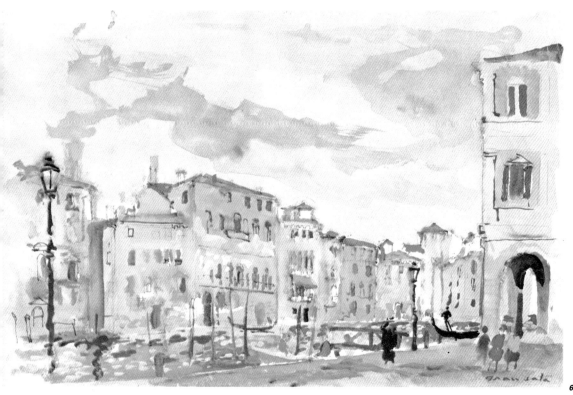

Fig. 69 Emilio Grausala, *Venice*, private collection. Grausala, a Catalan painter, moved to Paris in 1932 and became a part of the Second Spanish School of Paris, as it was called. He generally painted with oils, but on some trips and in private he did small watercolour works painted with his proverbial gaiety and richness of colour.

69

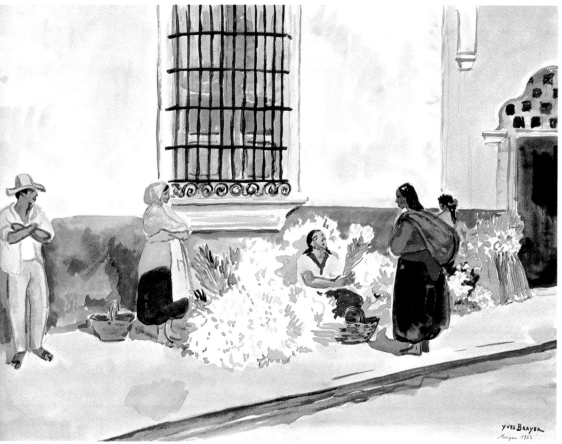

Fig. 70 Ives Brayer, *Flower Market, Mexico*. This work represents a modern concept of watercolour painting: a synthesis of form and colour, explaining the subject in an abbreviated manner without entering into details; a premeditated luminosity with a predominance of light colours over dark; and a richness of colours, also calculated to add to the transparency typical of watercolour. Brayer always paints with watercolour. He draws with great mastery, usually with lead pencil, and he always works with the model in front of him.

70

Watercolour painting today

Fig. 71 Ives Brayer, *Half-light at Baux-de-Provence*, private collection. As can be seen in this landscape, Brayer painted with conventional colours, attentive to the realism offered by the scene, attempting to capture the first impression suggested by the subject, applying pure watercolour techniques, enjoying 'the pleasure of playing with the white of the paper' – as he puts it himself – '*en utilisant juste une coulée de couleur, du bout du pinceau*' (*sic*).

Fig. 72 John Piper, *Bethesda, North Wales*, private collection. Piper is known as an excellent modern interpreter of the British landscape, which he rendered with an obvious mastery of technique and medium. In this landscape, for instance, he mixed watercolours with Indian ink, layering wet over wet, and using *frottage*, the dry-brush technique. He published a book of his work done in England and Wales.

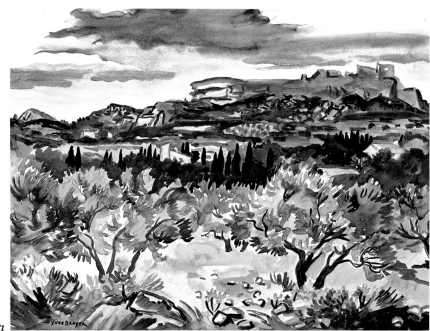

71

72

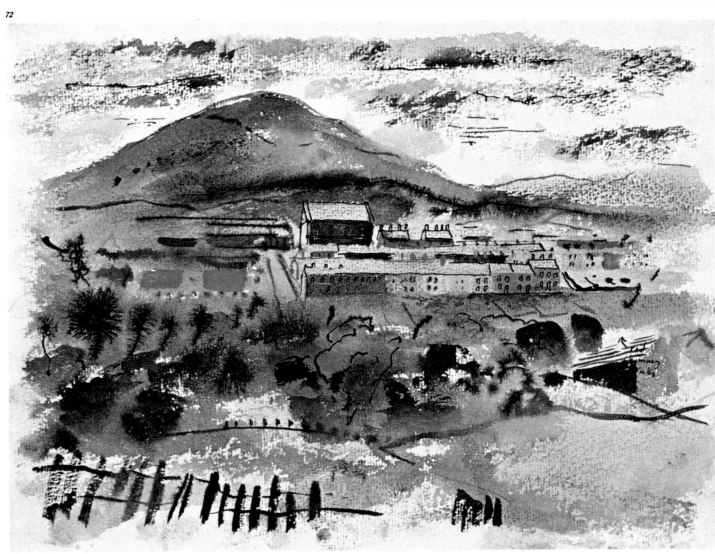

73

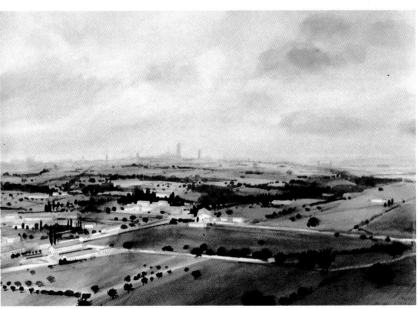

74

Fig. 73 Julio Quesada, *Landscape: Tamajón (Guadalajara)*, private collection. This is an excellent example of contemporary watercolours, as the Spanish artist, Julio Quesada, is so capable of exemplifying. He paints in his own way, with a very personal vision and interpretation; with a sober but perfectly harmonized colour scheme; synthesizing, summarizing in a few exact, precise brushstrokes, which nevertheless capture the forms, the site, the fields, and the trees. But above all, he executes all this with an exceptional mastery of pure watercolour technique.

Fig. 74 Michel Ciry, *Segovia*, private collection. Michel Ciry decided to paint watercolours around 1960. Six years later, he obtained these results while painting in central Spain. In harmony with the Castilian landscape, Ciry paints with a subdued, warm palette, formed of ochres, siennas, and greys, interrupting the landscape with houses and roads that contrast with the black trees and the earth scorched by the sun. This painting is a good example of the synthesis of form and colour.

The 19th and 20th centuries in the United States

The American Watercolour Society was formed in 1866 with Samuel Colman as its president.

At that time watercolour was already popular in the United States. This was mainly because oil painters Thomas Eakins and Winslow Homer also used watercolour. Homer was a Bohemian loner who worked as a magazine illustrator, correspondent, and sketcher. During his travels he visited France, England, Canada, Bermuda, and Nassau. After the age of 40, he devoted himself entirely to painting. He had a special gift for choosing marine landscapes and then painting them with oils or watercolours and giving them extraordinary colour.

The end of the 19th century was a marvellous time for American watercolour. Maurice Prendergast depicted groups of people. Mary Cassatt lived the adventure of Impressionism in France. James Abbott McNeill Whistler was also an Impressionist. John Singer Sargent, the famous portrait and watercolour artist, though American, was born in Italy and educated in

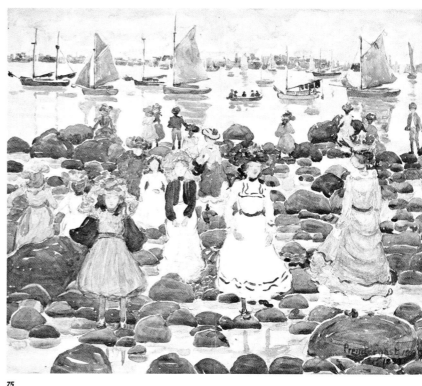

75

76

Fig. 75 Maurice Prendergast, *Low Tide, Beachmont,* Worcester Art Museum. Born in Boston, Prendergast went to Paris at the age of 21 when Impressionism was in full swing, so it is not strange that his paintings should be influenced by Manet, Monet, Renoir, Pissarro, etc. Curiously, Prendergast specialized in the subject of crowds, or groups of people in a particular situation, as in his painting *The Walk,* or in this one, *Low Tide*. In 1914, he returned from Europe to New York, where he exhibited with Los Pocho, a radical group that indirectly infused American art with new life.

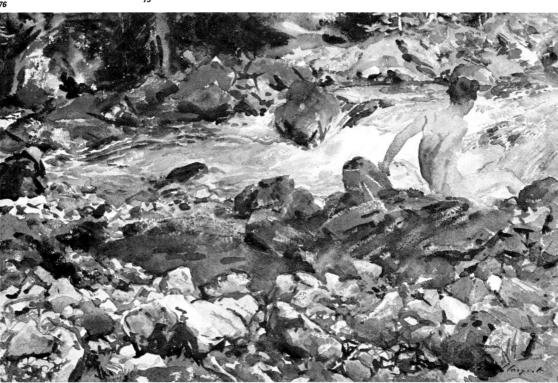

Fig. 76 John Singer Sargent, *Mountain Stream*, Metropolitan Museum of Art, New York. Painting his magnificent portraits in oils, Sargent was fabulous; painting with watercolours he was also extraordinary. At 18 he was in Paris studying under the painter Carolus, who inculcated him with a basic rule on synthesis that became Sargent's credo during his career as an artist: 'In art, anything that is not indispensable is prejudicial.'

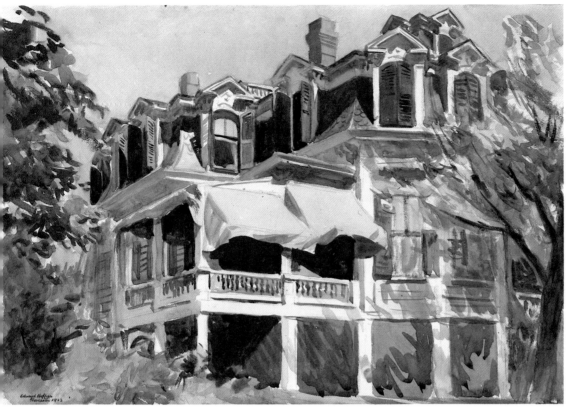

Fig. 77 Edward Hopper, *The Mansard Roof*, Brooklyn Museum, New York. When Hopper visited Paris at the age of 24, he was influenced by Post-Impressionism, but upon his return to America he shook off this influence to take up American Realism and specialize in urban scenes. In this watercolour, painted with admirable skill in the year 1923, Hopper cannot be defined as to style, but he gives us an excellent lesson on the effects of light and shadow, volume, colour, and watercolour techniques.

77

France. These four artists took the reins and led American art to its glorious finish at the end of the century.

During the 20th century, watercolour painting has achieved first place in the United States. It has thousands of fans and highly qualified artists too numerous to mention. We can cite a few examples to show how high the standards are. Figurative art is represented by Edward Hopper, Andrew Wyeth, Rowland Hilder, John Pike, and David Millard. The modern and even abstract styles are represented by John Marin, Georgia O'Keeffe, Lyonel Feininger, and Sam Francis.

History continues. Watercolour now has a place as a highly expressive medium. It has reached a level of quality and quantity that can be compared only with oil painting. The trends currently being followed with new techniques and styles could make watercolour painting even more exciting.

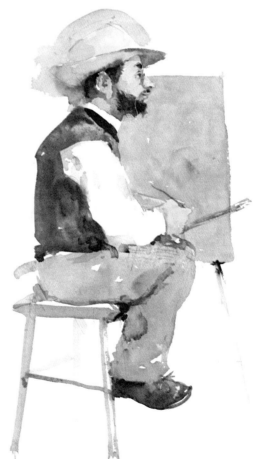

Fig. 78 Charles Reid, *Masculine Figure, Clothed*, private collection. I have chosen this watercolour by Reid as representative of the quality of a large number of amateur and professional artists who are presently painting watercolours in the United States. As can be seen, Reid is a great watercolour artist, and he has published several books on art and creativity.

78

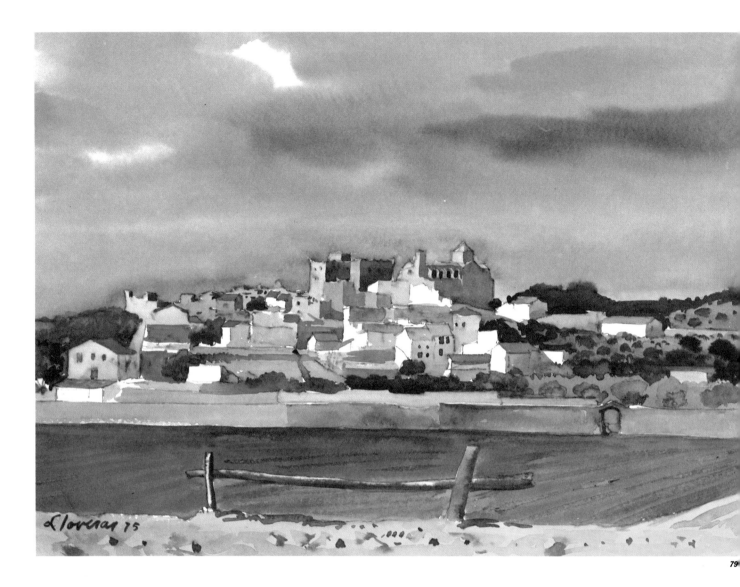

79

Fig. 79 Federico Lloveras, *Altafulla, Tarragona*, private collection. To conclude this brief history of watercolour I choose this simple landscape by my friend Federico Lloveras, recently deceased. He was a great artist of worldwide renown, who had painted in every corner of Spain, and all the cities of Europe and America. All his watercolours illustrated the ease with which he painted, as does the one shown here, which, characteristically, seems so simple, at first view. In an interview with Mr del Arco for *La Vanguardia*, he was asked how he managed to create this freshness, this feeling of 'a watercolour painted in just a few minutes'. Lloveras answered: 'I see a theme: I spend a lot of time studying, observing. Then I begin to paint – without hurry, very slowly, trying out, then hesitating. Because at first the subject dominates you, and you have to fight so that you dominate the subject. Once this happens, I can work securely; I know where and how to place every brushstroke. And then it seems as if I had painted the picture in a moment.'

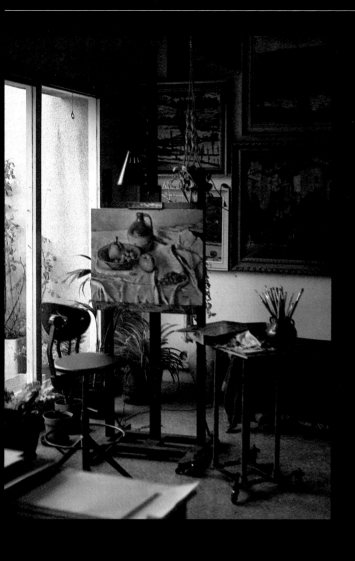

The painter's studio

'A small room captures the spirit; one should paint by the light of one window.'

Leonardo da Vinci (1452-1519)

The studio for painting in watercolour

The watercolour artist usually works outdoors. His favourite subjects are usually landscapes, seascapes, city streets, and squares. Nevertheless the watercolourist, like the painter of oils, also needs a studio for drawing, painting from sketches, still lifes, figures from nature, portraits...

To begin, all you need is a tabletop easel and another table to hold water jugs, brushes and paints, a sketch pad, a chair, a desk lamp, and a pair of portfolios in which you can store drawing paper and finished works.

The studio of many professionals is as simple as that in da Vinci's description. However, if one wants to invest in setting up a place to work very comfortably the following would be an excellent choice:

A room measuring 4 m square (about 12 feet square) with white walls and large windows with a northern exposure for working in daylight. A good choice for a table would be one whose top can be tilted at different angles. The chair should have an upholstered seat and back, at a height that can be adjusted at will, and metal castors for easier rolling. To keep supplies, such as jugs of water and a box of watercolours, close by, it is useful to have an

Fig. 81 The amateur, to begin, can install his studio in any room in the house. All that is needed is a table, a drawing board, and a chair. The artist can hold the watercolour paper at a slight incline by resting the board on the table with the help of a few books, or at a greater slant by resting it in his lap and against the edge of the table.

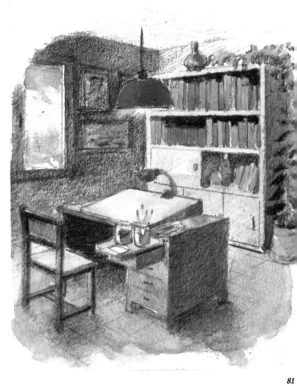

81

82

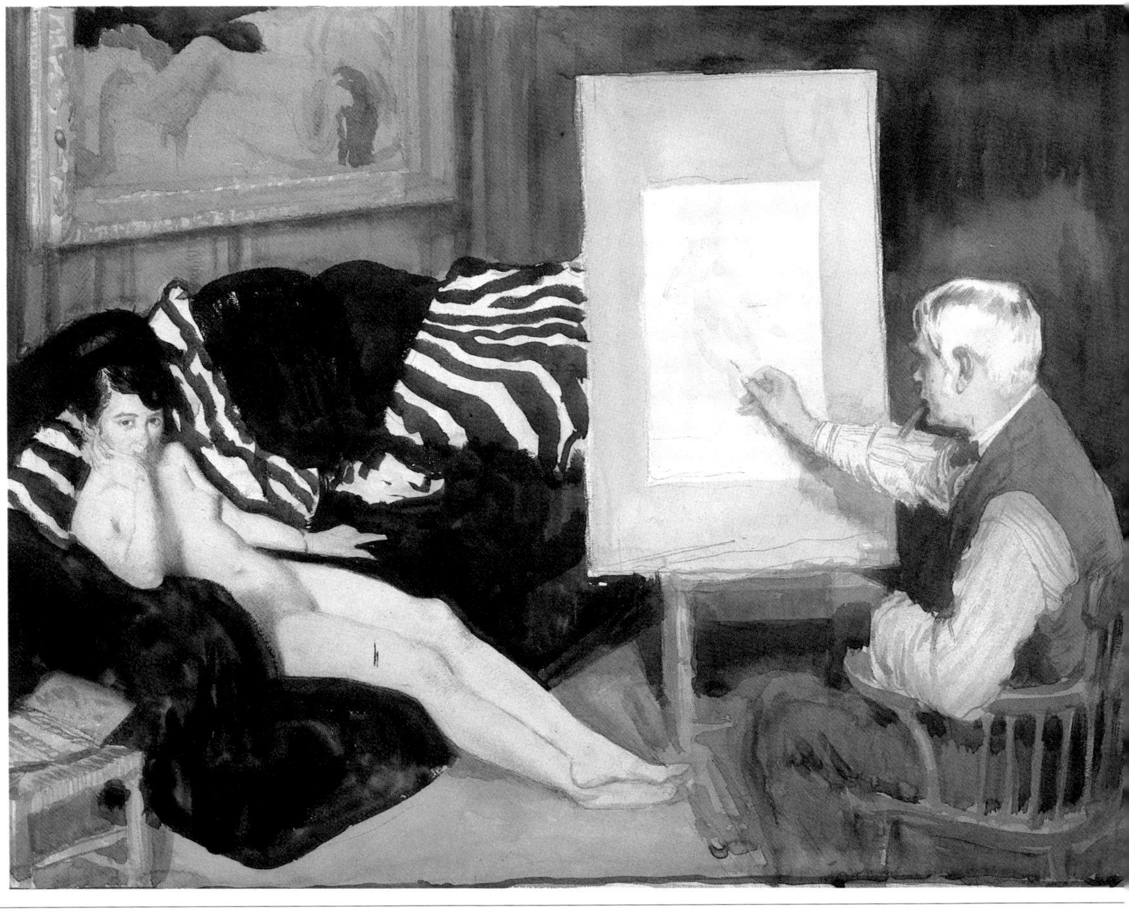

Fig. 82 Sir William Orpen, *The Model*, Tate Gallery, London. The Irishman Sir William Orpen offers us, in this magnificent watercolour, a partial view of his studio in London, apparently a small one to judge by this painting of 1911.

Lighting the professional studio

auxiliary table, also on castors. To paint you need a studio easel and a tabletop easel. A bookshelf wall unit and a plan chest are useful places to put away paper, sketches, first drafts, and the end product. A stand for file folders, a sink with running water, art books, a stereo, and a sofa or chaise-longue where your model can sit or where you can listen to music, read, or chat with friends are also nice to have.

The main source of daylight should come from large windows to the left of the work table if you are right-handed. It is wise to have blinds or curtains since they allow you to regulate the amount and type of light. Your electrical lighting should be powerful and evenly distributed, allowing the use of the studio for painting at night. It is wise to consult with an electrician and install at least one lamp with four fluorescent lamps. Two of these should give warm light and two cold light to imitate natural daylight. A table lamp should have an extendable arm and give off at least 100 watts. Finally, it is important to have light near the sofa and create an intimate spot for relaxing, listening to music, and talking.

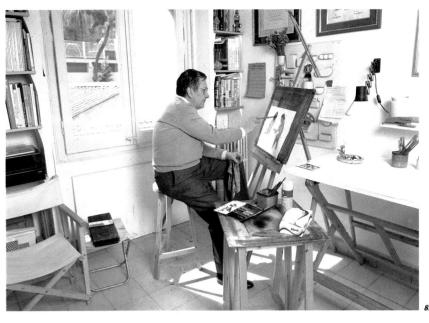

83

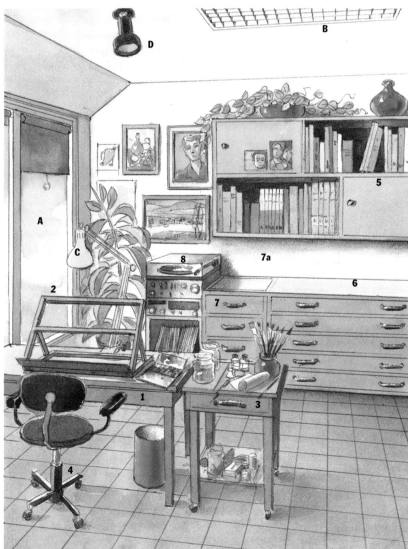

Fig. 83 Gaspar Romero's studio in his house in Barcelona. As you can see, the furniture is limited to a folding table with slanted top, a small side table, a studio easel of the classic three-legged type, and a stool for working partially seated.

Fig. 84 This is an ideal studio for watercolour painting: a room with white walls, 4 x 4 m (12' x 12'), with large windows facing north and the following furniture and lighting:

Furniture and tools

1: Table. *2:* Tabletop easel in the form of a lectern. *3:* Auxiliary table with wheels. *4:* Swivel chair, with adjustable height and wheels. *5:* Bookshelf. *6:* Plan chest. *7:* Set of drawers below the counter to store materials. *7a:* Light box – white glass with electrical fixture inside the top drawer, for tracing designs, looking at slides, etc. *8:* Stereo equipment. *9:* Sink or basin with running water (not shown in figure).
Lighting: A: Windows, daylight. *B:* Set of fluorescent lights. *C:* Table lamp. *D:* Auxiliary lamp.

84

Furniture and tools

The following is a list of the furnishings necessary for the studio of a professional watercolour artist.

A table for painting. This can be a regular office desk with drawers to keep boxes, brushes, and other materials. However, this type of table is only a temporary solution. Professionally speaking, it is best to work with a table designed specifically for drawing.

An inclined tabletop allows for a better view of the painting currently being worked on. For this purpose, please look at the classic folding table (fig. 88) which has been on the market for over fifty years. This style is known to young and old watercolour artists, but it has been outdated by more modern and functional designs. Modern tables include those used for technical drawing and architectural drafting, which are also useful for artistic drawing and painting. They are made of formica with metal hardware and have functional designs and elegant lines (figs. 87, 89). The table in fig. 89, custom-made, has two independent sets of drawers and a slanted tabletop. This allows for the drawers to be separated and the table size to be increased on both sides. Please note in the same figure that the depth of the drawers allows for a board to be placed on one of them

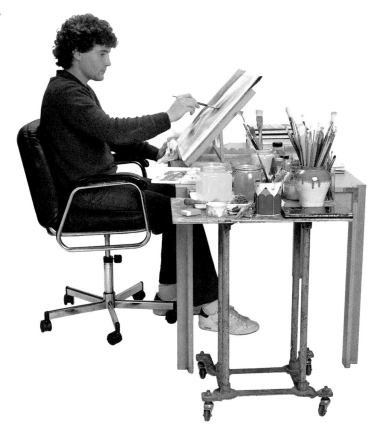

85

Fig. 85 These are the pieces of furniture that are really indispensable for working in the watercolour studio: the standard drawing table, a lectern-type tabletop easel, a small side table, and a comfortable swivel chair with wheels and adjustable height. Paints, brushes, jars with water, paper, etc.

Fig. 86 The classic drafting table with a top that can be slanted as desired – in use for over a hundred years – is still found in the studios of many professional watercolourists.

Fig. 87 The modern table, like this 'pioneer' by the maker Americana, in the United States, can be both elegant and functional, as seen in this picture. It has a top that can be tilted at any angle, drawers for extra materials, bars to rest the feet on, and other features.

86

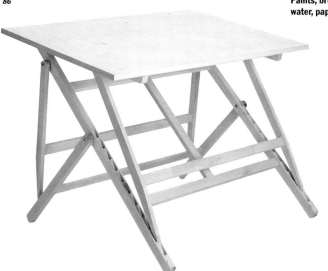

87

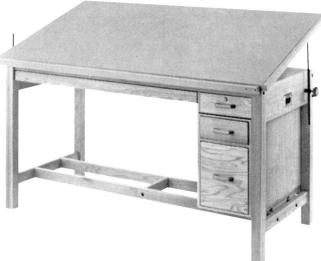

to form an auxiliary table. This will substitute for the second table mentioned earlier as a place to put water, brushes and colours. Other necessary objects include a tabletop easel like the one to be seen in fig. 85 and a classical three-legged easel.

It is necessary to have a smaller table on which to place water, paper, brushes, sponges, and paper towels. This can be a special piece of furniture with springs, shelves, and all kinds of drawers. If it also has a tilted board it is possible to paint without any table (fig. 88). It is even possible to use a normal table or a contraption such as the one I use. This consists of a standard typewriter table with a board on top (fig. 90). Regardless of the style you choose, this second table should have castors or wheels. This way it can be easily transported to the drawing table or easel you are currently using.

A professional studio also needs a stand like the one in fig. 91 on which one or two large portfolios with sketches or finished paintings can be left. This makes it easier to show your work to visitors and prospective buyers.

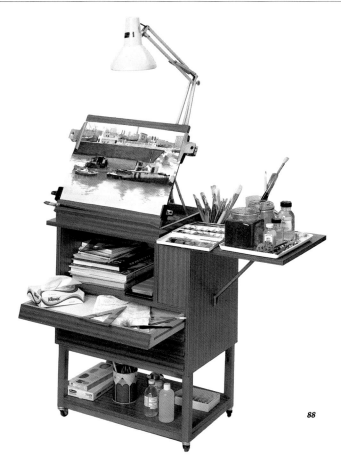

88

Fig. 88 Here is a marvellous invention that combines in a single piece of furniture the table, tabletop easel, a shelf that serves as an auxiliary table, two shelves to store materials, and three tray-drawers to keep paper, drawings, and watercolours (maximum size 32 x 50 cm). Equipped with wheels, it is at the very least a complete auxiliary table.

Fig. 89 Drawing table formed by two sets of drawers and a separate board as the desktop, allowing the table to be lengthened by moving the drawers out. The drawers are long enough so that one of them can be used as an auxiliary table by placing a board on top of it.

Fig. 90 Some time ago, using an old typewriter table and a simple wooden board that I tied to it, I made this sort of auxiliary table on wheels, which works just as well for oil painting as for watercolour.

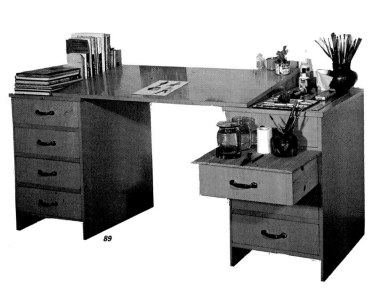

89

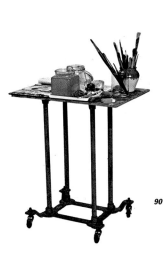

90

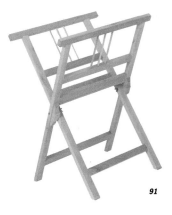

91

Fig. 91 The stand for large portfolios that the artist uses for keeping paper and completed work is essential in a studio, both to conserve the pieces and to show them to friends and clients.

Running water, wall unit, armchair...

Running water in the studio is not a must, but it does make life more comfortable. You will need water to paint and it has to be changed periodically. The reason why the source of water should be close by is because you also need it to wash the palette, the box, the brushes, and other things. You can even use one incorporated into the normal white sink with chrome tap. I installed one made of traditional ceramic and the result is quite pleasing.

If the studio is large enough, a complete wall unit may be a worthwhile investment. You can use the standard drawers to put away brushes, colours, palette, and jars. Tray-type drawers are the best place to keep your paper, future projects, sketches, drawings, and finished watercolours. This unit should also have a table with a large enough surface to fold, cut, and mount the paper.

You will need to have two or three boards with a thickness of 6 mm and two standard sizes, about 65 × 80 cm and 70 × 100 cm.

I recommend that you have a comfortable chair. It should be on castors with upholstered arms and back and adjustable height, similar to those used in offices. Painting is a tiring procedure. Do not forget that inspiration and creativity are still on speaking terms with comfort.

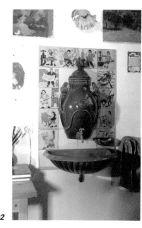

92

Fig. 92 **Running water is needed in a studio, but instead of an ordinary sink and tap, I installed this decorative basin of old-fashioned porcelain at very little extra cost.**

Fig. 93 **You can work in your studio with the traditional round wooden three-legged stool but I recommend drawing and painting on a comfortable swivel chair with adjustable height and wheels. You'll see that it's worth it.**

Fig. 94 **There should be at least two large sturdy portfolios in the studio and two or three 6 mm (1/4")-thick plywood boards, two of them 65 x 80 cm (26" x 32") and one 70 x 100 cm (28" x 40").**

Fig. 95 **Notice this piece of furniture, with one section serving as a bookshelf and another as a counter, and tray-drawers to store blank paper, sketches, designs, and original watercolours that are finished or in progress. A set of drawers can be added to this table to store materials and tools. One of the top drawers can be fitted with a piece of clouded glass with two fluorescent lamps inside and used as a tracing table, or for looking at slides, etc.**

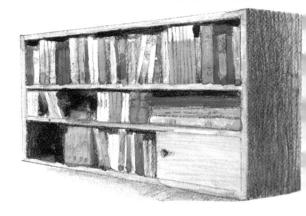

93

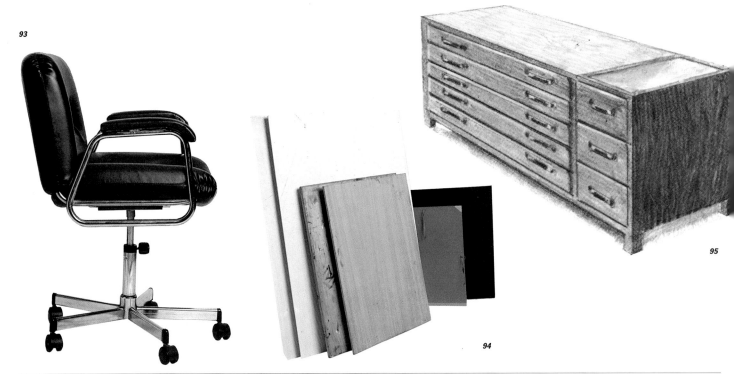

94

95

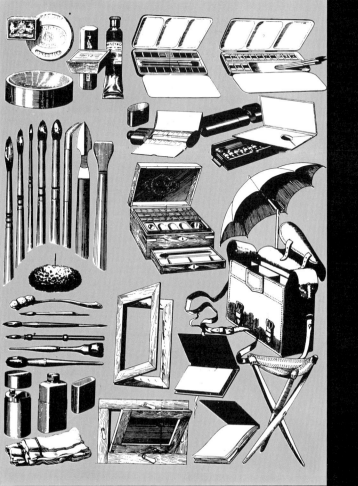

Materials

The easel

Most easels used in oil painting are also useful for watercolour painting. There are some like the tabletop easel that have been designed specifically with the watercolour artist in mind. Every easel for watercolours needs a supplementary wooden board to hold the paper. This is not necessary if the paper is attached to a board or rigid block made especially for painting in watercolour.

Among professionals there is no set or agreed-upon angle at which their drawing pad should be tilted. Some work outdoors with the board lying flat on the ground; others prefer the aid of an easel for tilting the board the way they want it. Indoors the situation is similar; some work on their desk which is slightly tilted, others use a tabletop easel set at a 4° angle, while there are those that use a conventional easel, which places their work perpendicular to the floor. It is my belief that a 45° angle is the most appropriate for developing adequate watercolour techniques.

Fig. 97 Special tabletop easel for watercolour painting. The design is almost identical to that of a traditional studio easel like the one shown in fig. 102, with the exception of its smaller size of 60 cm. It can be tilted at any angle, for painting in a vertical position or at a greater or lesser slant.

Fig. 99 A portable metal, folding easel, highly recommended for watercolour painting because of its compact solid mechanism that makes it possible to slant the arm as desired, to hold the board or pad of paper firmly in place.

Fig. 100 Portable easel for watercolour painting, made of wood, similar to the one in fig. 99, also foldable, but with the addition of a small board on which the watercolour palette can be placed. The inclined arm of this model is not as sturdy or steady as the one on the previous easel.

Fig. 101 Traditional easel with its own case, in common use in Europe and America for oil or watercolour painting. The top can be slanted as desired, and all the materials and tools needed for watercolour painting can be carried in the case. This stylized model is slightly narrower and lighter than the standard model.

Fig. 102 Traditional studio easel with a tripod and an adjustable height tray, but smaller than the traditional model for oil painting.

Figs. 103, 104 Studio easel that can be used for oil or watercolour painting thanks to its slanting top. It is solidly and functionally built, and takes up less space than the traditional studio easel (fig. 103 shows it folded).

Fig. 105 Finally, this is the best known and most commonly used studio easel for oil painting. It can also be used for watercolour painting provided the board is in a vertical position, though this may not be the best angle.

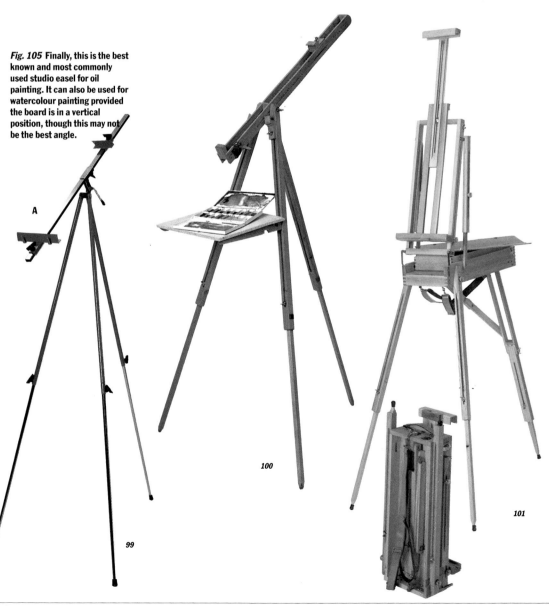

A

100

99

101

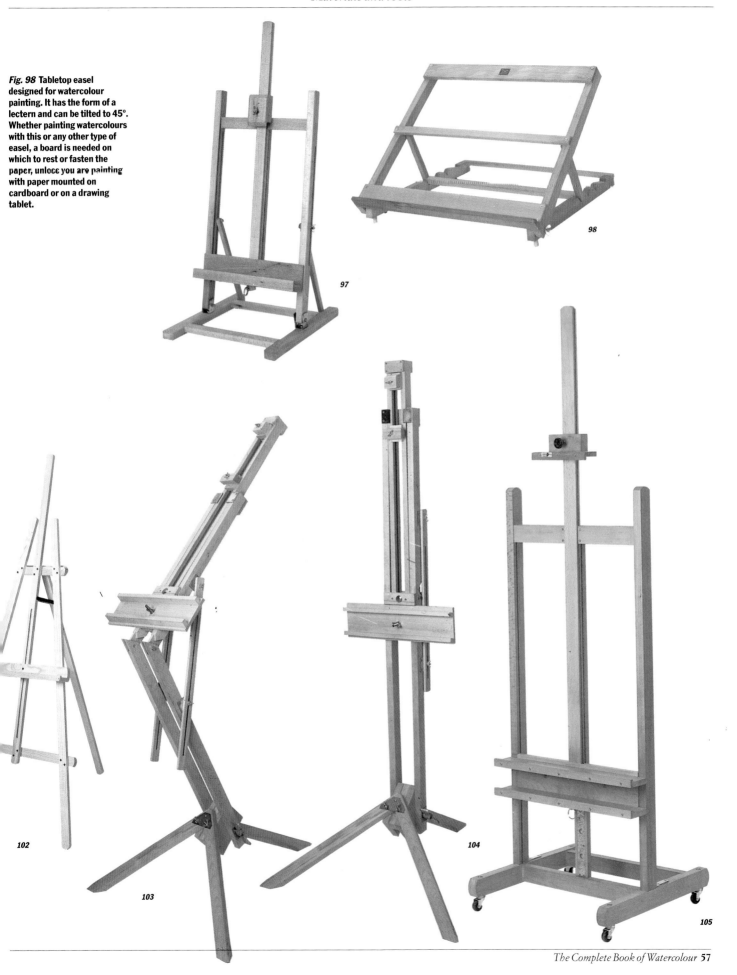

Fig. 98 Tabletop easel designed for watercolour painting. It has the form of a lectern and can be tilted to 45°. Whether painting watercolours with this or any other type of easel, a board is needed on which to rest or fasten the paper, unless you are painting with paper mounted on cardboard or on a drawing tablet.

Paper for watercolour painting

In watercolour painting the choice of the right paper is very important. There is paper made of wood pulp which is made by machines or moulds, and has a medium quality. Papers of the best quality contain 100% rag and are handmade with great care given to how they are glued. This last process determines the paper's quality and how it will stand up to the many layers of watercolour applied. The highest-quality paper is quite expensive but there is an intermediate quality made by some companies that is acceptable. High-quality papers can be distinguished by the mark of the manufacturer somewhere on the paper either stamped in relief, or as the traditional watermark, which can be better observed by holding the paper up to a light.

There are three basic textures of paper that are suitable for watercolours:

A *Fine-grain paper*

B *Medium-grain paper or semi-rough*

C *Coarse-grain paper or rough*

Fine-grain paper is pressed while hot to straighten it. However, it does maintain certain ridges that are needed for watercolour to adhere. This is why a completely flat paper is not well suited for this art form. Fine-grain paper is very good for drawing and painting with watercolour if the artist is an expert at controlling outlines, fusions, gradations, and wet contours, since the finer the grain the faster the paint will slide and dry. Although this is not an easy paper to work with, it does increase the luminosity of colours.

Medium-grain paper has ridges which make it unnecessary to work at very fast speeds. Its position between the most difficult and the easiest paper makes it ideal for the beginner. Beginners should wait a while before trying other grains of paper.

Coarse-grain paper prepared for watercolour painting offers an accentuated degree of small holes dispersed regularly but asymmetrically throughout the paper. These holes retain and accumulate the wet watercolour paint so that it takes longer for them to dry. They also make it difficult for the beginner to work with watercolour. However, for the professional, they offer a better control of moisture and of the watercolour paints themselves. In theory this paper takes away the brilliance associated with watercolour because each hole acts as a miniature shadow. However, in practice this darkening of the painting is hardly perceptible. All these papers have a front and a back which should be taken into account because the front has a better finish. The easiest way to know which side is which is that the grain in front is asymmetrical while on the back the grain has a more regular texture and can even form a small design or diagonal pattern.

Fig. 106 To distinguish between drawing paper and good-quality watercolour paper, machine- or man-made, manufacturers stamp their dry mark in relief in one of the sheet's corners, or they print their logo with the traditional watermark, which can be seen by holding the paper up to the light. (A list of internationally known manufacturers of drawing or watercolour paper appears on the next page.)

106

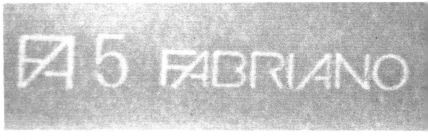

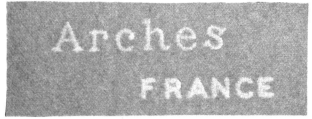

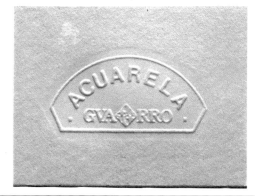

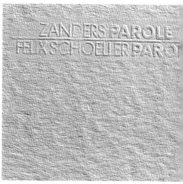

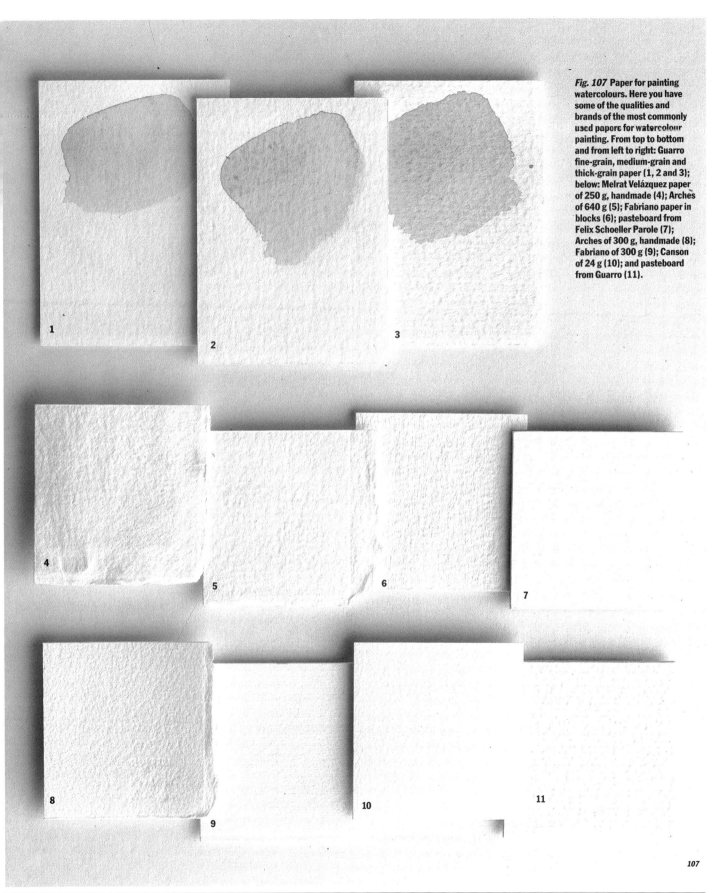

Fig. 107 Paper for painting watercolours. Here you have some of the qualities and brands of the most commonly used papers for watercolour painting. From top to bottom and from left to right: Guarro fine-grain, medium-grain and thick-grain paper (1, 2 and 3); below: Melrat Velázquez paper of 250 g, handmade (4); Arches of 640 g (5); Fabriano paper in blocks (6); pasteboard from Felix Schoeller Parole (7); Arches of 300 g, handmade (8); Fabriano of 300 g (9); Canson of 24 g (10); and pasteboard from Guarro (11).

107

Paper for watercolour painting

The unit used for measuring paper is the ream, which is 500 sheets, regardless of their size. The weight of the ream and its conversion to grams per square metre of paper determine how thick the paper actually is. We therefore have very light paper of 45 g, cardboard of 370 g, and other sizes in between.

You can buy paper in single sheets of specific measurements. Papers also come mounted on cardboard to eliminate the possibility of warping produced by the moisture of the watercolour paints and water. This paper is usually found in blocks of 20 or 25 sheets, glued to one another by all four corners, thus forming a compact unit that keeps its shape while one is painting.

Watercolour papers come in a large selection of sizes, from pads small enough to stick in your pocket, to large sheets for landscape painting. These sizes differ from country to country according to individual manufacturers. Britain has six different sizes from the small Royal Half (381 × 559 mm) to the large Antiquarian (787 × 1346 mm).

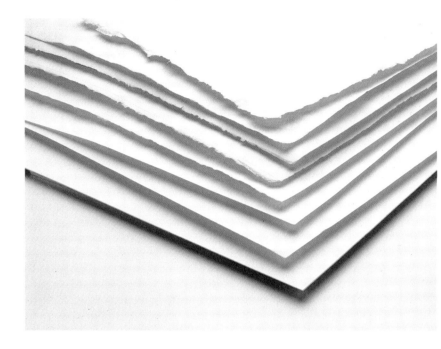

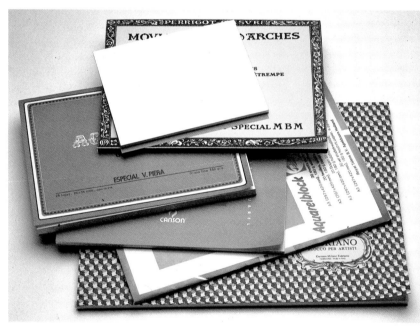

Manufacturers of quality paper for use in watercolour painting

Arches
Grumbacher
Strathmore
Winslow
Winsor & Newton
Watchung
R.W.S. (Royal Watercolour Society)
Guarro
Canson & Montgolfier
Fabriano
Schoeller Parole
Whatman

Fig. 108 Drawing paper or watercolour paper is sold in individual sheets, in sheets attached to cardboard, or in pads. Some of this paper has the irregular edges that indicate it is handmade. Other sheets have regular, even edges, an indication that they are machine-cut. Watercolour paper is also sold glued to thick, sturdy cardboard, eliminating the need to mount it on a board or use a back-up board. Drawing and watercolour papers are not, unfortunately, made in universally accepted standard sizes. But there is a great variety of sizes available to suit your needs and preferences.

Fig. 109 Most paper manufacturers make pads of 20 or 25 sheets attached to a thick piece of cardboard and 'bound' with plastic glue on all four sides, forming a compact block with the sheets taut, thus eliminating the problems of curling or warping caused by the moisture of the paints.

Stretching the paper

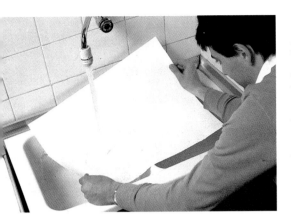

How to stretch the paper over the wooden board: To paint on a sheet as taut as a drum, without ripples, creases, or puckers caused by the watercolour's moisture, follow this procedure:

Fig. 110 Take the sheet of watercolour paper in both hands and hold it under running water, wetting it completely for about two minutes.

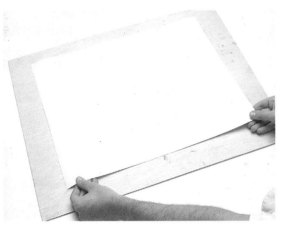

Fig. 111 Transfer the soaked paper immediately to a board and, while it is still wet, stretch it a bit with both hands.

Fig. 112 Immediately, without delay, tape one of the edges with a strip of gummed tape (paper on a roll 2 to 3 cm – or ³/₄" to 1" – wide).

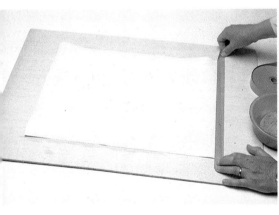

Fig. 113 Continue to tape all four sides of the sheet of paper with gummed tape and then leave everything to dry, keeping the board and paper in a horizontal position, without trying to speed the drying process with mechanical or forced means (in the sun, with dryers or heaters, etc.). After four or five hours, when the paper is dry, you will be able to paint on a smooth, taut surface that will not wrinkle no matter how much water your paints require.

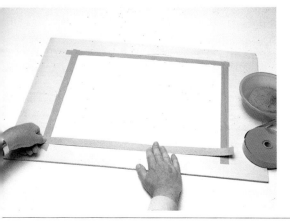

Fig. 114 The paper can also be stretched by moistening it and fastening it with metal staples from a staple gun such as decorators use.

Fig. 115 We should add, finally, that thanks to the remarkable thickness of watercolour papers sold today by most manufacturers, many professional artists skip stretching their paper and simply fasten it down with drawing-pins or metal clips, without wetting it first.

If you paint on paper weighing less than 200 g per square metre, you will find that the wetness of the watercolour will make the paper warp. To avoid this you must first mount and tense the paper. This is done by wetting the paper under the water tap and allowing it to stretch on a tabletop for a short while. Then the paper should be taped so that, as it dries and shrinks, it will remain flat and tense and not be affected by water.

In practice, however, most professionals skip the above-mentioned steps because they work with cardboard-like paper or with a block of mounted paper. Both of these eliminate the problems of warping. A professional friend of mine said: 'We hardly ever use the method of wetting the paper and taping it to the board. I just secure the paper with drawing-pins and it is ready.'

For those perfectionists who always like to use the correct methods, we present with figures and text the most frequently used methods of mounting watercolour paper.

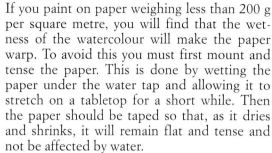

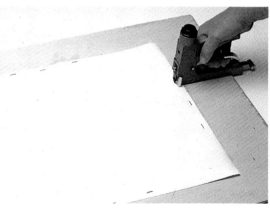

114

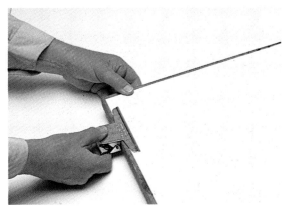

115

Watercolour colours

The colours used in watercolour painting are vegetable, mineral, or animal pigments mixed together with water and gum arabic. Honey and glycerine are added to prevent thick coats of paint from cracking as they dry, and a preservative is added to keep the paint fresh longer. You can paint using these four types:

Tablets of dry watercolours

Tablets of moist watercolours

Tubes of creamy watercolours

Jars of liquid watercolours

The tablets of dry watercolours are usually associated with an inexpensive product. They come in round button-like shapes and you have to use your brush firmly to obtain colour from them.

The tablets of moist watercolours are of professional quality and come in white plastic square boxes. To make the wet watercolours, the manufacturer increases the amounts of honey and glycerine and uses pigments of higher quality so that the colours dilute faster. Moist watercolours come in metallic boxes with 6, 12, 14 or 24 tablets, but they can also be bought individually.

Creamy watercolours in tubes are also of professional quality. They dilute instantaneously in water and give the same transparency as moist colours in tablets. They are available in boxes of 6 and 12 tubes and the ones with a capacity of 8 cm3 are the most popular. You can also buy refill tubes.

Lastly we have liquid watercolours, which come in glass jars. They are commonly used by illustrators and to a lesser extent in artistic watercolour painting to provide backgrounds or gradated washes.

The professional artist uses both moist watercolours in tablets and creamy watercolours in tubes. It is difficult to choose or give advice as to which one is the best. I think it depends on skill and what one is accustomed to. The finished product will be the same.

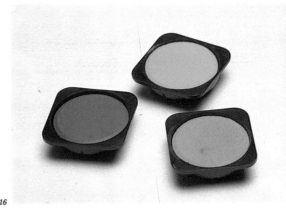

Fig. 116 Dry watercolours of an inexpensive type. These come in palette boxes with 6 or 12 colours. Some makers supply individual refills for separate colours.

116

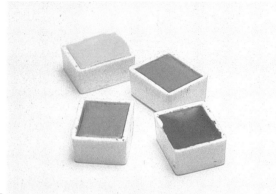

Fig. 117 Pans of moist watercolours, used by professionals. These are easily diluted in water and offer an extraordinary quality and intensity of colour. They come in palette boxes of 6, 12, 14 or 24 different colours, and refills for individual colours are available.

117

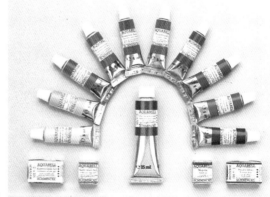

Fig. 118 Tubes of creamy watercolour also used by professionals. Their consistency is similar to that of oil paints. They have the advantage of dissolving immediately, with the same intensity and transparency as the moist watercolour tablets. They come in metal tubes in several sizes in palette boxes that generally hold 6 or 12 colours. Separate colours can also be obtained.

118

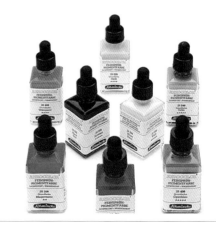

Fig. 119 Jars of liquid watercolour for professional use, especially for illustrators. These are similar to aniline pigments, with great strength and intensity, and are occasionally used in artistic watercolour painting for backgrounds or wide gradations of colour. They come in boxes of 6 or 12 bottles, and refills are available.

119

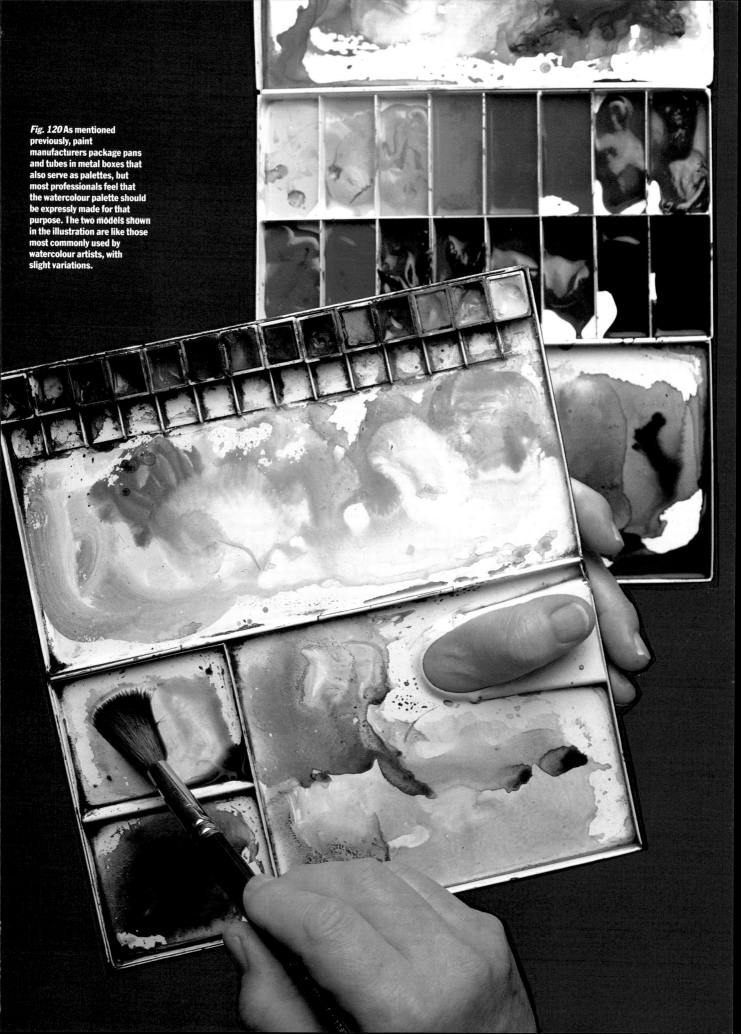

Fig. 120 As mentioned previously, paint manufacturers package pans and tubes in metal boxes that also serve as palettes, but most professionals feel that the watercolour palette should be expressly made for that purpose. The two models shown in the illustration are like those most commonly used by watercolour artists, with slight variations.

Watercolour colour chart

As you can see, this colour chart offers 81 colours plus China white. Another colour chart, by Winsor & Newton, offers 86 different colours including 14 yellows, 9 reds, 11 blues, and 10 greens. You do not need such a variety of colours to paint, but in art as well as in school, 'each teacher has a preferred text'. I use three classic blues: cobalt blue, ultramarine, and Prussian blue. The colour chart presents a large variety of colours enabling artists to study, experiment, and finally choose their own spectrum of colours. As we will see on the following pages, this does not clash with the idea of a standard palette used by professional artists.

Please note that here, as in all other colour ranges, two to five stars represent a greater or lesser degree of permanence, with five stars indicating the most permanent. We know that crimson, madder lakes, Prussian blue, olive green and all yellows except cadmium yellow have a low rating on the permanence scale. This is based on how long they last when the watercolour painting is exposed to direct light for some time. If you visit the National Gallery in London, you will appreciate watercolours painted over 150 years ago that have not lost the luminosity of their colours. The manufacturer's warning about how permanent colours really are is to be taken into account, but one should not worry excessively about it.

One must take into account the fact that watercolours lose between 10 and 20% of their intense colour between the time they are applied and the moment they dry. This colour can be regained through the use of fixatives. We will discuss this later on.

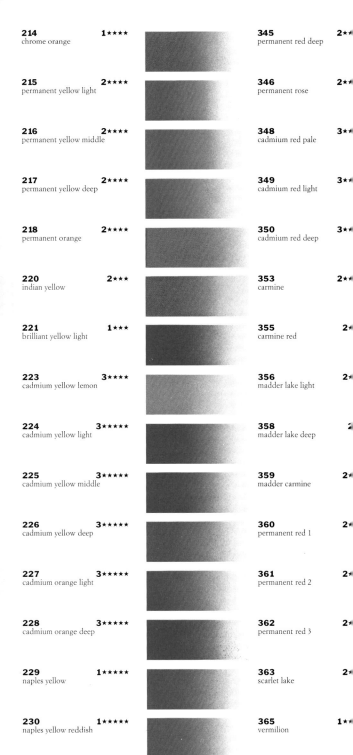

214 chrome orange	1★★★★	345 permanent red deep	2★★
215 permanent yellow light	2★★★★	346 permanent rose	2★★
216 permanent yellow middle	2★★★★	348 cadmium red pale	3★★
217 permanent yellow deep	2★★★★	349 cadmium red light	3★★
218 permanent orange	2★★★	350 cadmium red deep	3★★
220 indian yellow	2★★★	353 carmine	2★★
221 brilliant yellow light	1★★★	355 carmine red	2★
223 cadmium yellow lemon	3★★★★	356 madder lake light	2★
224 cadmium yellow light	3★★★★★	358 madder lake deep	2
225 cadmium yellow middle	3★★★★★	359 madder carmine	2★
226 cadmium yellow deep	3★★★★★	360 permanent red 1	2★
227 cadmium orange light	3★★★★★	361 permanent red 2	2★
228 cadmium orange deep	3★★★★★	362 permanent red 3	2★
229 naples yellow	1★★★★★	363 scarlet lake	2★
230 naples yellow reddish	1★★★★★	365 vermilion	1★★

121   **The figures 1, 2 and 3 indicate the price groups**

Fig. 121 **This colour chart has been reproduced and published with special permission from the firm of Schmincke.**

480 mountain blue	2★★★★	**516** green earth	1★★★★★	**650** english red deep	1★★★★★
481 cerulean blue	3★★★★	**517** green lake light	2★★★★	**651** golden ochre	1★★★★★
483 permanent violet	2★★★★	**518** green lake deep	2★★★★	**653** burnt green earth	1★★★★★
484 phthalo blue	2★★★★★	**519** phthalo green	2★★★★	**655** yellow ochre 1	1★★★★★
485 indigo	1★★★★	**520** hooker's green 1	2★★★★	**656** yellow ochre 2	1★★★★★
486 cobalt blue imit.	1★★★★	**521** hooker's green 2	2★★★★	**657** burnt yellow ochre	1★★★★★
487 cobalt blue light	3★★★★★	**522** cobalt green light	3★★★★★	**658** brown madder	2★★★
488 cobalt blue deep	3★★★★★	**523** cobalt green deep	3★★★★★	**660** raw sienna	1★★★★★
489 cobalt violet deep	3★★★★★	**524** may green	2★★★★	**661** burnt sienna	1★★★★★
490 magenta	1★★★	**525** olive green	1★★★★	**662** sepia brown tone	1★★★★
491 paris blue	1★★★★	**526** permanent green light	1★★★★	**663** sepia brown	1★★★★
492 prussian blue	1★★★★	**527** Permanent green deep	2★★★★★	**664** brown pink	1★★★★★
493 purple violet	2★★	**528** prussian green	1★★★★	**665** green pink	1★★★★★
494 ultramarine finest	2★★★★★	**529** sap green 1	2★★★★	**666** pozzuoli earth	1★★★★★
495 ultramarine violet	2★★★★★	**530** sap green 2	2★★★★	**667** raw umber	1★★★★★
496 ultramarine blue	1★★★★★	**531** vermilion green light	1★★★★	**668** burnt umber	1★★★★★
497 glowing violet	2★★	**532** vermilion green deep	1★★★★	**669** van dyck brown	1★★★★★

Watercolours commonly used

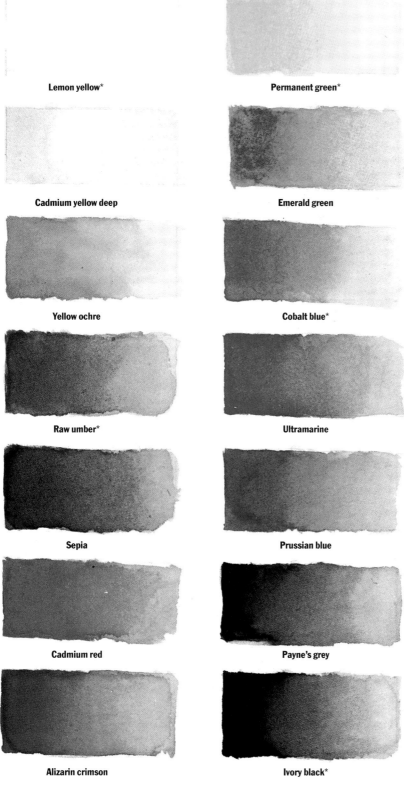

Lemon yellow*

Cadmium yellow deep

Yellow ochre

Raw umber*

Sepia

Cadmium red

Alizarin crimson

Permanent green*

Emerald green

Cobalt blue*

Ultramarine

Prussian blue

Payne's grey

Ivory black*

The English masters of the 18th century, Cozens, Girtin, and even Turner, used a limited palette of only five or six colours. You do not really need more than that to depict what surrounds you in nature. Actually, all you need to make new colours is the appropriate mixture of red, yellow and blue. However, let us be practical and see what other colours can enrich our palette.

While researching which colours are most frequently used, we found that most manufacturers sell watercolours in boxes of 17 tubes. The manufacturers answered our question and we are able to accept their choices because they know what sells. Their assortment of colours is not chosen haphazardly and most beginners start with this same range. With time, professionals determine their own palette, which will be adapted to their style and interpretation. Until you reach that point, let me explain a somewhat universal colour assortment.

The basic colours which are found in all prepackaged assortments are cadmium yellow or cadmium yellow deep, yellow ochre, cadmium red, alizarin crimson, emerald green, ultramarine, and ivory black. You just have to add some blues and a grey like Payne's grey, which to me is an indispensable colour. The following is a list of the most commonly used colours:

Fig. 122 Following a logical line of reasoning we believe that this selection of colours represents the most commonly used by the professional artist. To limit the number even further, the colours indicated with an asterisk could also be eliminated: lemon yellow, raw umber, permanent green, cobalt blue, and ivory black.

WATERCOLOURS COMMONLY USED

*Lemon yellow**	*Permanent green**
Cadmium yellow deep	*Emerald green*
Yellow ochre	*Cobalt blue**
*Raw umber**	*Ultramarine*
Sepia	*Prussian blue*
Cadmium red	*Payne's grey*
Alizarin crimson	*Ivory black**

122

Tempera colours (gouache)

Gouache or tempera colours have a great similarity to watercolours and therefore merit a discussion in this book. Temperas are diluted with water and you need the same type of brushes and paper as you do with watercolours. The main difference between temperas and watercolours is that the former has a larger quantity of pigment or coloured earth, the binding agent is glue, and the lighter tones are obtained by the admixture of white pigment.

Because of this difference we observe the following:

Watercolours have a distinctive transparency. Temperas are characterized by their opaqueness.

Temperas are opaque, thick, covering paints that allow you to use light colours over dark colours. If you dilute temperas with a lot of water, the resulting product is somewhat similar to watercolours. I would like to emphasize that the major characteristics of temperas are their opaqueness and their matt finish. They remind one of some oil paintings.

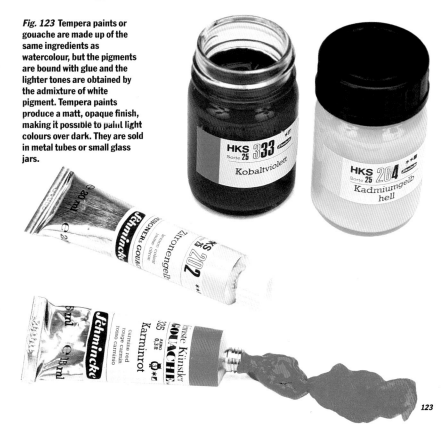

Fig. 123 Tempera paints or gouache are made up of the same ingredients as watercolour, but the pigments are bound with glue and the lighter tones are obtained by the admixture of white pigment. Tempera paints produce a matt, opaque finish, making it possible to paint light colours over dark. They are sold in metal tubes or small glass jars.

123

124

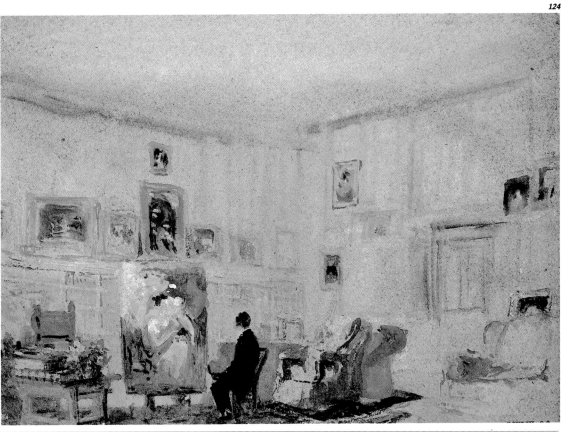

Fig. 124 Joseph Mallord William Turner, *Petworth Interior*, sketch on grey paper, British Museum, London.

The palette box

Most of the metallic boxes that watercolours come in also double as a palette for mixing colours. These boxes are made of iron enamelled in white. They have a series of concave divisions that are square or rectangular and allow you to mix the different colours separately. In some boxes you can separate the tray with the paints and this leaves you with a mixing palette of two or three trays. Some varieties even have a hole for your thumb or a ring that allows you to hold the palette with one hand while you mix colours with your other hand.

Professionals normally use palettes like the one shown on page 63. There are two styles, each suited to a different type of watercolour. This allows you to use the palette most appropriate to moist watercolours, tablets, or creamy watercolours. If you do not have a palette, a white china plate will do. Many artists also use an 'auxiliary palette' which is a piece of white watercolour paper where they try out the desired effect before applying it to the painting.

All colour charts and many of these palette boxes also have a thick white, similar in texture to temperas, called China white. What is the reason for and use of this white? After all, the basic principle of using watercolour is to work with the paper's white. This question must remain unanswered. There may be some unorthodox artists who use it to create a certain play of light in profiles or reflections, or for the white of a ship's ropes or small white wild flowers. But it should not be used – it is like cheating! As you will see from your reading of this book there are other methods that can be used to achieve the effects, reflections and so on created by white, without breaking the rules of good watercolour painting.

Fig. 125 **Miniature set with case, palette box, brush, and a small jar for water (the closed case measures 9 x 11 cm, 3.5" x 4.5"; it can be carried in a pocket with a small pad of paper to do notes while travelling in the country, etc.**

Fig. 126 **Palette box with dry watercolour cakes of the grade called scholastic. Underneath the tray of colours there is a ring that can be used to support the box with the thumb as if it were a palette.**

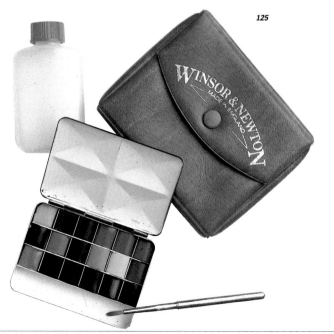

125

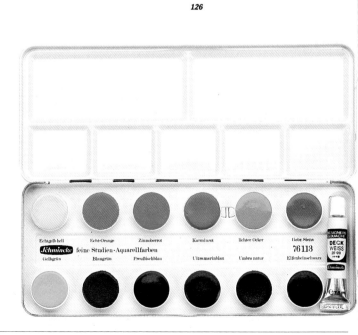

126

Fig. 127 Large palette box with 24 pans of moist watercolours. The tray with the colours can be separated from the metal box, leaving more space to mix colours. In the centre tray a rivet (A) can be seen which secures the ring for holding the palette with the thumb. When the session is over, the tray with paints is replaced in the box and the set can be folded and closed.

Fig. 128 Palette box with 12 tubes of professional-quality watercolour. The tubes can be taken out of the box and the box can be used as a palette. It has a rivet to secure the ring for holding the palette.

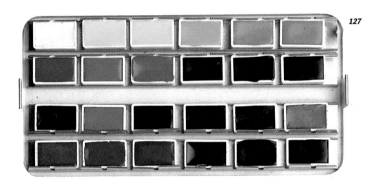

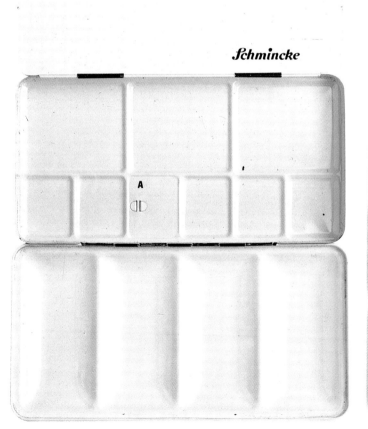

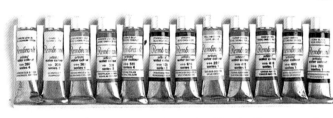

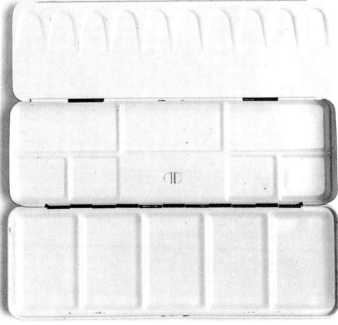

Moisteners, masking fluid, fixatives, and more

129

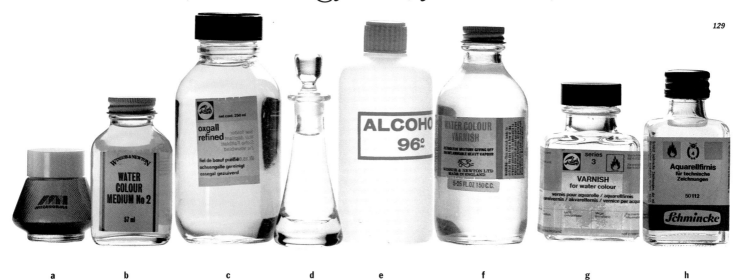

a   b   c   d   e   f   g   h

The only liquid that is absolutely necessary for working in watercolour is tap water. There are, however, a few liquids, such as moisteners and astringents, that improve the quality of the water you will be working with. There are also products such as masking fluid that allow you to achieve special effects. The following paragraphs describe these products and their characteristics.

Masking fluid: This product is especially designed to mask off the small areas that create a special brilliance, a twinkle, or a linear form such as a tree trunk or a thin branch. You apply it with a brush and allow it to dry. This creates a waterproof film which you can later remove with your finger or a normal rubber. To apply the masking fluid, use an old brush that can be cleaned with ethyl alcohol. Open spaces can also be masked off prior to painting by using white wax.

Medium number 2: This is a solution of acidified gum that should be added to your water with an eye-dropper. It will eliminate all oily traces from the water and give the colours greater intensity, shine and transparency.

Refined oxgall: This is a moistening product that you mix with the water to increase the clinging power and flow of the colours. Pour a small amount of the refined oxgall into half a litre of water.

Glycerine: When you paint outdoors on a very sunny or windy day your watercolours will dry faster than expected. This problem can be avoided by adding some glycerine to your water. This method of prolonging the drying time should also be used when you need the painting to dry slowly.

96° alcohol: Sometimes you will find that you need to speed up the drying process. This usually happens on wet, rainy days or if you are painting by the seashore. The solution to this problem is to add some alcohol (96° proof) to the water. It is known that 18th-century British artists added cognac or gin to their water instead of pure alcohol. This could make you wonder what they actually did at Monro's school!

Varnish: Almost all manufacturers of watercolours produce a special varnish. This product is used by some artists to protect and add brilliance to their paintings. Many professionals do not believe in using varnishes because watercolours should have a matt finish. I know that some artists add the varnish in layers and only in certain areas, particularly on dark colours so they will appear less intense and offer less contrast when they dry out. We recommend that you do not use many layers of varnish in order to avoid giving the watercolour the shiny finish of a plastic-covered print.

Fig. 129 Here is a series of auxiliary products for watercolour painting. From left to right: a) masking fluid for masking off open spaces prior to painting; b) medium to prepare the water; c) refined oxgall, as a moistening agent; d) glycerine to mix with the water and slow the drying of the paint; e) alcohol of 96° proof to mix with the water to speed drying; f), g), and h) varnish for the watercolour once it is completed. From a professional point of view, the masking fluid, medium and watercolour varnish are the most essential.

Water

There is no uniform criterion among artists on how many (one or two) or what type (glass or plastic) water jars should be used when painting outdoors or in the studio. Some artists use two jars, the first to loosen the paint and the second to wash the brush. Another school of thought believes that when you work with one jar you are 'dirtying' the brush and this will ultimately help you by making your colours blend better. Artists who work outdoors like to use plastic jars for obvious reasons. They do not want to risk breaking a glass one. Personally, I am no lover of plastic and always use glass containers.

Regardless of the material you choose, the jar must hold between half a litre to a full litre (a pint to a quart) of water and have a wide mouth. Marmalade or mayonnaise jars fill all these requirements.

It is quite useful to have a hairdryer in your studio to quickly dry a specific area of your painting. How can you solve this problem outdoors where there are no electrical outlets? Many artists carry cigarette lighters with them and place the flame near the wet section to make it dry faster.

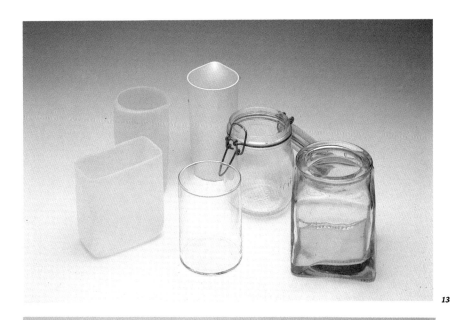

130

Fig. 130 Here are some suitable containers for water: glass for the studio and plastic to carry along and avoid breakage. In either case, the container should hold at least a litre (quart) of water and it should have a wide mouth.

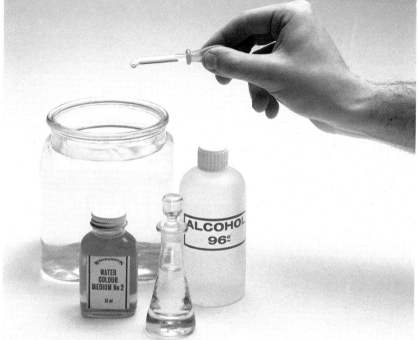

131

Fig. 131 The liquids on the preceding page, auxiliaries to watercolour painting, must be mixed with water with the exception of the masking fluid, which is applied directly to the watercolour with a brush. For mixing with water, it is a good idea to have an eye-dropper on hand and to establish for yourself the exact quantities needed.

Fig. 132 When working in the studio, a method commonly used by professionals to speed the drying of the watercolours while working is to use an electric hairdryer on the wet area.

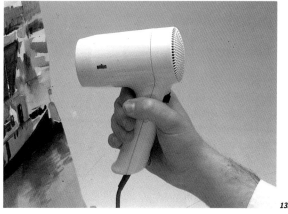

132

Brushes for watercolour painting

The brushes used for painting watercolours have a wooden handle covered with shellac to which a metal band is attached. This band serves to hold the hair itself in place.

Brush quality is determined by the animal hair used. The following types are available:

Sable-hair brushes

Mongoose-hair brushes

Ox-hair brushes

Japanese deer-hair brushes

Synthetic brushes

The best brush available is made with sable hair. The hair comes from the tails of Kolinsky sables that live in Russia and China. The high price of these brushes is due to the fact that it is very difficult to make them. In order to lower the price, some manufacturers sell a brush made from a mixture of red sable and ox hair (which comes from the ox's ears). One step down in quality we have mongoose-, squirrel-, or ox-hair brushes. The Japanese round brushes are excellent for painting oriental-style watercolours called Sumi-e, but they are no better than other brushes. There is another Japanese brush, fan-shaped and perfect for painting rays of sunlight and wide graduated washes, that is very inexpensive. In the last few years there have been many synthetic brushes. These are quite inexpensive and well shaped, but cannot compare with the qualities found in sable-hair brushes. The sable brush has sponge-like characteristics: it can absorb water and colour, bend to the slightest manual pressure, and yet maintain its perfect point.

Watercolour brushes come in different widths and are numbered from 00 to 1 to 2...up to 14 for sable-hair brushes and 24 for ox-hair brushes. These numbers are usually printed on the brush handle. The handle with the metal band measures about 20 cm in length.

To paint in watercolour, you need three sable-hair brushes in sizes 8, 12 and 14 and a size 24 ox-hair brush. We also recommend the use of a wide Japanese brush, a synthetic round sponge and a small natural sponge.

Fig. 133 This is the minimum assortment of brushes needed for watercolour painting: three sable brushes, nos. 8, 12 and 14, and an ox-hair brush, no. 24.

133

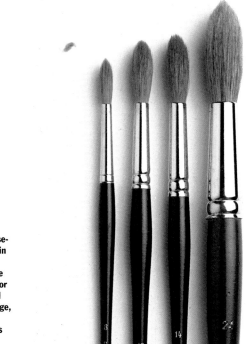

Fig. 134 Here are some additional brushes to complement those in the preceding figure: a Japanese-style hake brush, a sponge in the shape of a roller, and a small natural sponge. These three items are necessary for achieving backgrounds and gradated washes. The sponge, which by the way must be natural and not synthetic, is also used to blot water or, occasionally, to paint.

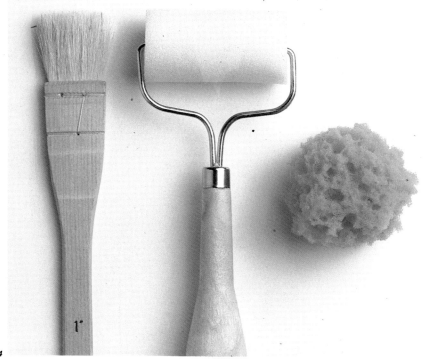

134

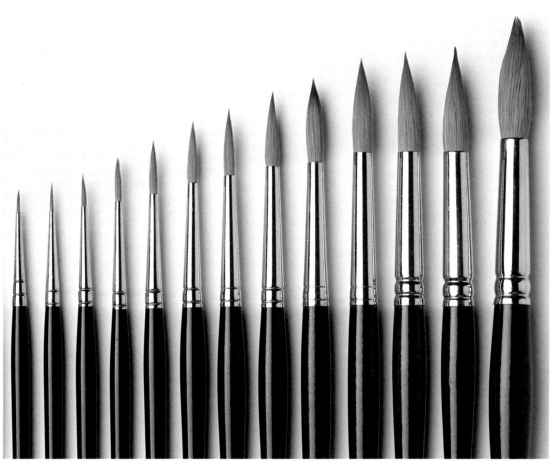

Fig. 135 This picture shows a complete assortment of sable brushes, from numbers 00 to 10, plus 12 and 14.

Fig. 136 Other kinds of brushes available besides sable include the following, from left to right: 1 and 2: Wash brushes, typically French, of squirrel's hair, suitable for backgrounds and gradations. 3 and 4: Japanese brushes with bamboo handles and deer's hair. 5 and 6: Round synthetic fibre brushes for students. 7: Mongoose-hair brush, stiffer than sable. 8: Special sable brush for drawing fine lines. 9: Fan-shaped boar's-hair brush for rubbing and scraping. 10 and 11: Ox-hair brushes used by many professionals, especially the higher-numbered ones.

135

136

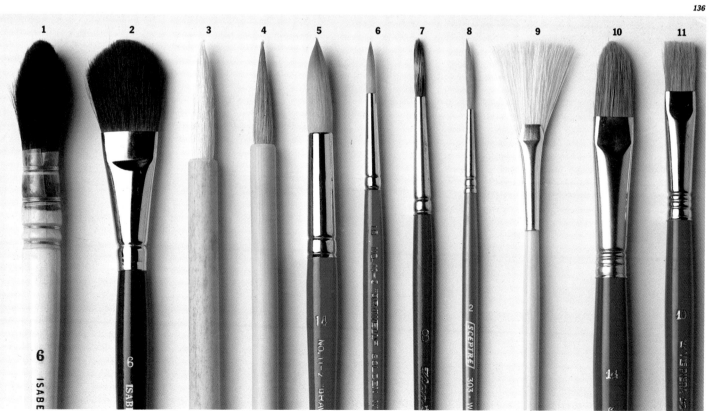

Brushes: their use and care

In watercolour as in oil painting, there are two ways of holding the brush. The first is just like a pencil only higher up and the second is with the handle in your fingertips (see figs. 137, 138, and 139). In both cases the distance is greater than the one normally used with a pencil, but it allows you to move the brush more freely, lengthens the arm, and lets you look at the painting from afar.

We have already said that brushes are expensive but with proper care a sable-hair brush can last for years. The following rules should be carefully observed:

1. Never allow your brushes to stay in water for hours.
2. When you are done using them wash your brushes carefully with soap and water if necessary.
3. Rinse them well and drain out the excess water.
4. Then with your fingertips, or better still between pursed lips, shape the point and allow it to dry in a jar with the hairs facing up.

When you are painting outdoors do not carry your brushes in your pocket or throw them in a box with other materials, a procedure which would be fatal to the hairs of the brush. Carefully roll the brushes in some cardboard or other stiff paper that will keep their shape, so that the brushes are immobile and the hairs protected from damage.

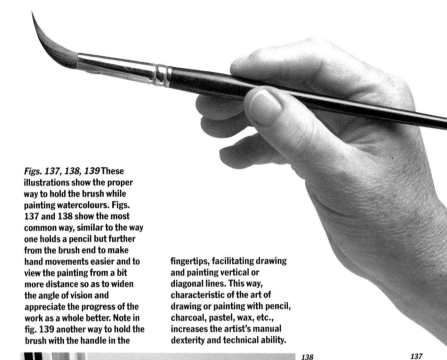

Figs. 137, 138, 139 These illustrations show the proper way to hold the brush while painting watercolours. Figs. 137 and 138 show the most common way, similar to the way one holds a pencil but further from the brush end to make hand movements easier and to view the painting from a bit more distance so as to widen the angle of vision and appreciate the progress of the work as a whole better. Note in fig. 139 another way to hold the brush with the handle in the fingertips, facilitating drawing and painting vertical or diagonal lines. This way, characteristic of the art of drawing or painting with pencil, charcoal, pastel, wax, etc., increases the artist's manual dexterity and technical ability.

137

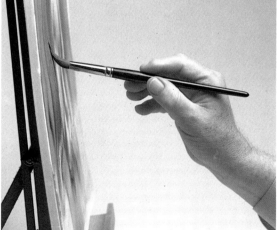

138

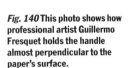

Fig. 140 This photo shows how professional artist Guillermo Fresquet holds the handle almost perpendicular to the paper's surface.

139

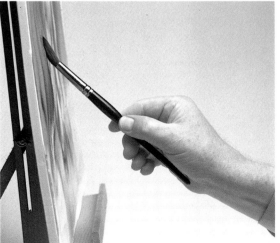

140

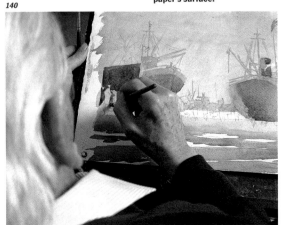

Other materials

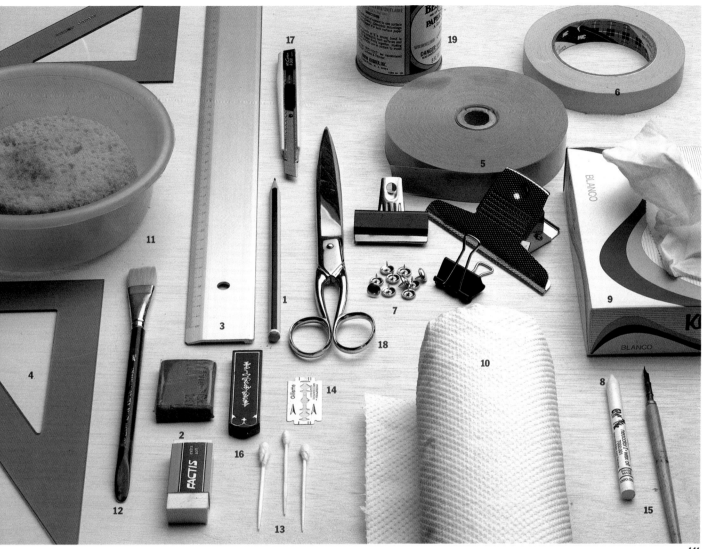

141

Fig. 141 In addition to basic materials such as paints, brushes, and paper, the watercolour artist uses a series of auxiliary tools that are shown in this picture. Their description and uses follow. **1:** A regular no.2B lead pencil for watercolour drawing, or a higher quality HB pencil. **2:** Normal soft white rubber and one in dark grey, or one of similar quality to clean with. **3:** Metal ruler 50 to 70 cm (20" to 30"). With a metal ruler, any type of blade can be used for cutting without danger of ruining the ruler. **4:** T-square

(not shown) and triangles. **5:** Roll of gummed tape, 2 or 3 cm (1" or 1¹/₂") wide for mounting and stretching the paper as explained in figs. 110 to 113. **6:** Roll of adhesive masking tape, used to frame the painting before beginning to work. The tape is positioned like a frame, and comes off easily when finished, leaving the edges perfectly clean and sharp. **7:** Drawing-pins to hold down and stretch the paper when it is thick, thus avoiding the laborious traditional mounting and stretching with damp paper, gummed tape,

etc. **8:** A stick of white wax to mask off areas to be left blank before painting as will be explained later in the text. **9:** Tissues to blot the brush before and after rinsing and to absorb moisture, water, or gouache in small or large areas. **10:** Roll of paper towels, for the same use as the tissues, especially for blotting or squeezing out the brush when it is full of water or paint. **11:** Plastic dish and moistened synthetic sponge to remove some of the colour or moisture from the brush by holding it against the sponge.

12: Brush with a special bevelled plastic handle to scratch and draw or to make light-coloured, open spaces while the painted area is still moist (this type of brush is imported from Japan). **13:** Cotton swabs for use in freshly painted areas, while still damp, to dry and absorb paint, leaving light-coloured areas. **14:** Razor blade to scratch and open up spaces when the watercolour has dried. **15:** Holder and nibs for drawing with Indian ink. The following items should also be mentioned: reed, black

ballpoint, and black or grey finepoint marker, used interchangeably by the professional artist on occasion to draw lines or emphasize forms during the final stages or finishing touches of a watercolour. **16:** Indian ink in stick form (it may also be liquid, in a normal jar) for drawing with the pen or reed. **17:** Utility knife for cutting paper with the aid of the metal ruler. **18:** Large scissors for cutting paper. **19:** Container of Cow gum or special glue to glue paper to cardboard or wood before or after painting.

Other materials

Watercolour painting demands a great many materials and tools that the artist must carry with him whenever he paints outdoors. It therefore becomes important to have a box, case or bag in which one will be able to carry colours, brushes, palette, sponge, paper towels, jars, liquids, and a long list of other things. In view of this need many manufacturers produce elegant cases with basic materials but which, despite their high prices, do not entirely solve the problem.

The solution would be a box or case for oil painting which you can adapt for using with watercolour, or an easel with a case incorporated such as the one seen in fig. 101, or the special one in fig. 142, reproduced here by courtesy of Ceferino Olivé, a professional watercolour artist.

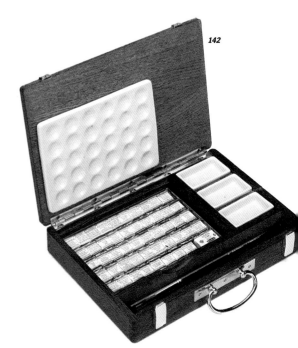

Fig. 142 Beautiful case of varnished hardwood, with metal catches and decorations, for carrying paints, brushes, ceramic palettes, and other materials and tools when painting outdoors.

Fig. 143 Typical case for oil paints, adapted for carrying watercolour materials and tools.

Fig. 144 This is a box designed by the professional watercolourist Ceferino Olivé. It measures approximately 75 x 52 cm (30" x 21"), making it possible to carry watercolour paper, a piece of plywood, a folding easel with tripod and a plastic water jar, in addition to paints, palette, brushes, sponge, etc.

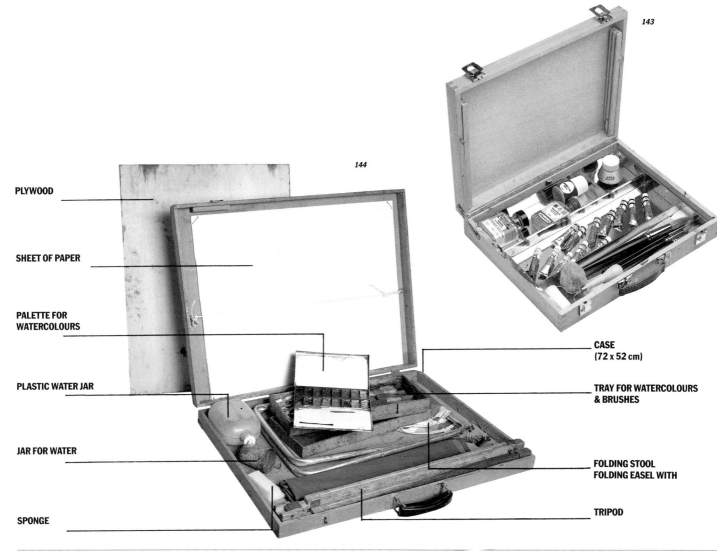

PLYWOOD

SHEET OF PAPER

PALETTE FOR WATERCOLOURS

PLASTIC WATER JAR

JAR FOR WATER

SPONGE

CASE (72 x 52 cm)

TRAY FOR WATERCOLOURS & BRUSHES

FOLDING STOOL
FOLDING EASEL WITH

TRIPOD

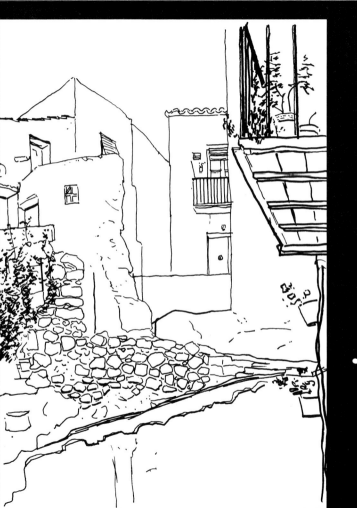

Drawing:
the
foundation
of
watercolour

Cube, cylinder, sphere

Peter Paul Rubens, aside from painting close to a thousand beautiful paintings, and producing thousands of drawings and sketches, also wrote a book. The book was titled : *Treatise on the Human Figure*, and in it Rubens dictated a definitive norm in the art of drawing. Rubens said:

'The basic structure of the human figure may be reduced to the cube, the circle, and the triangle.'

Almost 250 years later, Paul Cézanne reiterated Rubens's idea, amplifying it to include all subjects in nature. He told it to Monet, to Pissarro, to Vuillard, to Picasso, to everyone; in April 1904 he put it in writing in a letter to his friend Emile Bernard the painter. Cézanne told him:

'Everything in Nature is modelled after three fundamental shapes: the cube, the cylinder, and the sphere. It is necessary to learn how to draw these simple figures so that afterwards one will be able to do whatever one wants.'

This is right, it's true.

If you are able to draw a cube (or rectangular prism), a cylinder, and a sphere perfectly well, you will be able to draw everything you are capable of seeing: the table, the chair, the glass, your hand, your face, a figure, a landscape, everything – because these and all forms may be fitted into and structured upon these 'simple figures'.

May I request that you draw these basic figures. In doing so, you will be practising all the problems of the art of drawing, namely: the perspective of the forms, the problems of dimensions and proportions, chiaroscuro (the effects of light and shadow). After having finished this study, try to draw perceived or imaginary shapes starting out from the cube, the cylinder, and the sphere. I have done it here as if I were just beginning, remembering Rubens and Cézanne. I can assure you that, despite being so simple, the experience is magnificent.

Fig. 146 As Cézanne said, 'all the forms of all objects can be reduced to cubes, cylinders and spheres'. To draw these basic forms with a lead pencil or charcoal is, without a doubt, an extremely worthwhile exercise.

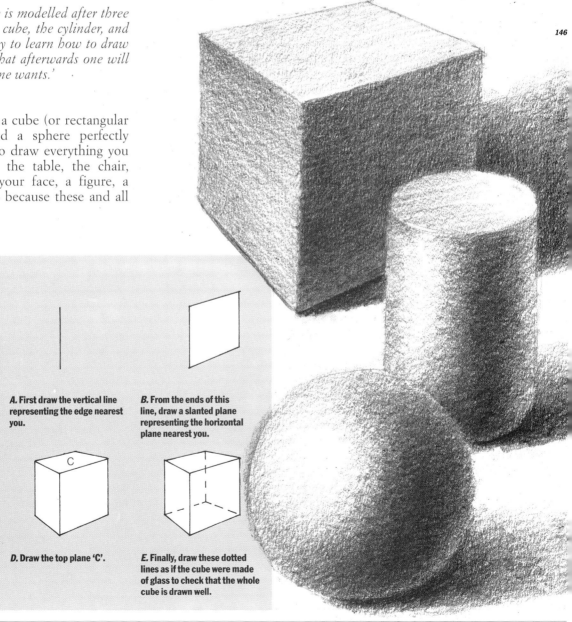

146

147

Fig. 147 The cube or rectangular prism helps indicate a linear or oblique perspective, the rules of which we will review in the following pages. For the moment, let us review how to draw a cube from an oblique perspective.

A. First draw the vertical line representing the edge nearest you.

B. From the ends of this line, draw a slanted plane representing the horizontal plane nearest you.

C. Next, draw the lateral plane 'B'.

D. Draw the top plane 'C'.

E. Finally, draw these dotted lines as if the cube were made of glass to check that the whole cube is drawn well.

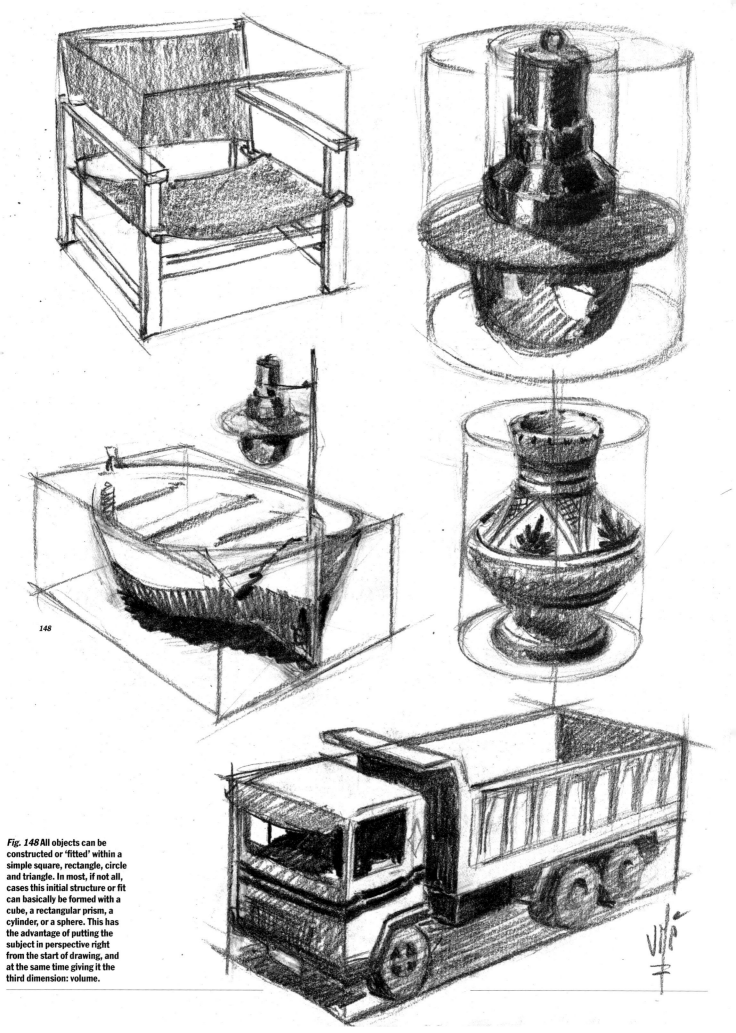

Fig. 148 All objects can be constructed or 'fitted' within a simple square, rectangle, circle and triangle. In most, if not all, cases this initial structure or fit can basically be formed with a cube, a rectangular prism, a cylinder, or a sphere. This has the advantage of putting the subject in perspective right from the start of drawing, and at the same time giving it the third dimension: volume.

148

Fit, dimensions, proportions

John Singer Sargent, the virtuoso American portrait painter, renowned for his extraordinary watercolours, taught the following basic principle repeatedly to his students at the Royal Academy:

'You must always cultivate the power of observation.'

This is the key to constructing: the ability to calculate dimensions and proportions in order to draw. In a word: calculate, observe, compare, resolve. Let us take the example of the two roses and small vase drawn on the following page. With the aid of a pencil, the handle of a brush or a ruler, we first calculate the total height and width of the model (fig. 149). Realizing that, in this case, the height and width are practically the same, we draw a square, into which we may 'fit' the model (fig. 150).

Now we compare some basic dimensions: the height of the small vase in relation to the total height of the model (A-A); the width of the flower on the upper right corner compared to the total width (B-b-B) of the picture. We try next to reduce and condense the box of the model. Assisted by the above calculations, we find a shape which conforms to these calculations (fig. 151). Next we imagine vertical and horizontal outlines which locate the shapes, distances, and proportions within the larger form (fig. 152). And at the same time, we study the spatial shapes of the empty spaces as in A, B, and C of fig. 153. Thus, we have taken on the problem, as Sargent described it, observing the model, calculating, and comparing.

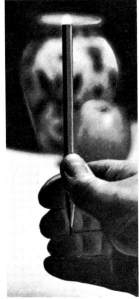

149

Fig. 149 The model's basic structure or 'fit' is determined by measuring and comparing its height with its width. These measurements are taken facing the model, arm extended, holding a pencil or brush handle in your hand. First the pencil is held vertically, to measure the height, then horizontally to measure width. Finally the relationship between the two measurements is calculated – for example, they may both be the same, or one may be double the other.

Fig. 150 Measuring the subject with a pencil or brush makes it possible to find its proportions, facilitating its 'fit'.

Fig. 151 Here, I can draw a more definite structure or fit within the rectangular box.

Fig. 152 In this or any model, vertical or horizontal lines can be imagined that pass through basic or reference points and allow you to situate and proportion forms, filling out the drawing.

Fig. 153 Another aid for estimating sizes and proportions is to try to imagine solid shapes in the open spaces (A, B, C). These are like moulds that allow you to situate and define the actual shapes of your subject.

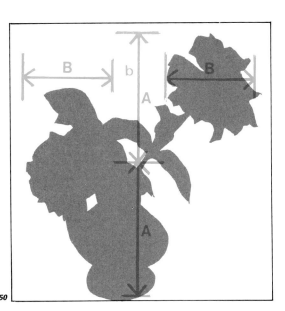

150

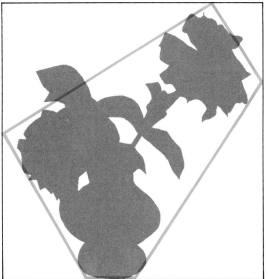

151

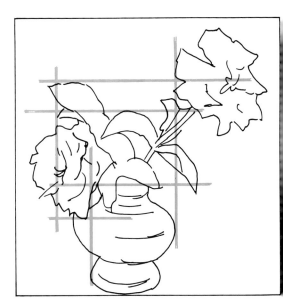

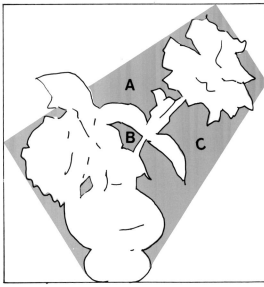

Fig. 154 It is certainly not easy to reduce the shape of a model like this one to the form of a cube, but in this, as in all cases, the drawing can be started with an overall box, square or rectangle, measured beforehand with a pencil or brush as explained in fig. 149. This basic form is then further broken down into smaller boxes inside the first one, with imaginary reference lines and points, and by trying to 'see' shapes corresponding to the empty spaces, as explained in figs. 150 to 153 above. Studying the composition, dimensions, and proportions of examples like this one is a good exercise to keep your ability to draw and paint with watercolours sharp at all times.

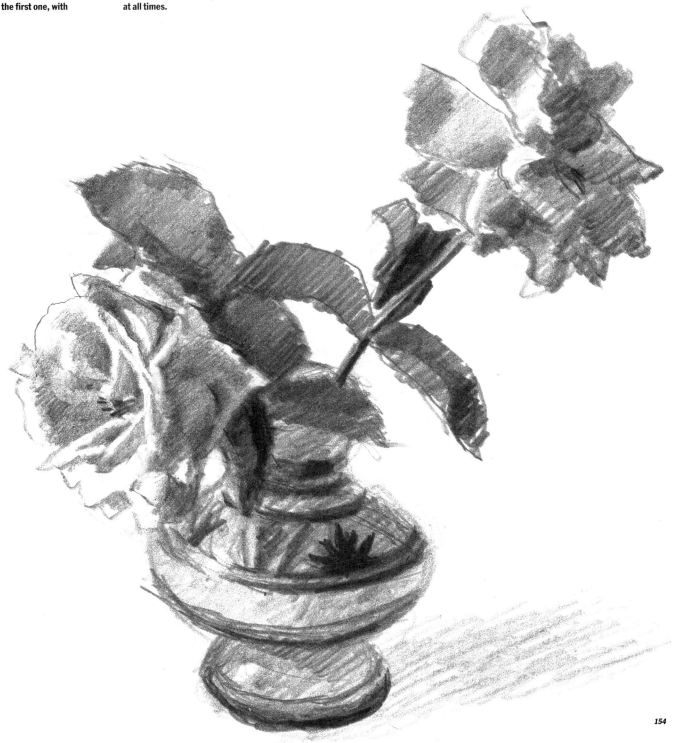

154

Light and shade: tonal values

Camille Corot, the artist and teacher, instructed Pissarro: 'You are an artist, you don't need any advice save this: you must study value above all.'

Values are tones; different tonalities are promoted by the effects of light and shade. Thanks to variation in values, we may represent the third dimension, that is the volume of forms, in drawing. One has to know the effects of light and shade – clarity, brilliance, shadow, projected shadow, chiaroscuro, and reflected light (fig. 155) – in order to evaluate tone. And one has to observe and compare carefully and constantly in order to achieve a perfect evaluation.

To evaluate is to compare.

To evaluate is to mentally classify the tonalities and hues of a form, constantly comparing in order to determine which tones are more obscure, which most clear, and which are the intermediate tones.

On this theme there is practice procedure you may carry out right now: build yourself a cylinder out of thick white cardboard or Bristol board and draw your own hand holding the cylinder as I have done here. Study the effects of the light and shadow, evaluate how the tones model the forms.

Fig. 155 Look at this drawing of a hand, my hand, as a study of the effects of light and shade and of tonal values, and note that the values are resolved with a limited spectrum of tones and that the volume of objects depends on the following effects:

A. LIGHT: illuminated areas where the colour is the model's own 'local' colour.

B. BRILLIANCE: obtained through contrast. Remember that 'a white is whiter the darker the tone surrounding it is'.

C. ACCENT: the darkest part of the projected shadow, between the penumbra or cast shadow and the reflected light.

D. REFLECTED LIGHT: on the extreme edges of the shaded part. It is accented when there is a light–coloured object next to the subject.

E. CHIAROSCURO: intermediate zone between the illuminated area and the area in shadow. The term chiaroscuro can be defined as light in shade.

F. CAST SHADOW: the whole shaded area opposite the illuminated section.

G. PROJECTED SHADOW: the shadow that appears on the surface that the body is resting on (I have not drawn it here).

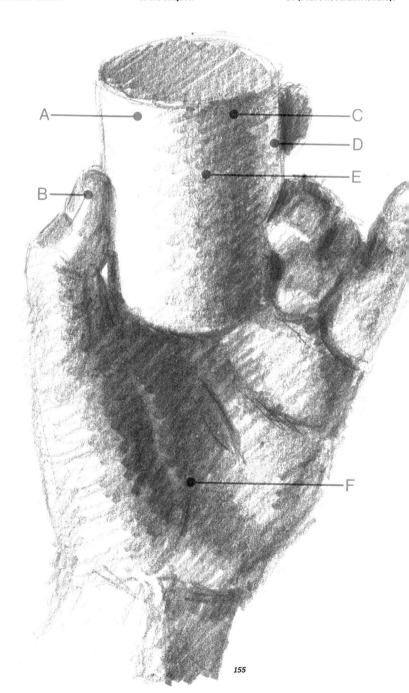

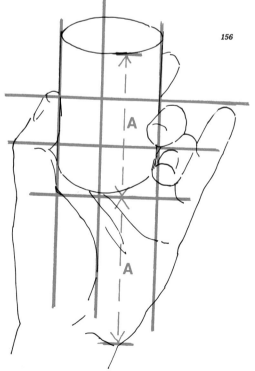

156

155

Doing a quick sketch

Here is a practical exercise, especially designed for the watercolour painter, the achievement of which demands – from my point of view – remarkable technical understanding and drawing ability.

I would like you to draw rapidly, without previous preparation, without outlines, boxes or other structures, using a permanent medium such as ink which doesn't allow you to go back and rework or erase. A fine-point marker or a black pen would be fine. Draw one or several objects seen from different angles – one of your own hands, for instance – and carry out the drawing linearly, without lights or shadows, using only a minimum of lines to represent the basic shapes and the most important details of the model. I know that it's not easy, but I believe that it is useful and applicable if you will keep in mind the reasons I will explain to you on the following page.

Fig. 157 **Your other hand may be the best model for this freehand sketch. Try it; it is an excellent exercise for people like you who want to learn to paint in watercolour.**

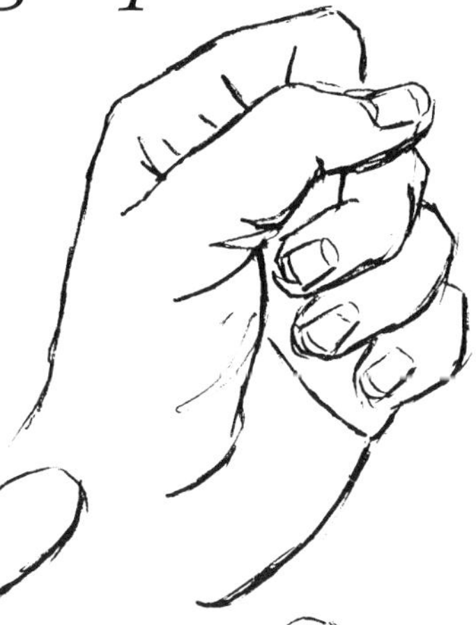

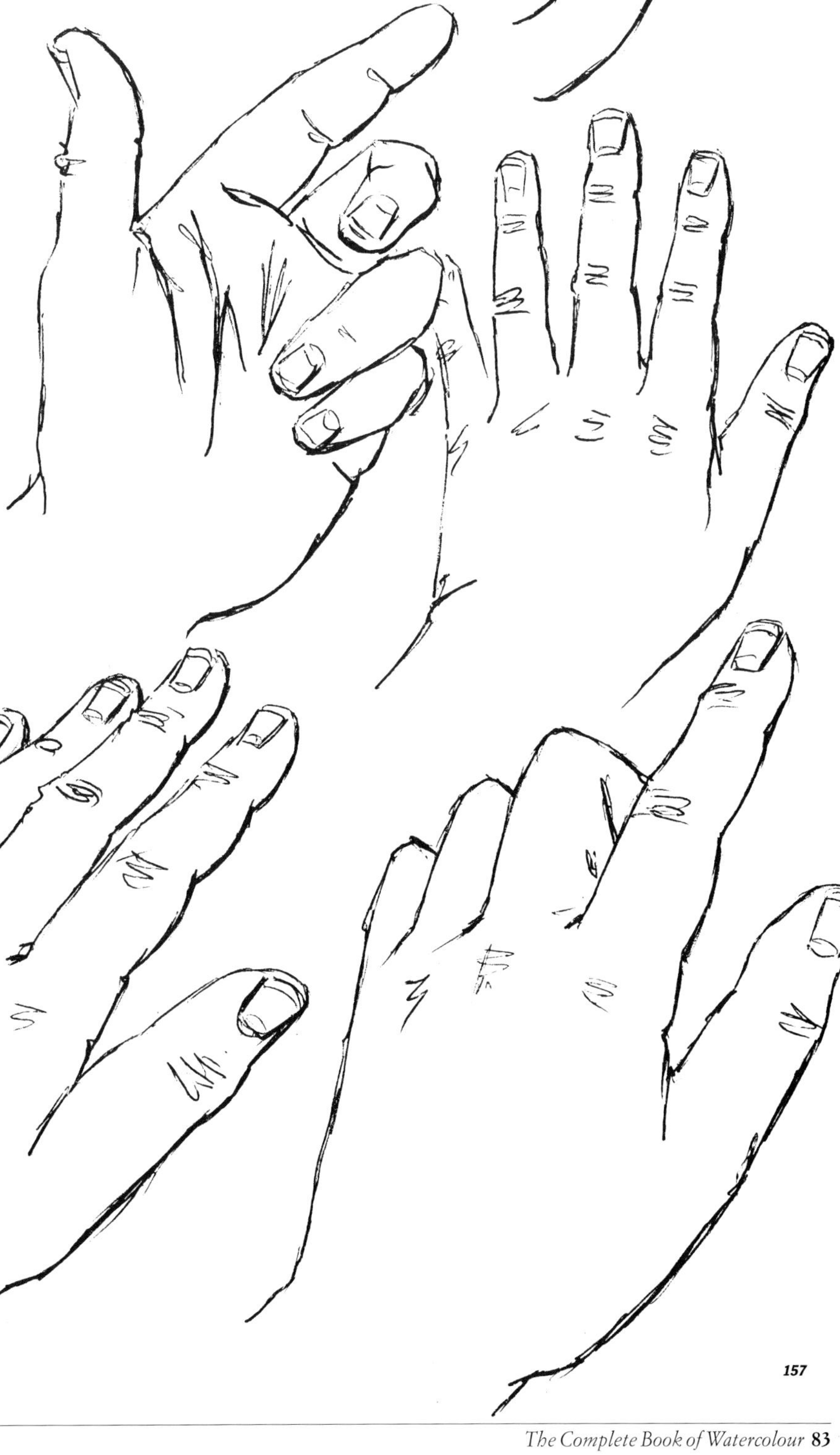

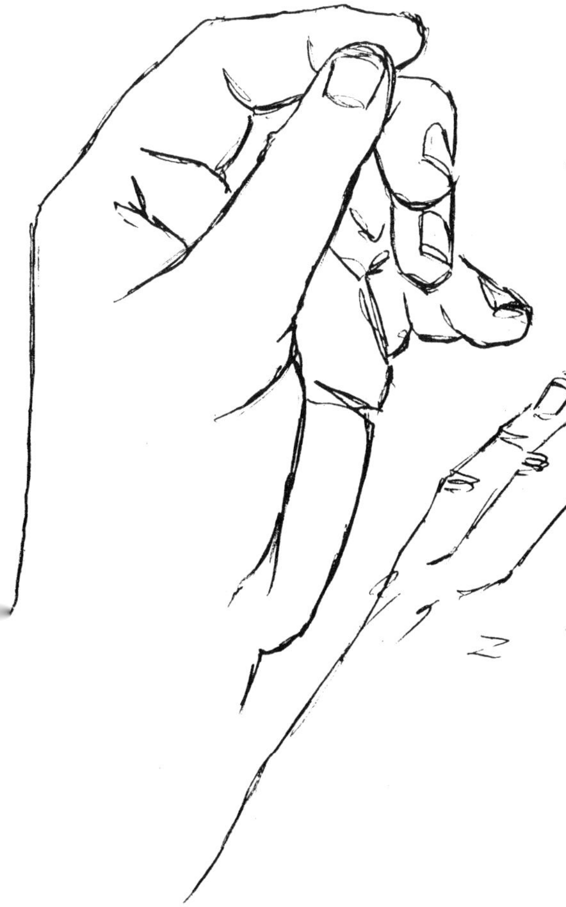

157

A special exercise

I assume that you are at home, sitting at your work table, or in your reading armchair, perhaps in your study. At any rate, may I ask you to look up in front of you and consider the possibility of drawing whatever you see before you. It may be necessary for you to go to another room in the house which offers more interesting drawing possibilities. At any rate, once you have found a setting which motivates you, draw it in a linear manner, eliminating light and shadow, and using a black pen.

I created this exercise at my work table in order to practise and explain how a drawing should be done from which you will paint a watercolour. Such a drawing should, first of all, be accurate and detailed so that later, while painting, you will not get lost. When painting,

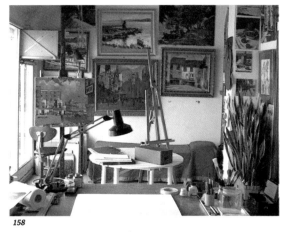

158

it should no longer be necessary to construct, so you may give all your attention to achieving hues, tonalities, and colours, that can make the watercolour into a masterpiece.

In the second place, the foundation drawing of a watercolour should be linear, without shadows or tones. But why? Well, because the interplay of lights and shadows should be explained with colours, not with the pencil. And this is due – let's not forget this – to the fact that watercolour is transparent. It is not difficult to imagine what would happen if we were to draw the shadows of this exercise in blacks and greys using a lead pencil and then paint on top of them. All the colours would be negatively affected, acquiring a grey and dirty tendency. (Unless one wishes to achieve this effect.) It should be pointed out that this exercise is simplified for practice purposes, but in actual work, a drawing for a watercolour should be done with a lead or graphite pencil, HB or B, in order to ensure that you make a less intense outline.

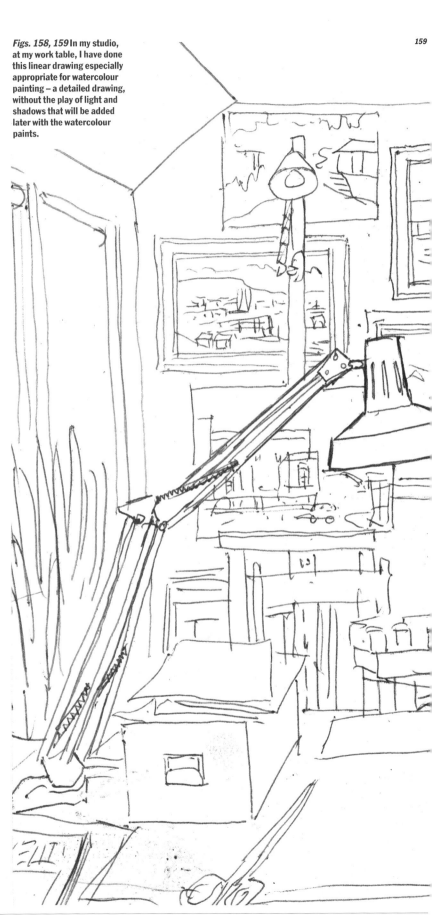

Figs. 158, 159 In my studio, at my work table, I have done this linear drawing especially appropriate for watercolour painting – a detailed drawing, without the play of light and shadows that will be added later with the watercolour paints.

159

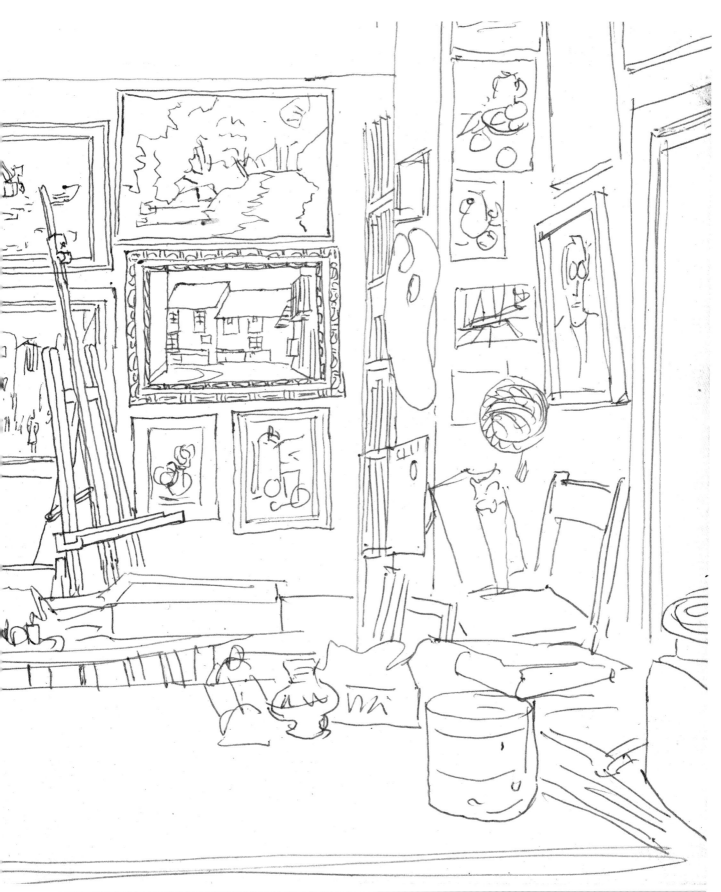

The right perspective

The themes of the watercolourist are often centred around streets and squares, buildings, suburbs, and sea ports, places in which the perspective plays an important role. The great English masters of the watercolour were experts in perspective. But after all, we are artists, not architects, and we are capable of viewing and capturing perspective by means of mastering only the basic rules which may be summarized as follows:

There are three kinds or classes of perspective:

1. *Parallel or vanishing-point perspective.*
2. *Oblique perspective or perspective with two vanishing points.*
3. *Aerial perspective or perspective with three vanishing points.*
(This last kind is rarely used in artistic painting and will not be commented on here.)

The *vanishing point* is the place where the lines or perpendicular intersections of the model meet. These vanishing points are always located on the *horizon line*, which is just at the height of the viewer's eye, whether standing, sitting or bending.

In *parallel perspective* the single vanishing point and the viewpoint coincide in the same spot on the horizon. In *oblique* and *aerial perspective*, the vanishing points and the viewpoint are points independent of each other, although they still meet in the same horizon line.

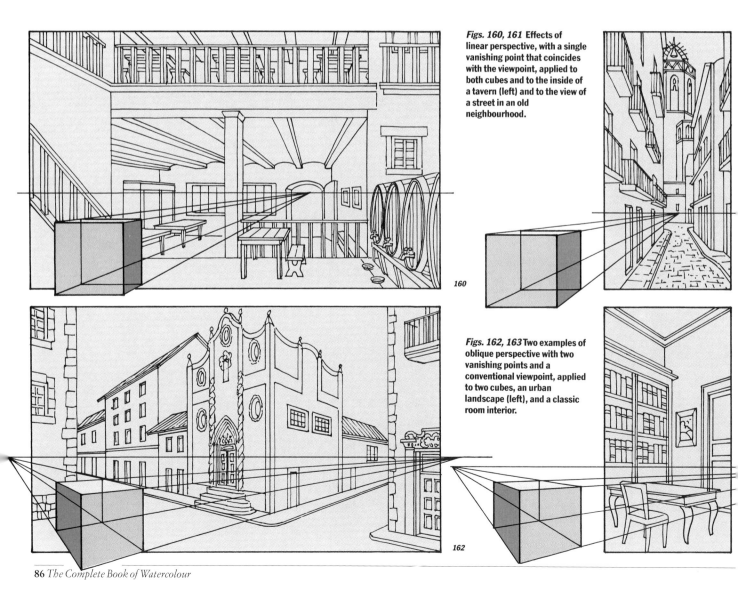

Figs. 160, 161 Effects of linear perspective, with a single vanishing point that coincides with the viewpoint, applied to both cubes and to the inside of a tavern (left) and to the view of a street in an old neighbourhood.

160

Figs. 162, 163 Two examples of oblique perspective with two vanishing points and a conventional viewpoint, applied to two cubes, an urban landscape (left), and a classic room interior.

162

Figures 160 and 161 show two examples of parallel one-point perspective. The first is applied to an interior, while the second looks at a typical street in an old neighbourhood. In figs. 162 and 163, you may find two applications of oblique perspective

Painting in watercolours such themes as the ones mentioned above, one often runs up against the problem of accurately dividing spaces or shapes that are repeated, such as the doors and windows of a house, a line of trees on a highway, or the arches of a cloister. For an expert painter, a problem of this kind doesn't represent any major difficulty. It is solved simply, calculating by sight. But I think it's good to know that there are a series of mathematical formulations that you can use. For example, you are painting the bars of an iron gate which from the front represent a symmetrical configuration. But to draw the gate in perspective, one has to calculate the perspective centre. Figures 164 and 165 show

the solution to this problem: an X-shaped cross with a vertical line down its centre was drawn (fig. 165) in order to obtain the perspective centre.

In figs. 166 and 167 you will find a really easy solution for solving the problem of dividing receding spaces which have repeated shapes, in this case, the cloister of an old church.

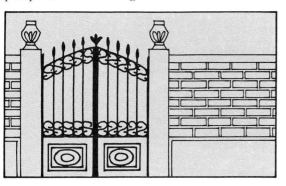

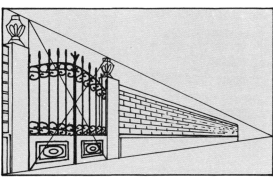

Figs. 164, 165 To put in perspective the centre of a model that, seen from the front, is symmetrical (fig. 164) you just need to draw the figure's square or rectangle in perspective and then find its perspective centre by drawing an X.

Fig. 166 (Above right) This picture shows how to divide spaces in depth and perspective.

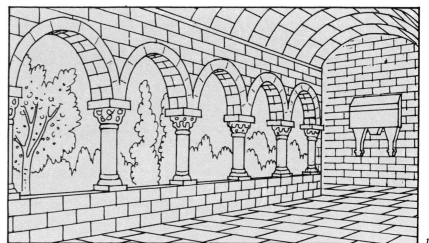

166

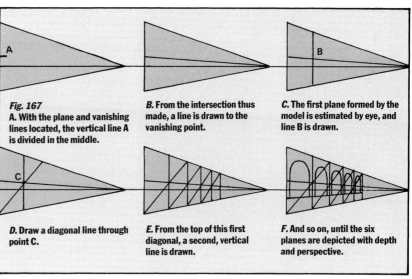

Fig. 167
A. With the plane and vanishing lines located, the vertical line A is divided in the middle.

B. From the intersection thus made, a line is drawn to the vanishing point.

C. The first plane formed by the model is estimated by eye, and line B is drawn.

D. Draw a diagonal line through point C.

E. From the top of this first diagonal, a second, vertical line is drawn.

F. And so on, until the six planes are depicted with depth and perspective.

167

The right perspective

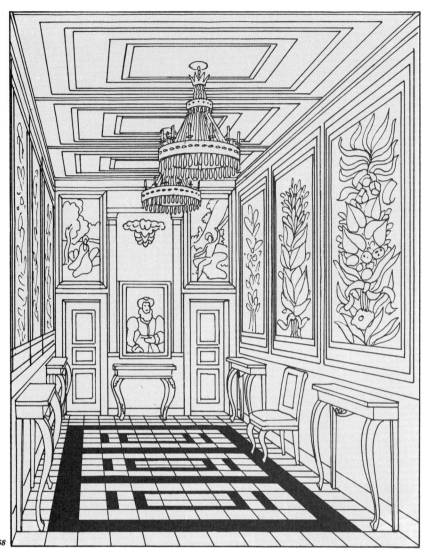

168

In the drawing in fig. 168, two typical problems of the division of receding spaces are illustrated: a wall with a determined number of equal spaces within a space which is also *determined*, and a mosaic; both in parallel perspective, seen from a single viewpoint. Note in fig. 169 schemes A and B, the solution to the first problem was found by tracing a *ground line* and then dividing it into equal spaces (169 A). Diagonal lines were then drawn to vanishing point E, thus determining the depth of the calculated spaces. In regard to the mosaic in parallel perspective (fig. 170, A, B, and C), it is only necessary to calculate by sight the dimension of rectangle a-b and use it as a base. We then make a series of diagonals to the vanishing point, tracing the grid pattern of scheme C, which allows us to draw the mosaic in perspective.

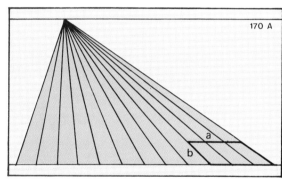

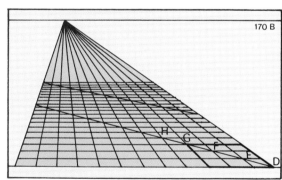

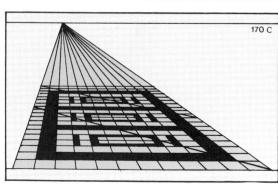

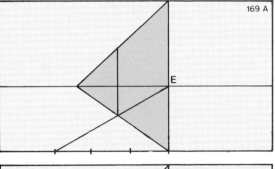

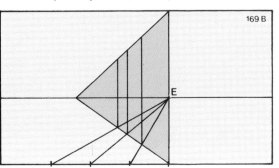

Figs. 168, 169 Here is the formula (A and B) for putting a defined number of equal planes into perspective within another defined plane, in this case, the right side-wall in the interior of the regal salon in fig. 168.

Fig. 170 In sketches A, B, and C of this figure, you can see the way to draw a mosaic in linear perspective from a single point, using a grid drawn in perspective.

1. *How to find the centre of a square in oblique perspective.*

2. *How to divide the depth of a given space into equal parts in oblique perspective (figs. 170 A and B).*

3. *How to draw a mosaic or grid in oblique perspective (figs. 171 A-F).*

Let me suggest that you try these perspective exercises on a larger scale than the figures here, at least double their size.

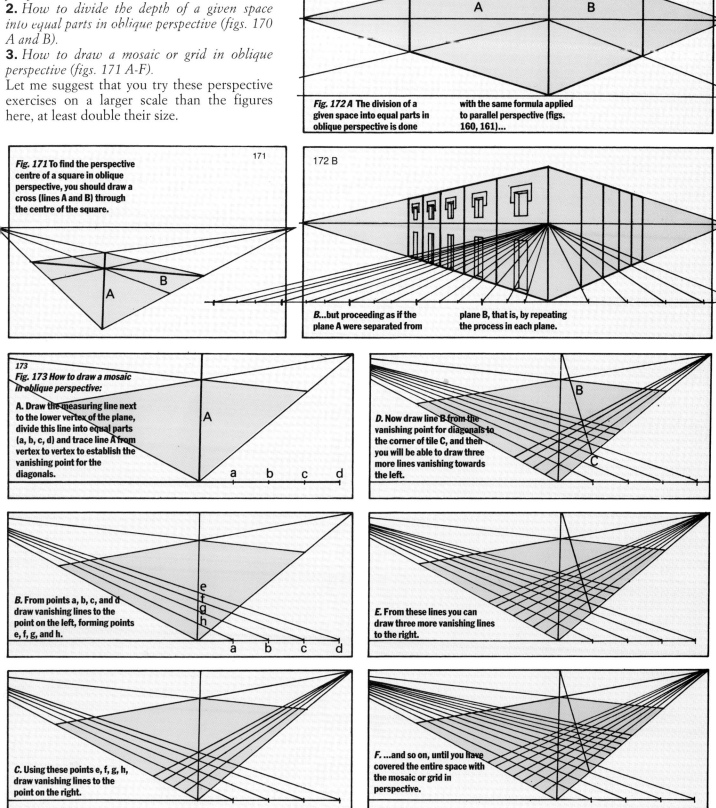

172 A

Fig. 172 A The division of a given space into equal parts in oblique perspective is done with the same formula applied to parallel perspective (figs. 160, 161)...

171

Fig. 171 To find the perspective centre of a square in oblique perspective, you should draw a cross (lines A and B) through the centre of the square.

172 B

B....but proceeding as if the plane A were separated from plane B, that is, by repeating the process in each plane.

173

Fig. 173 How to draw a mosaic in oblique perspective:

A. Draw the measuring line next to the lower vertex of the plane, divide this line into equal parts (a, b, c, d) and trace line A from vertex to vertex to establish the vanishing point for the diagonals.

D. Now draw line B from the vanishing point for diagonals to the corner of tile C, and then you will be able to draw three more lines vanishing towards the left.

B. From points a, b, c, and d draw vanishing lines to the point on the left, forming points e, f, g, and h.

E. From these lines you can draw three more vanishing lines to the right.

C. Using these points e, f, g, h, draw vanishing lines to the point on the right.

F. ...and so on, until you have covered the entire space with the mosaic or grid in perspective.

The right perspective

If you have studied and practised the exercises in perspective explained on the preceding pages, you will now be able to understand easily the last and possibly the most important technique of artistic perspective. It is to establish by eye the perspective offered by buildings, streets, and squares. Usually, in these cases, the vanishing points are outside the painting or the space in which the artist is drawing or painting. How do you make the windows, doors, rooftops and ledges of a street or square like the one I have drawn in fig. 174 appear in perfect perspective? Note the solution in sketches 175 A, B, and C, and keep in mind that this is a simple, practical technique for drawing freehand, without rulers or squares, the model in front of you.

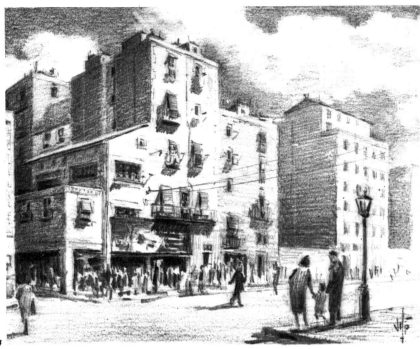

174

175

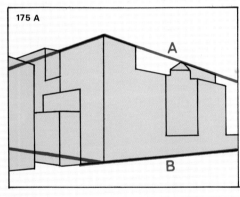

175 A

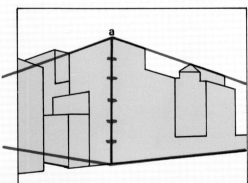

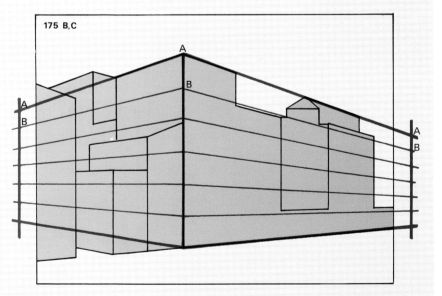

175 B,C

Fig. 174 Drawing or painting subjects like this, the perspective must be judged by eye, but there is a simple technique that can be applied that essentially solves all the difficulties.

Fig. 175 A The model is framed loosely, establishing with extreme care the angle of the basic lines that vanish to the horizon.
Then the vertical a is drawn, corresponding to the highest corner, and this line is divided into a specified number of equal parts, six in this example.

B. Now we will step out of the painting; at the paper's left margin, we draw another vertical and we divide it also into six equal sections.

C. Finally, we draw a new vertical, also outside the drawing in the right margin, divide it into six equal parts, and join point A with A, B with B, etc., forming a guide-pattern that enables us to draw all the model's parts in perfect perspective. The whole set of lines and measures for this technique, the verticals, their division into equal parts, and the sketching of a guide-pattern in perspective, must be done by eye and freehand, without a ruler or T-square. It is truly a technique for artists.

Aerial perspective, atmosphere, contrast

In addition to linear perspective, the artist should keep *atmosphere*, or aerial perspective, in mind. The author of *The System of the Arts*, Hegel, says in this regard that all objects in the real world show a variation in colour due to the atmosphere that surrounds them. The intensity of the colours is diluted with distances – this is what is meant by aerial perspective. Leonardo da Vinci, in his *Treatise on Painting*, followed a similar line of reasoning:

'The foreground should be finished in a clear and precise manner, the middle ground should be equally complete, but in a more vaporous way, more diffuse, and so on; depending on the distance, the contours should be softer, and forms and colours should disappear little by little.'

In a landscape with mountains in the background it is easy to verify this phenomenon of intervening atmosphere, noting that the nearest mountains offer more intense colour than those father away, and also noting that in the foreground there is more contrast of tone and colour and better definition than in the background. We could say, in summarizing these effects, that:

Contrast and definition decrease with intervening atmosphere.

As you know, when painting in watercolour, these effects of contrast and definition are obtained by diluting the outlines in the background with water, that is, by painting 'wet', while the foreground is preferably done 'dry'. Furthermore, contrast is increased by highlighting the light-coloured areas of the foreground with dark tones, recalling the classic rules of *simultaneous contrasts*:

The darker the tone surrounding it, the lighter a white or light colour appears to be.

Contrast can also be achieved by juxtaposing complementary colours, but we will leave this technique for later pages.

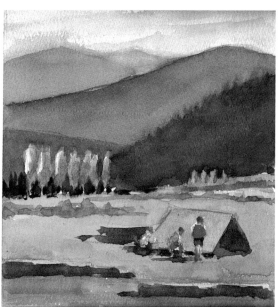

Fig. 176 In the city, on the sea, in the countryside, the intervening atmosphere softens the contrast and definition of the backgrounds, which offer less colour and appear greyer the further away from the viewer they are.

Fig. 177 The foreground is the darkest area and at the same time the clearest, that is to say, the foreground displays greater contrast and therefore greater definition. As we will see in the sketch, the farther away the planes are the greyer they are and the more contrast they lose. When these techniques are kept in mind, the painting achieves greater depth.

176

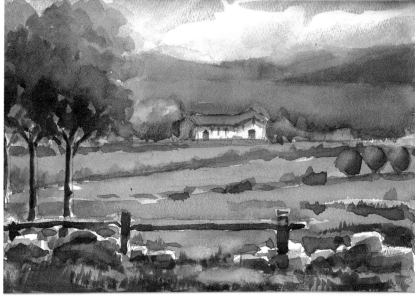

177

Fig. 178 The darker the tone surrounding it, the whiter a white appears. This law, called the law of *simultaneous contrasts*, can be appreciated in this example. The shine of ceramic B seems whiter than that of ceramic A because the tone surrounding B is darker.

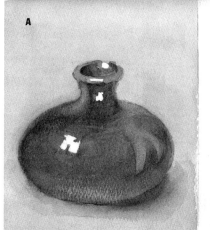
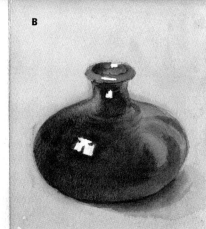

178

Plato's rule

To compose a watercolour painting…Yes, but first we should ask what is composition and, above all, how is a watercolour painting composed? To the first question – what is composition? – many artists and art experts have responded. Matisse, for example, the famous painter, wrote this fine definition: 'Composition is the art of arranging the various elements that the artist has at his disposal for expressing his feelings in a decorative fashion.' And Peter and Linda Murray, authors of *A Dictionary of Art and Artists*, published by Penguin, also define the term *composition* perfectly, saying that 'it is the art of combining the elements of a picture… into a satisfactory visual whole.' Fine, but HOW are these elements (which elements?) of the painting *arranged* or *combined* to express the artist's feelings and, at the same time, 'into a satisfactory visual whole'? There is no concrete answer to this question, only rules like those of Plato or Vitruvius that give us some guidance.

Plato was one of the great philosophers of ancient Greece, who taught his students as he strolled with them, as was the custom at that time. One of his students asked him one day how to compose a painting. Plato simply responded:

'Find and represent the variety within the unity.'

That is, find variety in the form, in the colour, in the situation, in the size and arrangement of the elements that make up the painting, so that this variety attracts the attention and awakens the interest of the viewer, inducing him to look and, finally, giving him the pleasure of looking and contemplating it. But be careful; when this variety is so great that it becomes disconcerting and disperses the attention initially attracted, the viewer tires and the painting ceases to interest him. The variety must be organized in some order and within a unity of the whole, combining the two ideas to establish:

UNITY *within variety*

VARIETY *within unity*

See the adjoining sketches and texts for an explanation of Plato's rule through pictures.

179

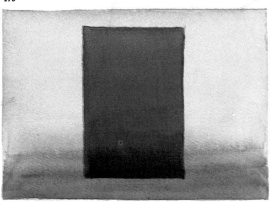

180

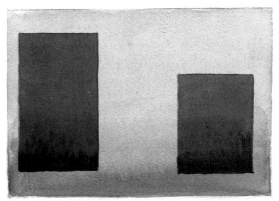

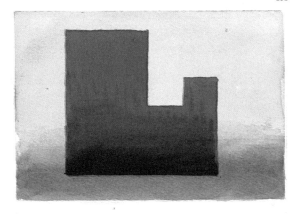

Fig. 179 Excessive unity. Colour and form offer few variants; the arrangement of the elements is static, symmetrical; the whole model displays too much uniformity, a lack of variety that can be monotonous and uninteresting for the viewer looking at the painting.

Fig. 180 Excessive variety. Here, on the other hand, an attempt has been made to diversify, varying forms, colours, arrangement and so on to such an extreme that the necessary unity has been lost, creating a dispersed composition that may cause the viewer to tire and lose interest.

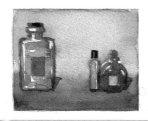

181

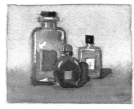

Fig. 181 Variety within unity. The painting's elements now offer variety in form, colour and arrangement and, at the same time, there is an order to these elements, a unity that creates a satisfactory visual whole.

Vitruvius's Golden Section

In the days of the Roman Emperor Augustus, an architect named Vitruvius studied the organization of forms and space from an aesthetic point of view. Vitruvius wondered even then what the perfect arrangement, artistically speaking, of a point or dividing line within a given space might be.

But let me explain Vitruvius's proposition to you with some drawings.

Imagine a given area – the painting – in which we are to place the principal figure of the picture. If we place this figure in the centre, we will obtain a symmetrical composition, appropriate for certain themes (solemn, majestic, religious, etc.) but without the variety necessary for modern composition. If we move this figure to one edge of the painting, the variety may become exaggerated. This is when the question arises as to where to place the figure. Vitruvius finally resolved this problem by establishing the famous *Golden Section* or *Golden Rule*:

'For an area divided into unequal sections to be agreeable and aesthetic, there should be the same relationship between the larger section and the whole as between the smaller and larger sections.'

The Law of the Golden Section

Let us imagine a segment whose total length is 5 cm.

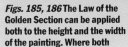

2 cm.   3 cm.

If we divide this area into two sections of 2 and 3 cm, we will see that according to Vitruvius's law, almost the same proportional relationship exists bet-ween the smaller portion (2 cm) and the larger one (3 cm) as between the larger section (3 cm) and the whole, or the entire length (5 cm). This is so because 5:3 is very similar to 3:2. If you reduce these simple fractions you will obtain similar results – almost 1.6.

Vitruvius thus found this numerical relationship in 'extreme and mean ratio', establishing that:

The arithmetical expression of the 'Golden Section' is equal to 1.618.

Practically speaking, when you want to find the division of a Golden Section, multiply the total length of the space by the factor 0.618. Look at the following examples:

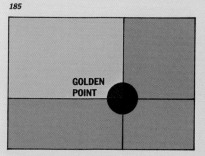

185

GOLDEN POINT

186

Figs. 185, 186 The Law of the Golden Section can be applied both to the height and the width of the painting. Where both sections cross, they form the golden point, considered the ideal place to situate the painting's principal figure.

By means of a simple change in the division of the segments, the golden point can be located in four different places.

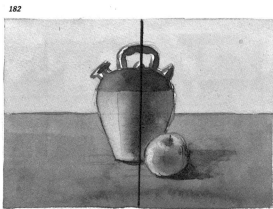

182

Fig. 182 Dividing the painting in the centre and placing its principal element right in the middle, we end up with a symmetrical composition, monotonous because of its lack of variation.

Fig. 183 Moving the painting's principal element to one side, the composition is asymmetrical, but it may present an excessive variation, detracting from the painting's aesthetic quality.

Fig. 184 Applying the law of the Golden Section to the height and width of the painting, we obtain a golden point that lets us situate the painting's principal figure in just the right place. Furthermore, this improves the placement of the level that limits the background (A), which we now situate at exactly the height of the Golden Section.

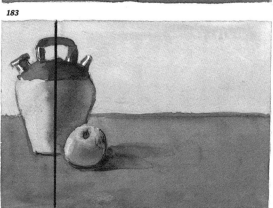

183

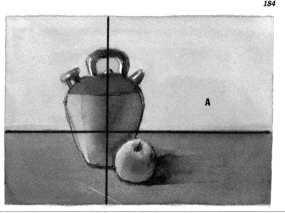

184

A

Compositional schemes

Here is another device that you can use to compose a painting: the device of *geometrical schemes*.

Scientifically proven, simple and eminently practical, this technique was established in practice by the German philosopher Fechner, who was the first to study the relationship between the physical and psychic effects of form. Fechner succeeded in proving, with surveys and statistics, that most people, when asked to choose between a series of geometric shapes, a series of natural shapes, and another series of abstract forms, prefer geometric shapes because of their simple, concrete configuration. C. P. Haas, an expert in images, offered the opinion that this truly bewitching power of geometric forms is a consequence of the principle of hedonism: 'Obtain the most satisfaction with the least effort', or the principle of muscular, nervous, or mental economy...

Let us hasten to explain, however, that geometric forms had already been in use in artistic composition for hundreds of years, first with the adoption of the triangle, a perfect scheme of symmetric composition and afterwards with the *diagonal scheme*, suggested and applied principally by Rembrandt, and associated with asymmetrical composition.

Well then, when it is time to choose the subject and determine how to frame it, try to find an overall form that corresponds to a particular geometric shape. And be sure that your watercolour will offer 'a satisfactory visual whole'.

Here are some examples of geometric shapes and their application to watercolour painting.

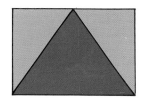

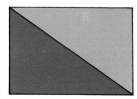

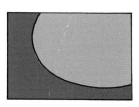

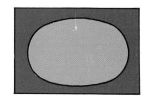

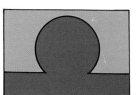

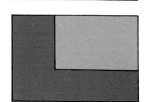

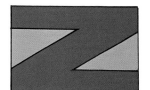

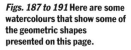

Figs. 187 to 191 Here are some watercolours that show some of the geometric shapes presented on this page.

187
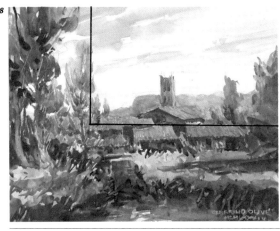

188

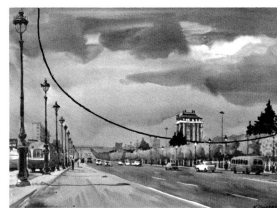

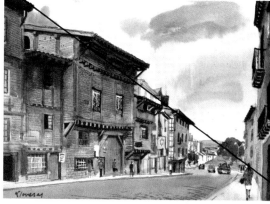

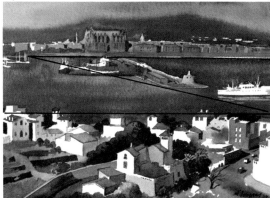

The third dimension

Representing the third dimension, or what amounts to the same thing – highlighting the effect of depth by showing the space intervening between one point and another – is also an important factor in the art of composing a painting.

Here, then, are the techniques that the artist can use to emphasize depth:

A Including in the painting a well-defined foreground: by painting a group of trees, a fence, or any other object of known dimensions and size in the foreground with the middle ground and beyond, mentally establishing in a mechanical way the distance between one plane and another, and as a result the painting's depth.

B Superimposing successive planes: when the foreground of a landscape shows some trees or bushes, some rocks or a fence, and includes in the middle ground beyond, say, the houses of a small town crowded together, and beyond that or in the background a taller building, a church or small mountain, we have a subject composed of *successive superimposed planes*, perfectly defined by Plato's formula of 'variety within unity', allowing us to represent and highlight the third dimension, depth.

C Painting in perspective: the third dimension is represented in drawings done in perspective: streets, squares, buildings, roads, rows of trees, etc. But the viewpoint, the framing that allows us to dramatize the effect of depth, must be chosen with forethought.

D Highlighting the contrast and atmosphere: these concepts are directly related to the different planes of the painting, to the impression of space and depth. It is a matter of remembering this technique and accentuating it when in front of your subject.

E Painting 'near' and 'far' colours: it has been shown that *warm colours* bring objects closer, while *cool colours* make them appear more distant. If you paint a spot of medium blue next to a spot of yellow, you will see that the yellow 'approaches', it is 'located' in the foreground, while the blue 'retreats', remains in a more distant plane. If you apply this formula of 'near' and 'far' colours to a painting, you will undoubtedly accentuate its depth.

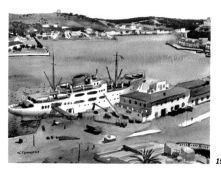

192

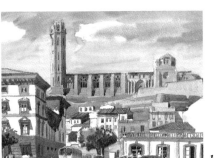

193

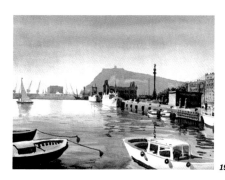

194

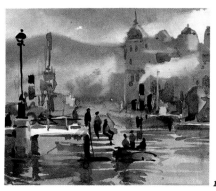

195

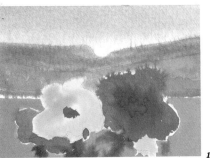

196

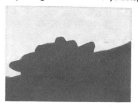

Fig. 192 Including an object in the foreground whose size and dimensions we are familiar with, as in this case of a tree, creates the idea of distance between the foreground and the rest of the painting, giving the painting a third dimension, that is, depth.

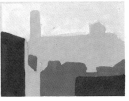

Fig. 193 Depth can also be found in landscapes like this one in which the superimposition (or overlapping) of successive planes (see the adjoining sketch) facilitates the representation of depth.

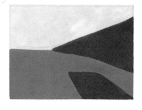

Fig. 194 Any effect of perspective, in a street, a building, a road with trees, etc., gives the painting the impression of a third dimension, a representation of depth.

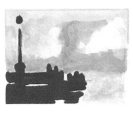

Fig. 195 Atmosphere and depth can be seen in paintings like this one, painted at eight o'clock in the morning, when the sun is rising and a golden mist surrounds the middle ground and background.

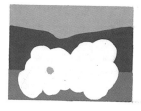

Fig. 196 Paint 'near' colours in the foreground, such as yellow and orange. In the middle and background, paint 'far' colours, such as greens and blues. In this way, you will highlight the depth almost automatically.

Composition in practice

Finally, once in front of the model, keep in mind these three important rules to improve your watercolour's composition:

1. Approach the subject just enough to create a centre of interest that 'explains' the content or reason for the painting. Don't paint empty spaces, minimizing the elements that are the real reason for the painting. Approach without fear!

2. To decide how to frame the subject, take a cardboard frame (fig. 198) with you that will enable you to choose the best point of view, and thus the best composition for the subject. Better yet, before beginning to paint, do a quick postcard-sized sketch suggesting the framing and composition of the subject.

3. Finally, don't be content with the subject as you first see it. Look at it from further to the right, from further to the left, stooping or climbing where you can, so that you have a chance to pick the best viewpoint.

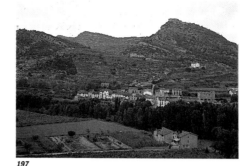

197

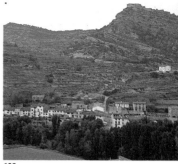

198

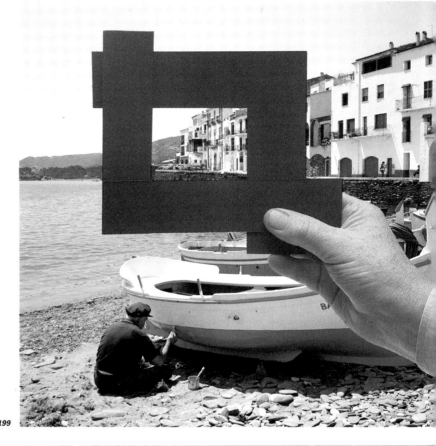

199

Figs. 197, 198 One of the most common mistakes made by the inexperienced amateur is to place himself too far away from the principal subject, losing the opportunity to emphasize the painting's centre of interest. Note the difference in these figures between staying far away or drawing near the subject.

Fig. 199 Get a cardboard frame painted black or covered with black paper. With this frame you will be able to study the framing of the subject before beginning to paint. Better yet, sketch a quick note with a lead pencil or watercolours to analyse the framing you have chosen and the composition in general.

Figs. 200, 201 Before beginning to paint, exhaust all possible points of view and framings. Try to get as much as you can out of these factors, which have such an impact on the painting's composition.

200

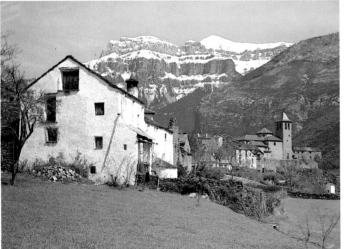

201

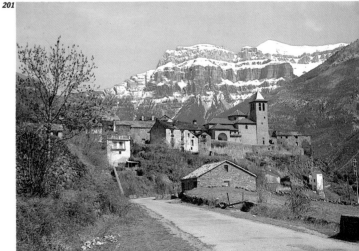

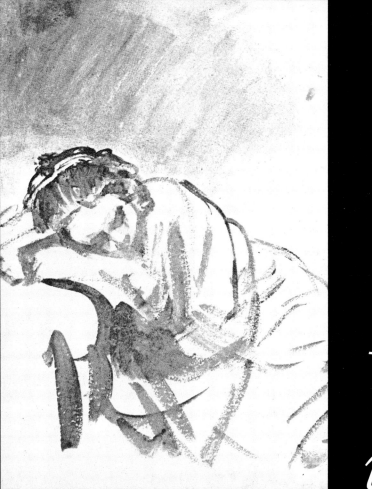

Wash:
warm-up

Characteristics and similarities

Learning to paint is always difficult. Painting watercolours is even more difficult. First of all, as in all the visual arts, you have to know how to draw very well. What's more, you must master colour, and the compositions and mixtures of colours. As if this weren't enough, you must also know the *craft* of watercolour painting. Well then, 'divide and conquer'. It is a matter of dividing these three basic problems and reducing them, in principle, to just two: drawing and craft. These two problems can be studied separately, without going into the problem of colour just yet, by practising gouache painting, a true first step towards watercolour painting.

The examples here of gouache painting, done by Nicolas Poussin and John Constable, painted in two colours, one sienna and one black (or Payne's grey), allow us to compare the characteristics and similarities of gouache and watercolour. In these landscapes, note the transparency of the gouache and the absence of opaque white; the whites here are actually the white of the paper masked off beforehand. The resolution runs from less to more, in other words, it was arrived at by superimposing dark layers over light, a typical characteristic of watercolour painting.

It is natural, therefore, for us to start these exercises by painting in gouache, and it makes sense to do it with colours as bright as red, blue, and yellow as we will see in a minute.

Materials needed

Watercolour paper (of good quality), heavyweight, as thick as necessary for mounting.

A drawing board.

Watercolour paints.

Two sable brushes, nos. 8, 12, or 14.

A wide 'paletilla' or wash brush, no. 20 or 24.

A piece of natural sponge.

A roll of paper towels.

Two jars for water.

A cup or pan to dilute colours.

Pencil, rubber, etc.

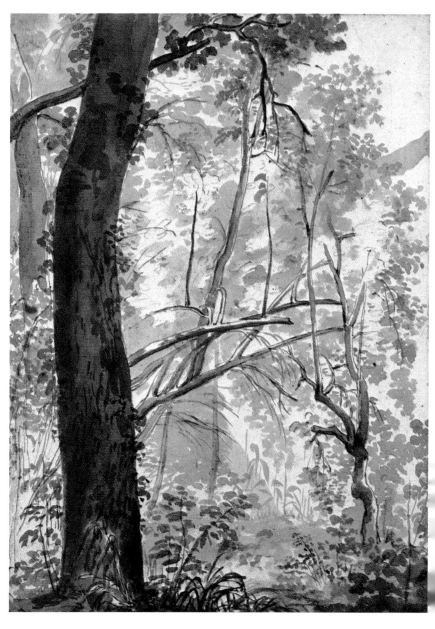

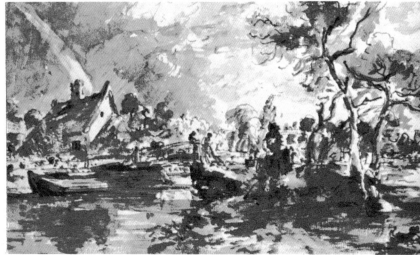

Fig. 203 Nicolas Poussin, **Scene in the Forest**, Albertina, Vienna.

Fig. 204 John Constable, **The Old Bridge at Flatford**, Victoria and Albert Museum, London.

First practical exercises

**Dry wash in
a medium tone**

Fig. 205 Place the board at a slight angle. On your paper, draw a square, approximately 15 x 15 cm (9" x 9") in pencil. Keep a scrap of paper ready for testing. In a small cup or one of the pans of the palette box, prepare a wash of a medium cobalt blue. Try to get a tone like the one in the example here. Load the brush with a lot of colour and begin by painting a band 2 to 3 cm (1" to 1¼") wide at the top of the square. Begin by painting from side to side horizontally. Work with a no. 12 brush. Be careful with the amount of paint – it should be enough to spread evenly as you paint but it should not be so much that it runs or drips.

205

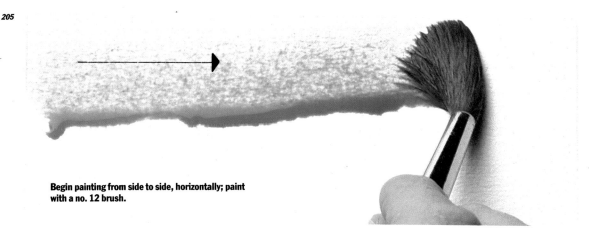

Begin painting from side to side, horizontally; paint with a no. 12 brush.

206

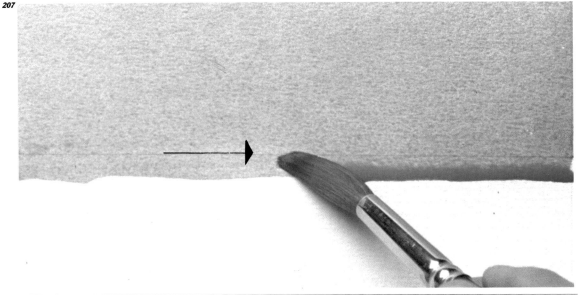

Fig. 206 Continue to maintain the moisture, working quickly. Keep displacing the wash, moving towards the bottom, painting horizontally, always leaving enough paint on the bottom edge. To control the accumulation of paint and to keep it from running, the board can be slanted as necessary.

Now paint vertically, from top to bottom, keeping the brush loaded so that you are always painting in wet.

207

Fig. 207 When you reach the bottom of the square you will have some paint accumulated. Quickly blot the brush with a paper towel and absorb the paint accumulated at the bottom until you have a regular, uniform tone over the whole square.
The perfect harmony and uniformity in the colour of a medium-tone dry wash basically depends on, first, the quality of the paper, second, the slant of the board, and third, the brush and the amount of paint on it. Of course, there is no chance of retouching or redoing it.

First practical exercises

Dry wash in different tones

Figs. 208 to 211 Here the object, as can be seen from the picture, is to paint four progressively lighter shades of carmine (crimson)- coloured wash.

First draw four rectangles 15 x 8 cm (9" x 3"). Use the colour rose madder or any crimson and keep a piece of paper handy for testing. Start with the darkest shade, loading the brush with intense but not opaque wash.

For both this shade and the following ones, keep in mind the instructions given on the previous page. The procedure is the same. The difficulty now rests in not only achieving washes of even tones but also obtaining a range of progressive tones. In order to do this, it is necessary to test the colour or more accurately, the tone, each time before beginning to paint. Be careful with the amount of paint necessary for each tone, keeping in mind that it is better to err on the side of excess than on the side of insufficient colour.

208

209

210

211

Dry gradated wash

Fig. 212 Sketch a square some 15 x 15 cm (9" x 9") and get ready to paint a gradated wash with the colour cadmium red, or vermilion, in the area specified. Have a scrap of paper on hand for testing and keep in mind that the success of a gradated wash in gouache or watercolour depends to a large extent on the quantity of water in the brush when you begin to paint. Begin by painting a band saturated with colour in the upper portion of the square.

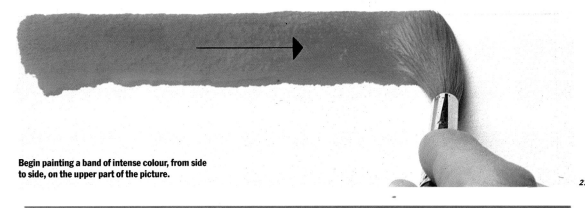

Begin painting a band of intense colour, from side to side, on the upper part of the picture.

212

Fig. 213 Quickly now: wash the brush, drain it slightly on the edge of the water jar and apply it to the bottom half of the red band, dissolving and gradating towards the bottom but painting from side to side at all times, horizontally. Put pressure on the brush to bring out more water, making sure that the colour does not accumulate when you lift the brush. Always paint horizontally. Move towards the bottom rapidly, putting pressure on the brush to release more water.

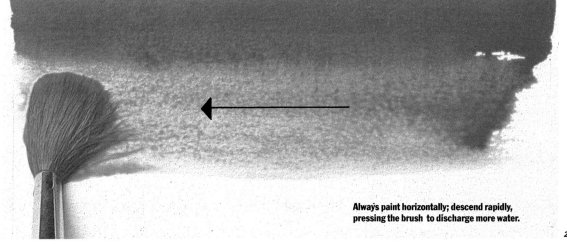

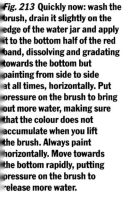

Always paint horizontally; descend rapidly, pressing the brush to discharge more water.

213

Fig. 214 Wash the brush again, drain it as before, and continue gradating until you get to the bottom of the square. You will probably have to wet and drain the brush during this final phase, controlling the amount of liquid, going over it, retouching it...but not too much, since if you paint and repaint, returning to the upper part of the wash, the difficulties increase and the gradation will not come out clean. You have to move quickly, measuring the water and working preferably with the bottom portion, which at this stage is the only area that allows for repeating and retouching.

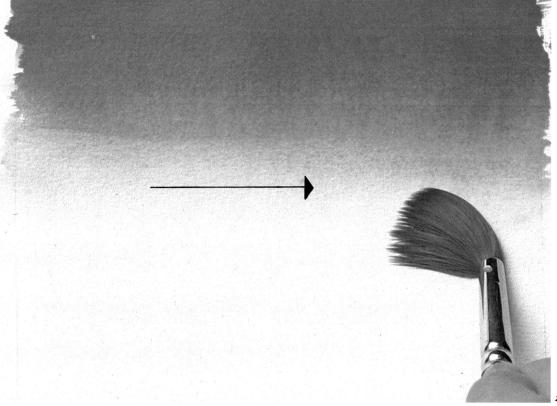

214

First practical exercises

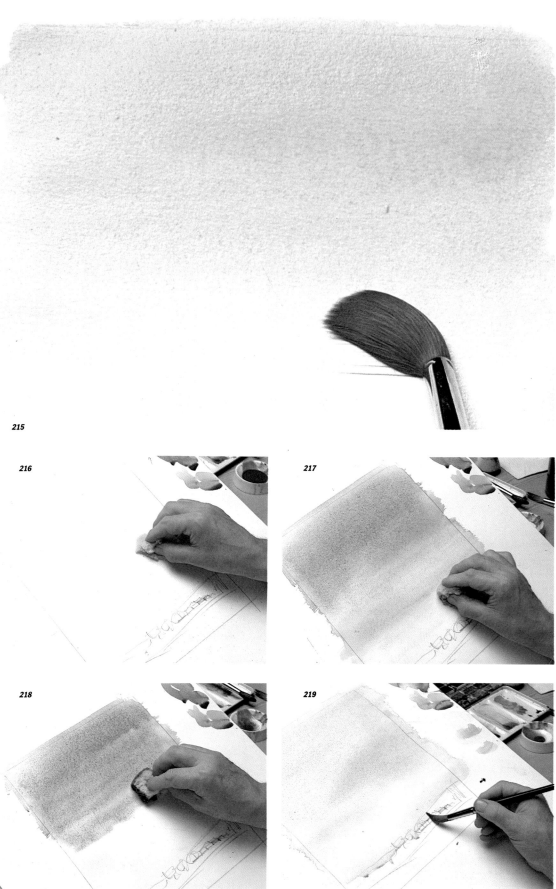

Wet gradated wash

Fig. 215 The first step is to moisten the square or area to be painted using a natural sponge (a small piece of sponge such as the one in fig. 216), or a wide, flat, Japanese-style brush like the one mentioned previously in the chapter on supplies. This wetting of the paper should be done by rubbing the sponge over the paper lightly several times so that the paper's fibre does not deteriorate, but will absorb the moisture without water remaining on the surface. You should be painting on a damp, but not wet, surface. Work with the paper slanted at a 60 to 75 degree angle. Load the brush with yellow ochre, with less water than previously, and paint the top band of the picture. Half rinse the brush quickly and continue gradating with quick strokes that do not alter the uniformity; move with spontaneity. Keep in mind that gradating the top part to the middle is the most difficult part. This is the hardest and most complicated exercise here, and you should not be surprised if it does not come out on the first try.

215

216

217

Painting with the sponge

Fig. 216 Prepare a cup with the amount of wash (cobalt blue with a little ochre) needed to paint a cloudy sky some 18 x 25 cm (7" x 10"). Wet the brush with clean water and moisten the paper with several strokes of the sponge and water.

Fig. 217 Squeeze out the sponge, load it with the colour prepared in the cup and paint, pressing lightly, from side to side, controlling the evenness, squeezing the sponge more or less to extract more or less colour.

218

219

Fig. 218 When you get to the bottom third, drain the sponge a bit, add a little clean water, and load it with gouache of a very light ochre colour only. Paint this slightly lighter colour, mixing it and gradating it with the still-wet previous colour, until you get to the horizon or the bottom edge of the rectangle.

Fig. 219 Still working wet, retouch the bottom part of the wash, controlling and retouching the evenness, absorbing gouache with the brush if necessary.

Techniques of watercolour

How to 'open up' white spaces by absorbing colour

In the next few pages I will ask you to paint in gouache using two colours. Since gouache is in many ways similar to watercolour, I would first like to go over some techniques for painting in watercolour. I begin with the method that is generally used by professionals to 'open up' whites, or to 'erase' paint so that the white of the paper is once more exposed.

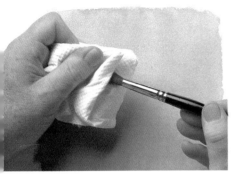

220

Wet: This is how to 'erase' still-wet wash and 'open up' white space.
1. Begin by washing the brush and draining it with the help of a paper towel. *2.* Apply the brush to the still-wet

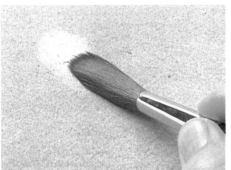

221

wash area, and you will observe that the brush absorbs the liquid and the colour underneath. *3.* If the white is not sufficiently light, wash the brush again, drain it once

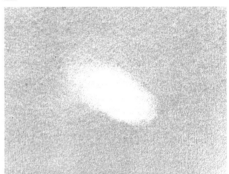

222

more with the paper towel and apply it again. By repeating this operation several times you can obtain an almost perfect white.

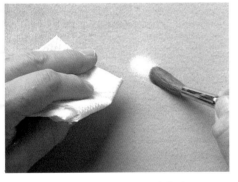

223

Dry: Here it is a matter of 'erasing' a wash that has already dried.
1. Begin by wetting the area with a brush and clean water. At the same time, rub gently with the tip of the brush, diluting and lifting the colour.

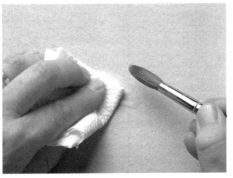

224

2. With a scrap of paper towel, folded in quarters or smaller, absorb the water applied previously. With this, you will begin to open up the white. Repeat the operation several times until you get a satisfactory white.

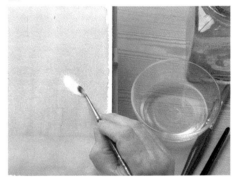

225

Extra help from bleach: To obtain a purer white you can use bleach diluted with water (half bleach, half water). But be careful. You should use a synthetic brush, the only kind that will withstand the corrosive effects of the bleach. Sable hair or others, such as ox hair or squirrel, will burn.

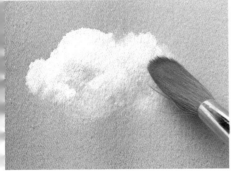

226

Comparing results: Wet: Undoubtedly the best of the techniques explained here, permitting even the painting of forms with gradated washes, forming for example the shapes of the clouds.

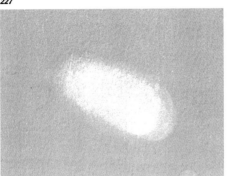

227

Dry: A laborious technique that, in the end, does not give good results. Absorption is more difficult with certain colours (carmine, emerald green, Prussian blue, and cadmium in general resist being diluted).

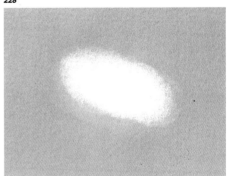

228

With bleach: This technique is also laborious, but the results are clearly good, as can be seen in this illustration. It is difficult perhaps if attempting gradated washes, since the bleach cuts the edges of the treated areas.

Techniques of watercolour

**How to reserve
whites ahead
of time**

In watercolour white is provided by the white of the paper; no white paint should be used. The ability of the good watercolourist is exhibited, among other things, by his knowing how to reserve the white areas ahead of time.

However, sometimes reserved areas are small, thin, or situated on top of a uniform background. The professional will generally use masking fluid or white wax, employing some of the various techniques explained here.

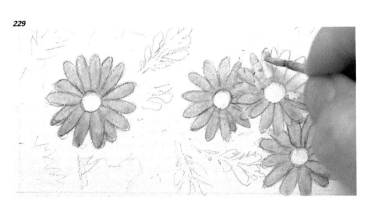

229

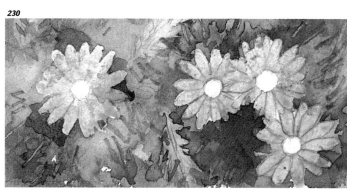

230

Reserving with masking fluid: *1.* Once the drawing is done and the area or forms to be masked off have been studied, one proceeds to paint them with masking fluid with a synthetic no. 4 brush. The masking fluid is of a light green or cream colour, so that you can see where it has been applied.

2. Once the areas are reserved with masking fluid, you can paint over and around them without any limitations. The masking fluid rejects the water of the watercolour and so continues to be visible.

231

232

3. When the artist is ready, the masking fluid is removed by rubbing it with a finger, uncovering the white paper. Naturally, this is done when the watercolour has dried.

4. Then the reserved areas can be painted with the colours, lights, and shadows of the model, following the normal procedures for painting. Masking fluid is a good aid, but it is not advisable to abuse its use, since it never gives the same quality as the white reserved with the brush while painting.

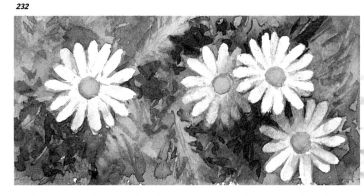

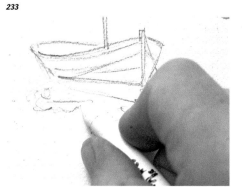

233

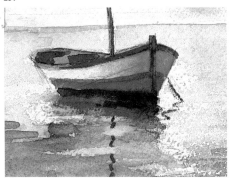

234

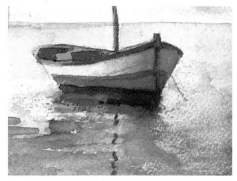

235

Reserving with white wax: **1.** White wax can also be used to reserve whites before beginning to paint. Once the drawing is completed and the whites that are to be reserved beforehand have been studied, you 'paint' them in with a white wax crayon, with more or less fine lines,

depending on the shapes chosen.
2. Then you paint around these reserved shapes or areas, knowing that you can paint on top of the wax since it will repel the water.

3. But be careful! If you go over the wax reserve again and again, it will finally absorb, either totally or partially, the liquid colour, and the effect of the reserved white will disappear.

Other techniques to 'open up' whites

The requirement that the white paper serve as white colour forces the artist to use a series of procedures for those cases in which the white was not reserved beforehand. These cases, usually unforeseen, are solved by the professional with some of the techniques which are explained on this page.

236

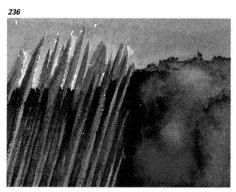

Scrubbing out whites in dry paint: 1. When you want a white in a dark area in an already dry watercolour painting, it is advisable to do it with a synthetic flat brush, no. 4, which has stiffer bristles than sable hair. Begin by moistening the area with lots of water.

237

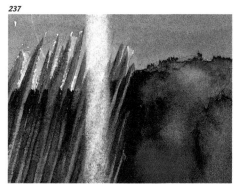

2. Let the water sit for a minute or two, allowing it to soften the paper and the paint, and then rub softly with a clean, rinsed brush until the deposited water begins to get cloudy with the loosened paint. At that moment, dry the area with a paper towel.

238

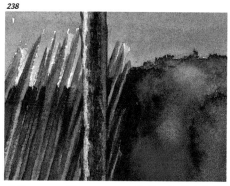

3. For a purer white you can resort to bleach, diluted with water and applied with a synthetic brush. Once the whitening is done you can paint again, retouching, creating shapes, etc.

239

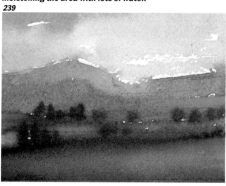

Scratching out whites in wet paint with a bevelled brush handle: 1. There has always been a need in watercolour painting to create white lines against a dark background. This must be done in a freshly painted area, while the paint is still damp and the colour is somewhat thick.

240

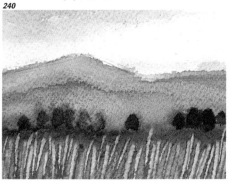

2. There are two ways to open up these white lines: one consists of tracing them forcefully and resolutely using the bevelled end of a special brush with a plastic handle and synthetic bristles, or...

241

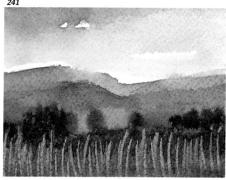

...with the fingernail. The other system, used by today's watercolourist and those of a hundred and fifty years ago, is to scratch and expose the white paper with the nail of the little or ring finger in the form and position illustrated in this figure.

242

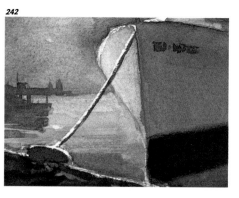

'Opening up' white spaces with a knife or blade (dry paint): The watercolour must be absolutely dry for this procedure. Here a white line can be etched from a dark background with the sharp edge of a mat knife, x-acto, or single-edge blade.

243

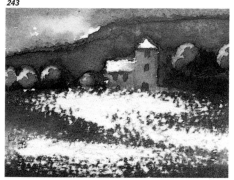

'Opening up' white spaces with sandpaper (dry paint): 1. With a small piece of very fine sandpaper (in this example 3/0 has been used) a perfect white can be 'opened up' by vigorously rubbing the chosen area (the paint must be completely dry).

244

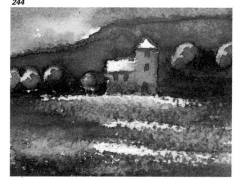

2. The success of a white obtained with sandpaper depends to a large extent on the quality of the watercolour paper. If it is thick and of good fibre it will survive and come out like new to be repainted on.

Techniques of watercolour

Textures

The 'frottage', the textured effects, the stains... The techniques of the watercolour are extremely varied and offer the possibility, within the purest forms of watercolour, of painting with systems, methods, and procedures that create diversity and style. We offer on this page some of these procedures, which I request you put into practice, in order to enrich and improve your technique, your confidence, and your trade in watercolour.

245

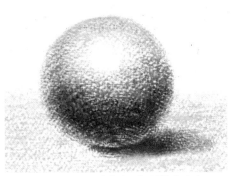

'Frottage' or rubbing with the brush: 1. This technique, also called dry brush, consists of painting with an almost dry brush which, when rubbed, reproduces the rough texture of the paper, as seen in this illustration.

246

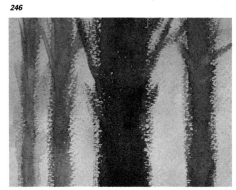

2. 'Frottage' can be applied at edges and contours in a casual or premeditated way, as in this example.

247

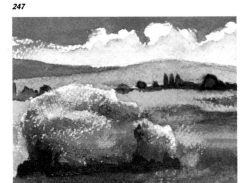

3. The dry-brush technique is also used to create contrast and to represent the rough texture of certain forms. In all cases, it is advisable to try this technique out on a separate sheet of paper before using it.

248

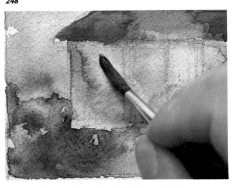

Textural effects with water: 1. Painting with the wet-watercolour technique, very rich textural effects can be achieved simply by loading the brush with clean water and applying it to a recently painted area that is still damp.

249

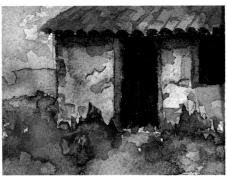

2. The spots and special effects which result from this wet-in-wet technique will suggest surprising textural effects to enrich the colour and style of your painting.

250

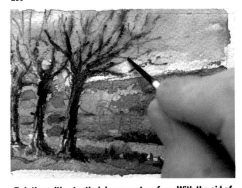

Painting with a toothpick on a wet surface. With the aid of a stick or toothpick loaded with the watercolour from a brush, you paint and draw, defining lines, tree branches, etc. The moist paper dilutes the paint from the small stick, making it run and creating an original modern idiom.

251

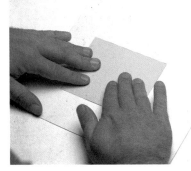

Transfer. 1. Transfer is a technique of pressing a recently painted and still-wet piece of paper against another piece of paper that may be white or painted, wet or dry. The pressure will transfer the wet area, creating an abstract configuration or texture on the receiving paper. Transfer is used for background walls, ground, hills, etc.

252

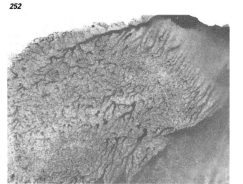

2. Example of transfer: the paper to be painted on was painted a light pink. The transfer paper was painted an even, dark pink that, when applied, left this abstract image.

253

3. Another example of mackle: in this case the receptor paper (the painting), was painted a light yellow background, and the printing paper (the mackle) was painted with a crimson wash. When pressed, it printed this image.

Textures and special effects

On this page we find some special effects, such as those obtained with turpentine and kitchen salt, which, when applied to the wet watercolour creates various textures and finishes that invite us to experiment, to invent, to create, and to discover a personal style, one's own visual language.

254

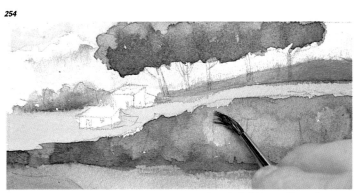

Textural effects with turpentine: 1. A synthetic brush is loaded with turpentine and brushed over a freshly painted, still damp area. When the turpentine comes into contact with the watercolour or gouache, light-coloured, irregularly-shaped spots are formed, creating special effects and textures.

255

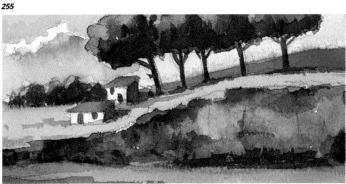

2. You can paint over areas treated with turpentine without difficulty, although it does not make sense to go over them with more watercolours to the point of eliminating or diminishing the effects achieved previously.

256 257

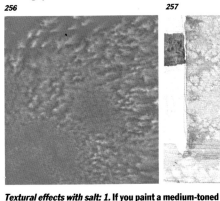

Textural effects with salt: 1. If you paint a medium-toned even wash and sprinkle salt on it while it is still damp, you will see that as the paint dries the grains of salt absorb the pigment and form some curious spots, light in colour, and diffused.

2. This effect can be used for the background, walls, ground, hills, etc. of a watercolour, creating special effects of surprising quality.

258

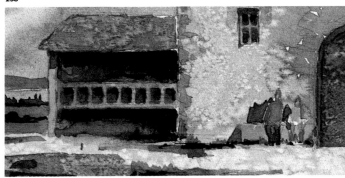

3. When this effect has been achieved in the areas treated with salt and the painting is dry, the grains of salt sticking to the painting can be removed simply by rubbing them gently with your fingers. In any case, you can paint over them without any problem.

259

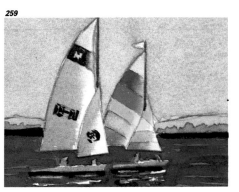

Gradated washes through dispersion or pointillism: 1. Here is an example whose sky has turned out too light, lessening the contrast between the ship's sail and the colour of the sky. For this and other cases, it may be interesting to paint a grey area or wash with an airbrush technique, but by hand.

260

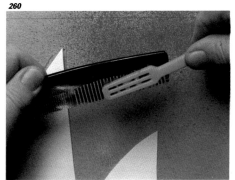

2. The technique of pointillism consists of dragging a toothbrush loaded with colour across the teeth of an ordinary comb. This dragging produces a spray of liquid watercolour. Naturally, beforehand, it is necessary to cut a paper pattern to cover the shapes that are to be reserved.

261

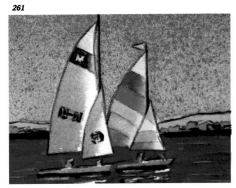

3. Final results, and finishing off with marker, ballpoint or Indian ink: Here are the results – the sky has gradually darkened, and the subject shows more contrast. Note further, the finishing black lines which have been added with a marker to emphasize some of the painting's contours and shapes.

Painting with two colours

This is an exercise that I request you put into practice: paint with wash techniques using only two colours, from a model made of a cube, a cylinder and a glass of water on a table, against a white Bristol board as the background. Did I say two colours? Well, they aren't two, but four colours, namely:

Cobalt blue
Burnt umber
Black
White

In the figs. 262 and 263, you will see the blue, the brown, the black – created by mixing the blue and brown – and the white, which is simply the white of the paper. But there are still more colours, an infinite range of tones, which you can see here. Therefore, considering the range of colours that this particular palette can create, we might say that we are going to paint without limitations, with many colours, much like the original, renowned English water-colourists who used only to add a red ochre, in order to obtain beautifully coloured paintings, and perfect colour harmonies. Looking at fig. 267 on the next page you will notice the illumination of the model created by the small desk lamp and the white Bristol board background; fig. 266 shows you the set-up.

Let me now ask you to construct the cube and cylinder out of lightweight Bristol board, following the design and measurements given in fig. 265. As for the glass, it doesn't matter if your glass is different from the model, but try to find a glass that, like the model, offers some decorative relief to make reflections and variations.

Without any more introductions, this is how I painted the model.

Materials:

The two above-mentioned colours.
Watercolour paper, 300 g, fine grain.
Lead pencil (normal) no. 2.
Kneaded rubber and white rubber.
Brushes of marten hair, nos. 8 and 12.
Masking fluid (liquid gum).
Absorbent paper.
Two containers with water.

262

263

264

Figs. 262, 263, 264 Only two colours are used in doing the practical exercises described on the following pages, cobalt blue and burnt umber. But in reality, you will also have the use of black produced by mixing the two colours, and the white of the paper. Observe, in these illustrations, the wide range of colours and tones that you can obtain using just the two colours mentioned.

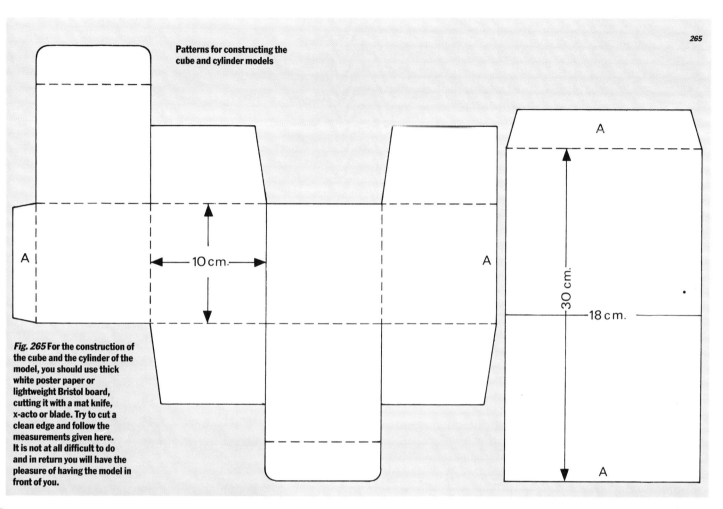

**Patterns for constructing the
cube and cylinder models**

10 cm.

30 cm.

18 cm.

A

A

A

A

265

Fig. 265 For the construction of
the cube and the cylinder of the
model, you should use thick
white poster paper or
lightweight Bristol board,
cutting it with a mat knife,
x-acto or blade. Try to cut a
clean edge and follow the
measurements given here.
It is not at all difficult to do
and in return you will have the
pleasure of having the model in
front of you.

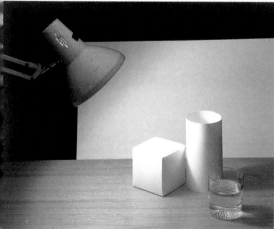

266

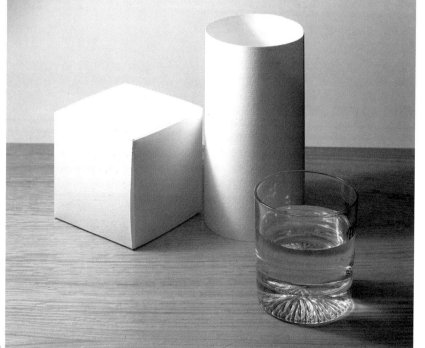

267

Figs. 266, 267 (Above) Note
the position of the model and
the type of lighting, coming
from the side, from the tabletop
lamp. Note the white Bristol
board behind the model as
background and, to the right,
the play of lights created by the
model.

Painting with two colours

First stage: drawing and reserving with masking fluid (Fig. 268) For this relatively easy drawing, I begin with the cylinder, noting that its height is equal to twice its width, while the left profile of the glass is just in the centre of the cube, and the diameter of the glass is slightly bigger than that of the cylinder, etc. As usual, I draw without shadows, using only line. Once the drawing is complete, I reserve the bright areas of the glass, by painting them with the masking fluid and synthetic brush. Notice in fig. 268 the small colour stains of the masking fluid which will allow me to find the reserved areas later on.

Second stage: painting the background (Fig. 269) Using clean water and a sponge I wet the surface of the paper to eliminate any possible residues of grease left by my hand while I was drawing. I wait for the moisture to dry before I wet the paper again, this time with the marten-hair brush no. 12, and only in the background area behind the model, following carefully the contours of the cube and cylinder. Watch out! Don't go past the line or the colour of the background will invade the shapes of the cube and the cylinder. Without allowing this new layer of water to dry, I paint the background warm grey, using a little more burnt umber than blue. I wait for a few minutes until this first paint wash dries. Then I paint the table, mixing blue and burnt umber with a predominance of the latter. But, pay attention: I don't paint with an absolutely regular and uniform wash. I mix the colours as I paint, at times mixing them on the paper itself, with the purpose of achieving a colour with slight variations.

Third stage: painting the cylinder and cube (Fig. 270) I go on to the cylinder. First wetting the visible part with water, reserving the part half hidden by the glass, and then painting over the still-moist area with a wash with a slightly bluish tendency. I charge the brush and, with a slightly zig-zagging stroke, I paint a dark stripe from the top to the bottom of the cylinder, still reserving the part hidden by the glass. Fast now! With the brush cleaned and a little wrung out, we have to dilute the previous colour in the shadowy area by degrading it as it moves towards the illuminated zone. I paint the side of the cube which is most in shadow, using a premixed wash. When the facing square has dried, I paint it a cold clearer grey colour.

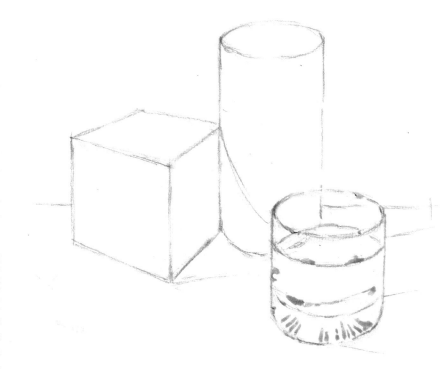

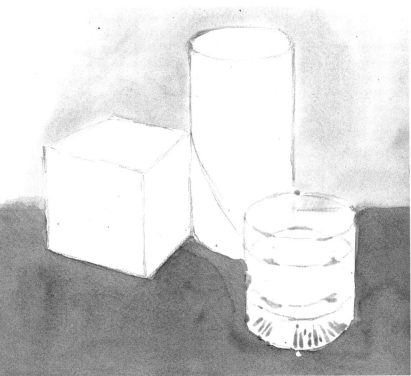

Fig. 268 The first stage of this two-colour painting exercise shows the drawing done in pencil and the small coloured spots of masking fluid, indicating the points where whites have been reserved.

Fig. 269 In this second stage, it is important to achieve the irregular colour of the table, with small variations that better reflect reality. The graded wash of the background, behind the geometric shapes, has of course been painted wet-in-wet.

Next, I paint the triangular shadow projected by the cube on the cylinder. And before it dries, soften the edges of the shadow so that it does not look so hard. I finally paint the shadow on the inside of the cylinder.

Fourth stage: the glass, shadows projected on the table, and some finishing touches (Fig. 271) I first paint with diluted gouache, indicating the construction form and slight variations of tone in the glass. While this dries I go to the background, darkening the area behind the angle formed by the edges of the cylinder and the cube, and paint wet-in-wet. Next I remove the masking fluid and retouch some of the uncovered white areas. I paint the shadows projected by the model on the table; when I reach the shadow of the glass, I have opened up a small spot of white to represent the light reflected by the glass's crystal surface. Finally, I work on the lights and shadows of the glass, thus finishing this study.

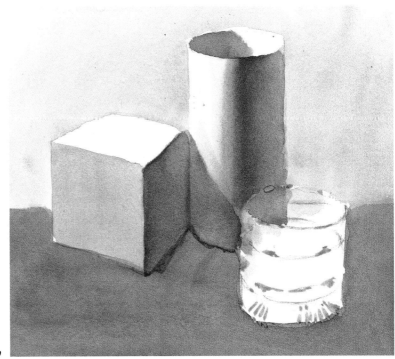

270

271

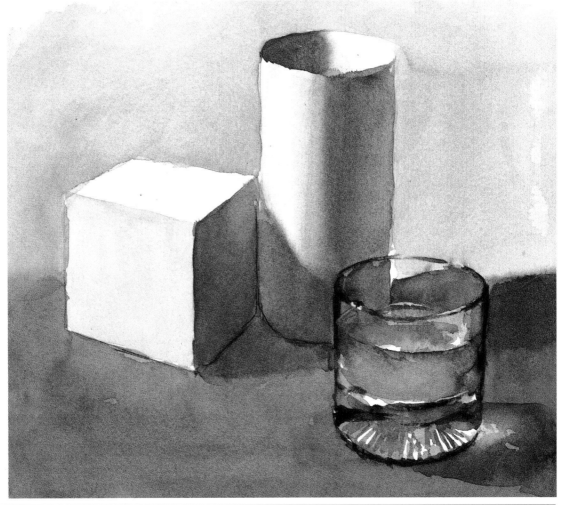

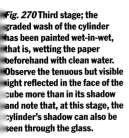

Fig. 270 Third stage; the graded wash of the cylinder has been painted wet-in-wet, that is, wetting the paper beforehand with clean water. Observe the tenuous but visible light reflected in the face of the cube more than in its shadow and note that, at this stage, the cylinder's shadow can also be seen through the glass.

Fig. 271 Removing the masking fluid by rubbing with the finger and uncovering the pure whites reserved previously is always a surprise...at times an unpleasant one because of the excessive contrast and the need to paint and retouch, to soften the harsh contrasts of the colour and the whites. Try, as I have done, to enrich the colour, diversifying tones and shades and painting blues, remembering that blue is visible in the glass, in the shadows, etc. Finally, note the black lines, drawn with ballpoint, that mark the bases of the cube and the inside edges, in the shadow, of the cube and the cylinder.

Examples in wash

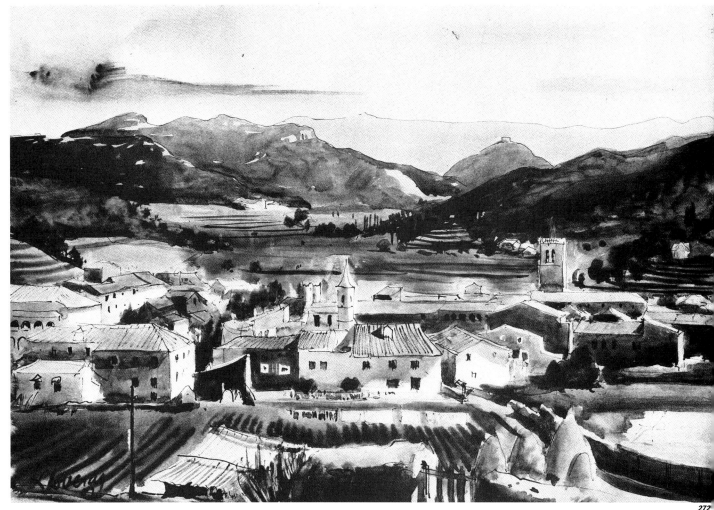

272

Fig. 272 Wash painting, even painting with only black watercolour or diluted Indian ink, offers ample possibilities for artistic expression. In addition, it is a perfect medium for getting started in the practice of watercolour painting. These pictures show an excellent wash painting of a landscape by Federico Lloveras, and a sketch I made of a child's head.

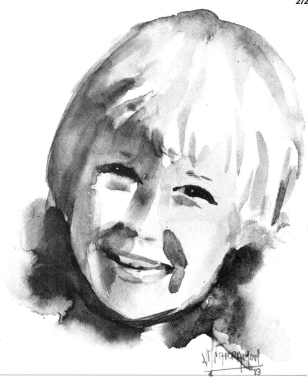

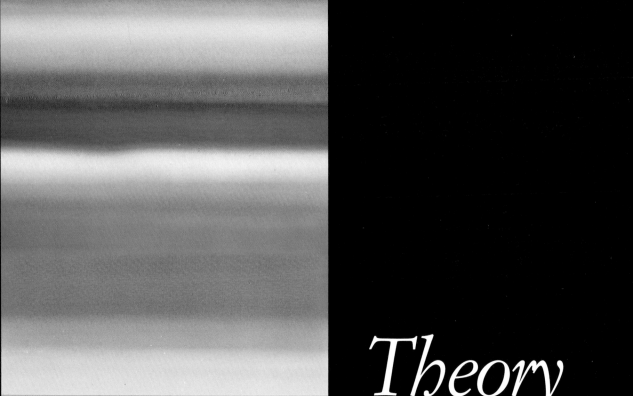

Theory

Primary, secondary and tertiary colours

To summarize:
Nature 'paints' with the *colours of light*. Newton, the physicist, reproduced the phenomenon of the rainbow: in a dark room he intercepted a light beam with a crystal prism, and was thus able to *decompose* the white light into the six colours of the spectrum. Young, another famous physicist, did the opposite: while doing research with coloured lamps, he was able to *recompose* light, obtaining white light. Besides this, he arrived at the important conclusion that the six colours of the spectrum could be reduced to three basic colours, from which he established the *three basic light colours*: green, red and dark blue. By mixing these three *light colours* in pairs, Young determined the *three secondary light colours*: cyan blue, purple, and yellow. To summarize: everything that you and I are seeing right now, is receiving the three basic light colours and, through extension, the three secondary light colours. Nature 'paints' with light colours.
In the studio we paint with pigment colours. Fortunately we paint with the same colours, with the difference that we change the primacy of some colours with reference to others, and we can thus say that:

Our primary colours
are the secondary light colours.
Our secondary colours
are the primary light colours.

Primary pigment colours (secondary light colours):

Yellow, cyan blue[1]*, purple*

Secondary pigment colours (primary or basic light colours), by paired mixture of the previous colours:

Red, green, dark blue

Pigment colour mixing is always supposed to *subtract light*, that is to say, to pass on from light to dark colours: if we mix red and green we get a darker colour – brown. We get black if we mix our three primary colours together. Physicists call this phenomenon *subtractive synthesis*. Light, in turn, 'paints' by *adding colours*: by adding a red beam to a green beam the amount of light is duplicated, and logically we obtain a clearer light, in this case yellow. This phenomenon is called *additive synthesis*.
Now look at the chromatic circle or table of pigment colours – our colours – derived from

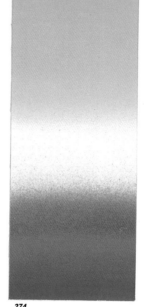

274

the three *primary* colours (P), which, mixed in pairs, produce the three *secondary* colours (S) which, if mixed again with the primary colours, make six more colours known as *tertiary* colours (T).
What we have seen and read up until now leads us to the following practical conclusions which justify our knowledge of the theories of colour:
– Light and the artist 'paint' with the same colours: the colours of the spectrum.
– The perfect coincidence between light colours and pigment colours permits the artist to imitate the effects of light as it illuminates forms and to reproduce, with great fidelity, all the colours of nature.
– In accordance with the theories of light and colour, the artist can paint all of the colours of nature, with only three primary colours: cyan blue, purple and yellow.

[1] The term 'cyan blue' does not appear in the colour charts for watercolour or oil paints. It belongs to the graphic arts and colour photography, and has been adopted for the present for the purpose of discussing colour theory. It corresponds to a neutral blue, very similar to Prussian blue when mixed with a tinge of white.

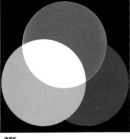

275

Fig. 274 The decomposition of light, discovered by Newton, gives place to the formation of the spectrum composed of six basic colours.

Fig. 275 Colours of light: additive synthesis.

Fig. 276 Pigment colours: subtractive synthesis.

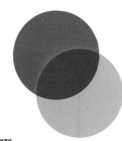

276

Complementary colours

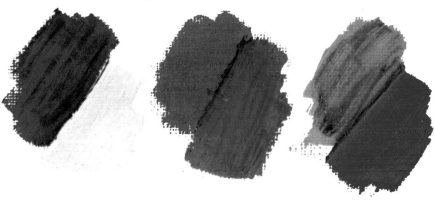

The chromatic colour wheel below shows that the colours are complements of each colour by pairing the colours one in front of the other. We thus see that:

Yellow *is the complement of* blue
Cyan *blue is the complement of* red
Purple *is the complement of* green
(and vice versa)

But, what is the use of knowing colour complements?
In order to create colour contrasts; to know, for example, that green next to red will make a really extraordinary contrast.
In order to paint with a different range of colours: a range of warm colours, cool colours, or broken colours, about which we will speak in the following pages.
In order to paint the colour of shadows, which we will discuss on the next page.

277

Fig. 277 The juxtaposition of complementary colours creates the maximum contrast of colour. The mixture of two complementary colours becomes a dusty black. When the mixture is not in the proper proportions, you get a range of broken colours, or a range of greyish colours when working with watercolours.

Fig. 278 Chromatic circle or table of pigment colours, in which the primary colours (indicated with a P) appear. Mixed together in pairs they yield the three secondary colours (S) which when mixed in pairs, one primary and one secondary, yield six tertiary colours (T). The smaller circle shows the paired complementary colours indicated with arrows. Below is the list and classification of these colours.

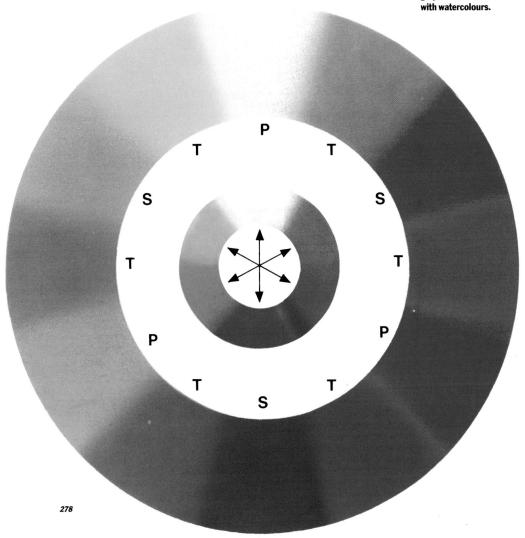

278

PIGMENT COLOURS

Primary
Yellow
Cyan blue
Purple

Secondary
Green
Red
Dark blue

Tertiary
Orange
Crimson
Violet
Ultramarine
Emerald green
Light green

The colour of forms; the colour of shadows

What's the colour of things?

Well, people say that bananas are yellow, that tomatoes are red, and that some flowers are blue, but in fact to us painters, these and all forms basically have three factors which determine their colour:

The local colour or colour of the object itself: the yellow of the bananas, the red of the tomatoes, that is to say, the intrinsic colour, not modified by light, shadow or the reflection of other colours.

The tonal colour: lighter or darker than the inherent colour, it is due to the effects of light and shadow that lighten or darken the yellow of the bananas, the red of the tomatoes.

The ambient or surrounding colour resulting from various factors: the colours reflected from the colours of surrounding objects; the colour of the light illuminating the forms which may be more or less orange, or blue; the intensity of the light; and the effects of the interposed atmosphere, which diffuses light and modifies colours, giving forms a greyish hue.

But in the end the colour of the form is there, in the model, and we have nothing to do other than observe carefully and follow its dictates. The biggest problem, the one that many amateurs (and some professionals) have not been able to grasp, is the colour of shadows. What's the colour of shadows? Is there a formula that would allow us to successfully solve the problem of painting the colour of shadows? I think so.

The colour of the shadow is constituted by:

1. *The colour blue, which is present in all darkness.*
2. *The local colour in a darker tonality.*
3. *The complementary of the local colour.*

Let's use some examples.

The colour blue, present in all darkness (fig. 279): this is certainly the most important of the three mentioned factors. Right from the beginning of the painting it is important to incorporate blue into the colour of the shadow.

The local colour in a darker tonality (fig. 280): the tonal colour, sienna appears in the shadow of yellow; carmine in that of red.

The complementary of the local colour (fig. 281): blue complements yellow; green complements red or carmine, and so on.

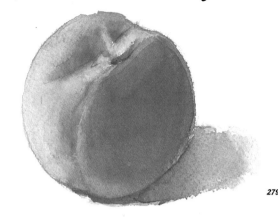

Fig. 279 If we could make a dissection of the colours that are in any shadow, we would see that, as in this peach, blue is present in all the colours, but in greater quantities in shadowed areas.

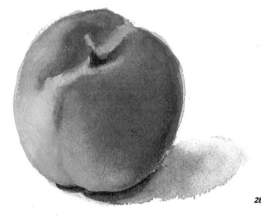

Fig. 280 In the same manner, the local or intrinsic colour is present in the shadow, but in a darker tone. Before Impressionism, which gave voice to this rule, artists achieved the colour of the shadows by adding brown or grey.

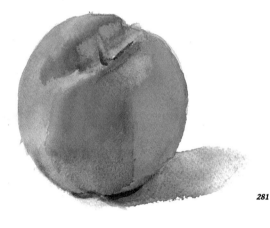

Fig. 281 Ever since the Impressionist movement, and following the laws of Chevreul, the complement of the colour of the object being painted is present in its shadow. If the intrinsic local colour is red, there is green in the shadow.

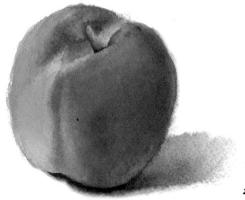

Fig. 282 Mixing the colours mentioned in the figures above gives us the colour of the shadows, with a marked approximation to reality. The artist will of course vary the proportions and quantities of colour to respond to his or her own style.

Colourists and value painters

How you mix these colours, what proportion of each you choose, depends on whether you want to paint in a classic or modern style – more classic if you accentuate the darker tonality of the local colour, and more modern if the tendency is bluer, mixing blue with the complement of the local colour. In either case, you will have solved the problem of the colour of shadow. That's what I hope.

Some artists paint almost completely with flat colour without shadow, especially in contemporary painting. Have you noticed this? These are the artists that André Lhote classified as *colourists*: 'those who rely mainly on colour'; those who, while painting outdoors, choose frontal illumination or diffused lighting without shadows, seeing and differentiating forms with colour reminiscent of the style of the Old Masters such as Fra Angelico, Hieronymus Bosch, the Brueghel brothers. And colour as form was a basic principle to the Impressionists and Fauvists from Van Gogh to Matisse to Derain, with their premeditated exploitation of colour, because, as Bonnard wrote, 'colour alone, without any help, is capable of representing mass and volume, and of expressing a pictorial climate'.

On the other side are the *value painters*, those artists who paint the model with lights and shadows, who use the natural shadow (shadow of the form itself) and the projected shadow to explain volume. In this group can be included all the classical painters and some as modern as Corot, Courbet, Nonell, and Dali. It seems obvious that the colourist is closer to the formulas and styles of the present – if it is true that 'there are neither good nor bad styles,' as André Lhote said, 'only good or bad ways of using them'. On the other hand there is no reason why one should follow a single formula: Picasso would sometimes paint with flat colour devoid of shadows, while at other times he would yield the role of protagonist to shading, modelling, mass, and volume. 'To paint? to draw?' Cézanne said. 'When the colour appears in all its richness, the form appears in all its plenitude.' But the question remains: you now know the two alternatives: will you then paint as a colourist or as a value painter?

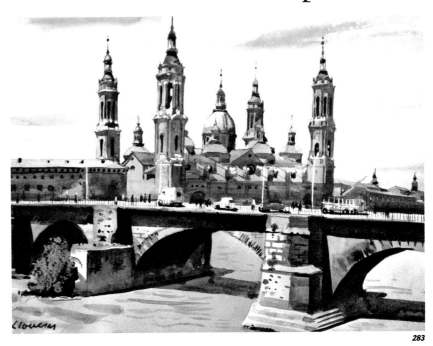

283

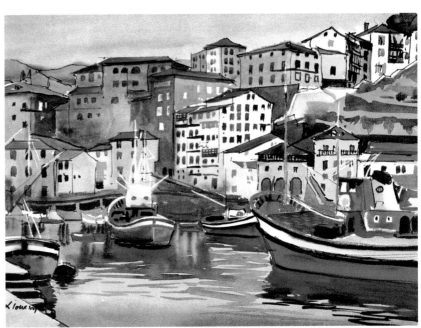

284

Fig. 283 Federico Lloveras, *El Pilar, Zaragoza*, private collection. An example of value painting. The artist attempts to achieve and explain the forms of objects through the use of light and shadow – a classical style of painting, used by most artists throughout the last century.

Fig. 284 Federico Lloveras, *Fishing Port in the North of Spain*, private collection. Here the same artist paints in the style of the colourist. Forms are not rendered by pattern or by the play of lights and shadow, but rather through the use of colour: the different colours of each house, each boat, each object. Modern painting contains many examples of the *colourist* interpretation, particularly among the art of the Fauvists and Expressionists.

Harmony

In 1840, at the age of sixty-five, Turner travelled for the second time to Venice, where he painted the best watercolours of his lifetime. They were, and still are, a marvel of technique, a fabulous mastery of water and colour, but above all, a masterly lesson on mixing and harmonizing colour. Looking at the extraordinary beauty of Venice painted with greys and blues, the great Constable said of Turner's work: 'He has been able to dye the atmosphere.' Turner did not arrive at these results by chance. It's certain that the concept of these famous watercolours responds to a preconceived idea of colour tendency or colour dominance, that Turner would then develop into a range of colours: 'A succession of perfectly organized colours or tonalities.'

In fact, a painting can be completely toned with colours of a blue tendency by using a *range of cold colours*; or it may be painted with a red tendency by using a *range of warm or hot colours*; in the same manner, it may offer a series of greyish tones and colours, through the use of a *range of broken colours*.

Fortunately for us artists, these colour ranges appear in the model itself, thanks to the fact that in nature there exists always, no matter what the theme may be, a *luminous tendency*, which causes a relationship between colours. At times, this tendency is very accentuated; for example, at daybreak on a foggy day when blue and grey dominate, or at sunset when everything is golden, yellow, and red. When the harmonizing of colours is not so evident, the artist must plan and organize; accentuate, exaggerate...imagine a colour tendency and hold onto it with a true obsession, from the moment he starts painting to the finishing touches.

Do it this way, and perhaps you too will be able to 'dye the atmosphere'.

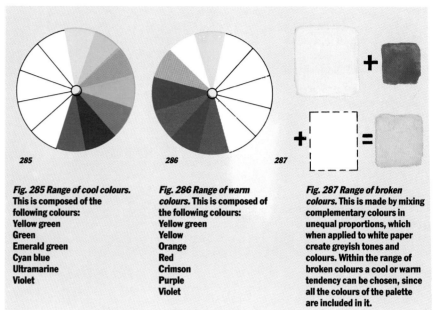

285   286   287

Fig. 285 Range of cool colours. This is composed of the following colours:
Yellow green
Green
Emerald green
Cyan blue
Ultramarine
Violet

Fig. 286 Range of warm colours. This is composed of the following colours:
Yellow green
Yellow
Orange
Red
Crimson
Purple
Violet

Fig. 287 Range of broken colours. This is made by mixing complementary colours in unequal proportions, which when applied to white paper create greyish tones and colours. Within the range of broken colours a cool or warm tendency can be chosen, since all the colours of the palette are included in it.

288

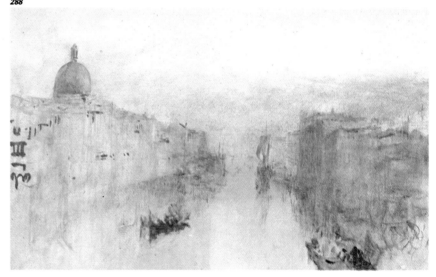

289

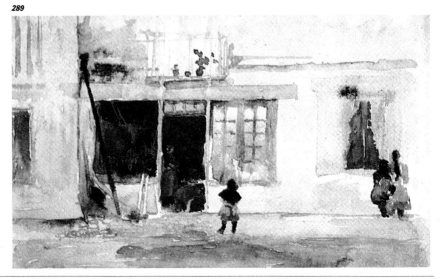

Fig. 288 Turner, *Venice: The Grand Canal*, Tate Gallery, London. One of Turner's watercolours, painted during his second trip to Venice, this offers an example of a range of cool colours.

Fig. 289 Whistler, *Grey and Green. A shop in England*, Glasgow University, donated by Birnie Philip. A good example of a subject painted with a palette of broken colours of greyish tendency.

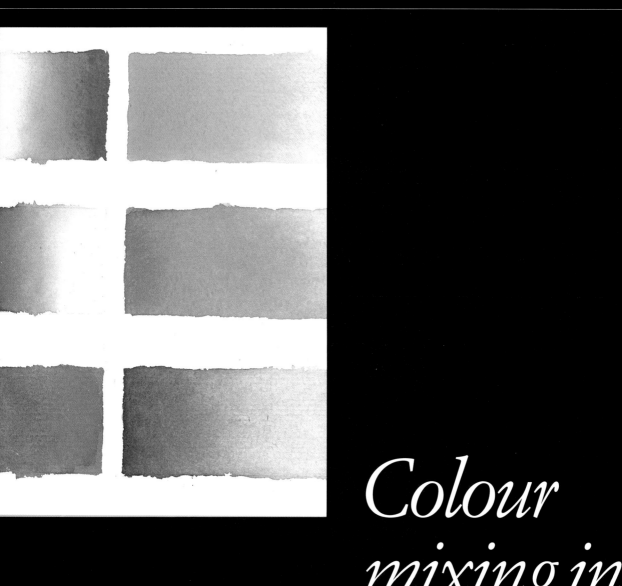

Colour
mixing in

Three basic colours

Light, colour, pigments, primaries, secondaries...
No, no. We're not going to continue talking about colour theories, but rather the practical application of these theories, which, as we said before, allow us to make the fabulous discoveries of Newton and Young so that we may:

Paint all the colours of nature with only three colours.

The three primary pigment colours – yellow, cyan blue, and purple – mixed in pairs, give us the secondaries, green, red, and dark blue, and all six, mixed in pairs, give us the tertiaries, and so on and on.
The equivalent in watercolour or gouache of these three magic colours is:

Cadmium yellow medium
Prussian blue
Alizarin crimson carmine
(Plus the white of the paper)

Fig. 291 Here is a watercolour note that I myself did painting with only three colours, cadmium yellow medium, Prussian blue, and rose madder.

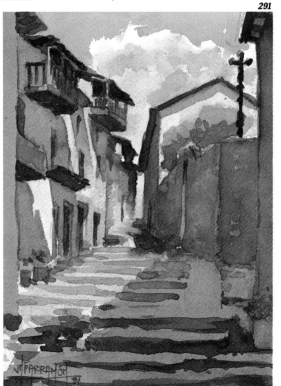
291

Fig. 292 A. Graded wash of cadmium yellow medium.

B. Graded wash of cyan blue.

C. Graded wash of alizarin crimson carmine.

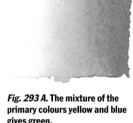

Fig. 293 A. The mixture of the primary colours yellow and blue gives green.

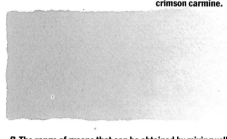

B. The range of greens that can be obtained by mixing yellow and blue is practically infinite.

Fig. 294 A. Mixing carmine and yellow, we obtain red.

B. Note the wide range of reds, oranges, and yellows that can be obtained by mixing crimson and yellow.

Fig. 295 A. Blue mixed with purple gives us an intense blue of violet tones.

B. With cyan blue and purple a wide range of carmines, purples and violets can be achieved.

Fig. 296 A. When the three primary colours are mixed together, they produce black.

B. This is the range of greys that is obtained with the black produced by mixing the three primary colours.

Warm colours

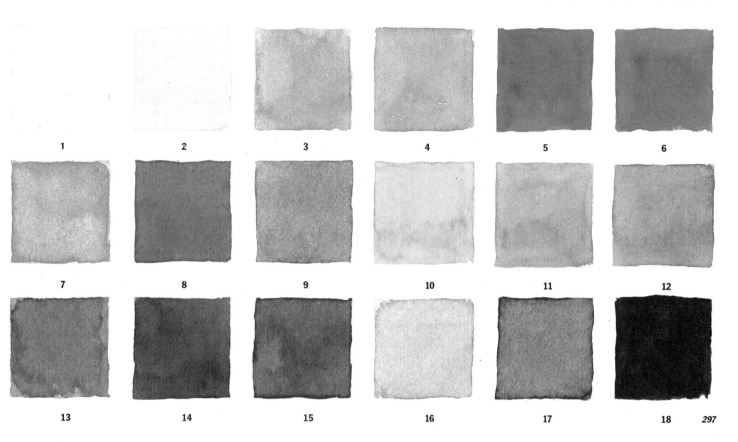

1 2 3 4 5 6

7 8 9 10 11 12

13 14 15 16 17 18 *297*

This exercise will serve as the preamble to a whole watercolour painted with these three colours.
You will need the following materials:
Medium-grain paper, 250 g or more, of good quality.
The three colours mentioned above.
Palette or palette-box.
Brush of marten hair no. 8.
Roll of absorbent paper.
Two containers with clean water.
Please read the following instructions referring to the numbered samples above: together they will provide you with instructions for mixing a vast range of colours.

1. *Lemon yellow:* Made with only cadmium yellow and water.
2. *Light rose yellow for skin tone:* Made with the above and a very small wash of carmine.
3. *Pink yellow:* The previous colour with a bit more carmine.
4. *Light orange:* Intense cadmium yellow with a little bit of carmine.
5. *English red:* Intense charge of yellow and carmine.
6. *Vermilion:* Intense charge of carmine with a bit of yellow.
7. *Pink:* Carmine with abundant water.
8. *Light carmine:* Wash of intense carmine.
9. *Purple:* Wash of carmine with a bit of Prussian blue.
10. *Light yellow ochre:* First a wash with more yellow than carmine; then add little by little a small quantity of blue.
11. *Dark yellow ochre:* Same as the previous, but increasing the yellow and the blue.
12. *Natural sienna:* First an orange (4 or 6 above) and, little by little, add blue.
13. *Burnt sienna:* Mix an intense purple; then add yellow.
14. *Van Dyck brown:* A thick mixture of intense blue and yellow; then add carmine until you achieve this warm dark maroon.
15. *Warm bottle green:* Charge of intense blue, a little carmine and yellow.
16. *Light grey of warm tendency:* Lots of water, a very light purple, and a clear wash of yellow.
17. *Dark grey of warm tendency:* Mix a dark purple of blue tendency; little by little add yellow.
18. *Black:* Thick amounts of blue and carmine will render an almost black colour; add a little yellow for a warm black.

Warm colours

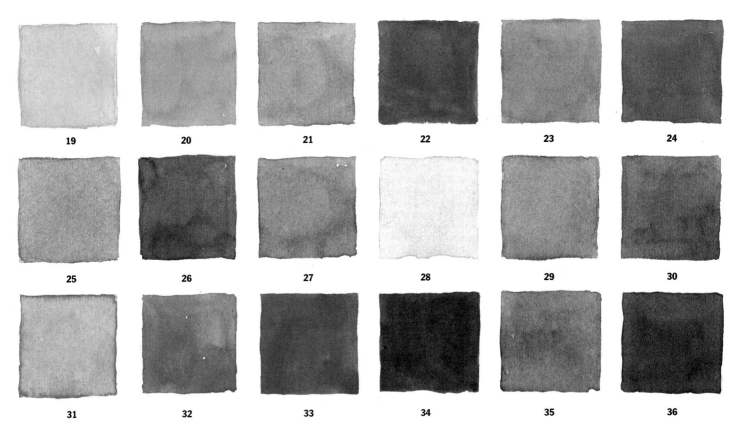

19   20   21   22   23   24

25   26   27   28   29   30

31   32   33   34   35   36

298

We continue painting with warm colours, but we now incorporate greens and even blues into our mixes, since in a range of warm colours nuances of cold colours may intervene, that is, 'cold' colours with a warm tendency. Thus, this green will reflect a bit of red or sienna, and here the blue will show a nuance of brown or carmine.

19. *Yellow green:* Wash of yellow with a bit of blue.
20. *Permanent green:* A neutral colour neither cold nor warm, which you may make simply with yellow and blue.
21. *Olive green:* The previous colour with a bit of carmine.
22. *Dark green or emerald green:* Undiluted blue and yellow, the latter in smaller quantities, plus a touch of carmine.
23. *Greyish blue:* A wash of blue mixed with a very light wash of carmine.
24. *Darker grey blue:* The same as above but increasing the amounts.
25. *Warm blueish grey:* First make a

wash of blueish green with lots of water, then add a wash of carmine.
26. *Dark warm grey:* The same as above but increasing the amounts.
27. *Khaki:* Blueish green and a bit of carmine.
28. *Warm clear grey:* A very clear watery wash of blue and green and a still lighter (more watery) wash of carmine. (It is preferable with colours as liquid as this one to mix on a clean palette or test paper.)
29. *Light purple:* A wash of carmine and blue with an addition of some very light yellow wash.
30. *Neutral grey:* A wash of all three colours in equal amounts, but with a little more blue.
31. *Dark yellow green:* Somewhat intense yellow, a little bit of blue, and a very light wash of carmine.
32. *Natural sienna:* The same composition as that in the previous colour, adding a bit of carmine.
33. *Venice red:* Identical composition as colour 32 with a bit more carmine.
34. *Burnt umber:* Now add a bit of blue wash to the composition of the

previous colour.
35. *Light burnt umber:* The previous colour with more water and a bit more blue, that is, clearing and dirtying at the same time.
36. *Dark neutral grey:* Mix a neutral grey like that in colour 30; slightly increase the amount of each colour.

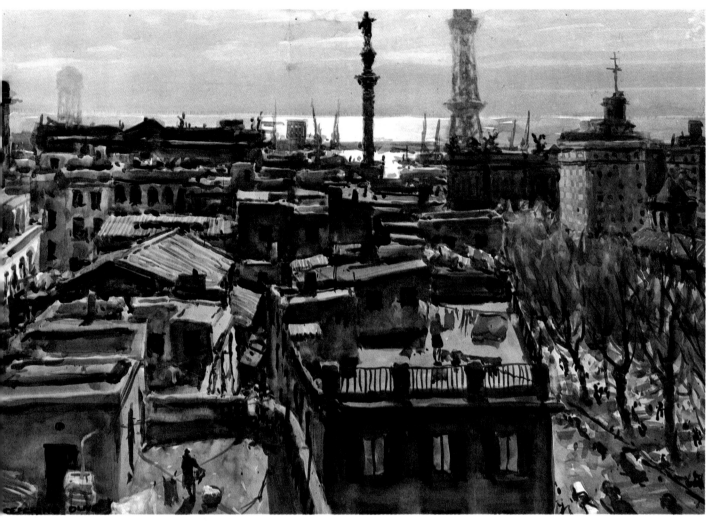

299

Fig. 299 Ceferino Olivé, *Plaza del teatro (Barcelona)*, private collection. A notable example of colour harmony in a warm range.

Cold colours

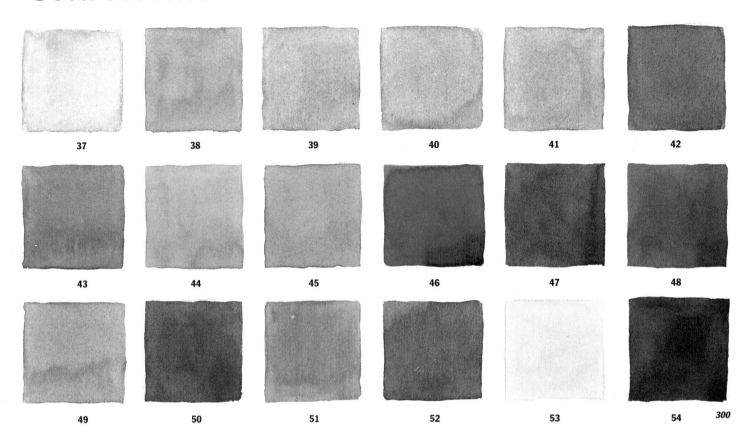

We are now going to mix a range of cold colours with greys, blues, greens and violets predominating, but without eliminating the yellow, reds and sienna which may exist in an ensemble of cold colours, provided they retain a green-blue-grey tendency.

37. *Light blue:* Simply a blue wash with abundant water.

38. *Sky blue with warm tendency:* A blue wash mixed with a very light yellow wash.

39. *Sky blue of red or carmine tendency:* A blue wash with abundant water, mixed with carmine wash.

40. *Medium neutral grey:* The three colours equally distributed, with a slightly larger amount of blue.

41. *Light cold grey:* The previous colour, increasing the blue a little.

42. *Dark cold grey:* First mix a purple of medium intensity with a heavy load of colour. Add a little yellow and neutralize again with carmine and blue.

43. *Medium blue:* Simply a wash of very intense blue.

44. *Meadow green:* Blue and a bit of yellow with a heavy load of both colours.

45. *Blue green:* Made of blue and yellow, loaded more with blue.

46. *Navy blue:* Prussian blue with much paint and little water.

47. *Violet:* Prussian blue and intense carmine.

48. *Blueish carmine (or dark carmine):* An intense wash of carmine with a little blue.

49. *Light earth green:* Compose an orange with yellow and carmine; little by little add blue.

50. *Dark earth green:* The same as the previous colour with increased amounts of each colour to make it darker.

51. *Dirty orange:* Mix yellow and carmine to make an orange, then add a bit of blue which will 'cool' it off.

52. *Sienna:* Compose a wash with carmine and yellow to make a light red; then add a bit of blue.

53. *Dark lemon yellow:* Can the colour yellow belong to a cold range? Yes. It is a yellow with blueish tendency, with a little bit of blue, which gives us a yellow closer to the cold range.

54. *Cold black:* A thick load of Prussian blue, a smaller quantity of carmine, and a little yellow. Increase the blue if necessary in order for the blue tendency to become evident.

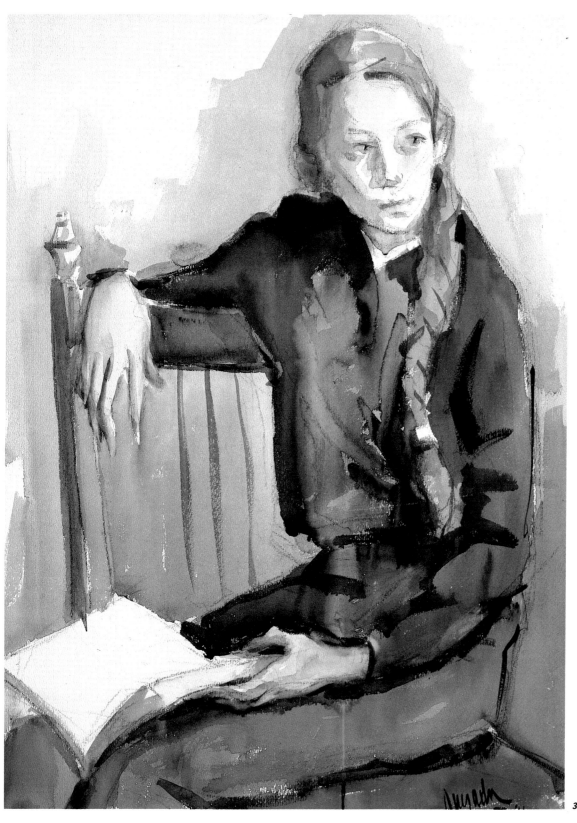

Fig. 301 Julio Quesada, *Niña Venezolana*, private collection. A magnificent example of colour harmony using a range of cold colours.

301

Broken colours

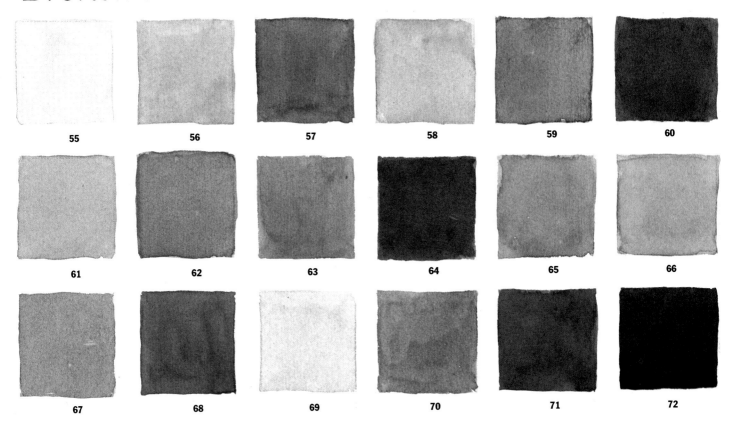

Here we have a range of broken colours, worn-out colours, close to grey or 'dirty' colours. Some colours, you will remember, are the product of the mixture of two complementaries in unequal amounts and white. In watercolour the white is the paper, so the first part of the formula is enough.

55. *Light yellowish grey:* Using plenty of water, mix blue and carmine to make a violet blue, then add a bit of yellow (violet blue or purple is the complementary of yellow).

56. *Medium yellowish grey:* The same composition, with higher amounts of colour.

57. *Dark yellowish grey:* This is a good colour to practise the combination of complementaries mixed in unequal proportions. On the one hand the blue and the carmine when mixed give us the violet blue, and on the other, the complementary yellow is added in smaller quantities. When we add the white of the paper,

the broken colour appears.

58. *Light grey carmine:* Make a light green and add a wash of carmine.

59. *Medium grey carmine:* The same as the previous procedure, increasing the amounts slightly.

60. *Dark grey with a carmine tendency:* Make a very clean green with a heavy load of colour and slowly add carmine until you get to this colour.

61. *Ochre:* Begin with a clean orange wash; then mix in blue in increasing amounts until you arrive at this colour.

62. *Olive green:* Mix a clean green in a medium intense wash; little by little add carmine until you arrive at this colour.

63. *Light sepia:* Mix a brilliant green with enough paint and slowly add carmine.

64. *Intense sepia:* As previously but using more colour and finally adding either a little more blue or carmine.

65. *Greyish blue:* A blue wash with

little carmine and even less yellow.

66. *Broken green yellow:* Begin with a very clear yellow wash; add a wash of carmine and blue.

67. *Broken sky blue:* Prepare a very clean blue wash and add a very clear wash of carmine and yellow.

68. *Greyish blue:* The same colours as previously but in a more intense wash.

69. *Light neutral grey:* Mix washes of the three colours, adding in layers on the test paper, so that the three colours interact in equal proportions.

70. *Medium neutral grey:* Like the previous procedure, using larger quantities.

71. *Payne's grey:* A neutral grey with blueish tendency, this is made with intense blue, a bit of carmine, and less yellow.

72. *Neutral grey:* Intense thick blue, to which is added a bit of carmine and a bit less yellow. Test it before painting, because the actual nuance is not appreciated without seeing it on white paper.

'Special' colours

Sometimes amateurs with little experience will ask: is there a special colour to paint silver or gold? What colour should one mix in order to paint glass?

Let me answer these questions by saying that there aren't special colours to paint silver, there isn't a gold colour, nor is there a colour to paint glass objects.

Glass does not have colour: To paint a glass object is more complicated than painting a cube but not more difficult. If anything, it is more laborious (painful), more time-consuming. You have to observe the model attentively and consciously; you have to study the forms, transparencies, tonalities, and colours. 'One has to stupidly copy everything,' as the great Michelangelo used to say. There is no secret, or any special ability: the colours we see through a crystal object or reflected on their surfaces, are as concrete as those of a table or an apple. What happens is that these surfaces appear to vary in brightness and are broken by reflections; this slightly modifies the tonality of certain colours, and sometimes promotes small deformations, but that's all.

And the colour gold does not exist: If we had to determine the local colour of gold, we would certainly choose yellow ochre to begin with. But gold without brilliance or reflections would stop being gold. The colour gold is the result of an ensemble of nuances, stains and small degradations, that can go from white to black (depending on the colours that the gold may reflect), passing through carmines, greens, siennas, ochres, reds, yellows, blues.

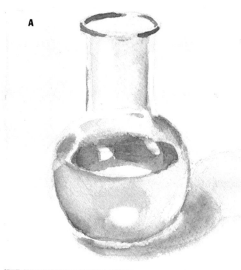

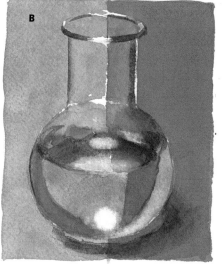

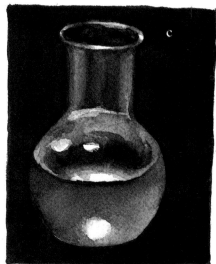

Fig. 303 Glass has no colour. This glass receptacle (A) is white because it is placed in front of a white background which we see through the transparent glass. The same receptacle, placed in front of a red and orange background (B), appears to have these colours, with the edge of the colours slightly deformed by the shape of the receptacle. Against a black background, a glass object (C) is physically recognized by the reflections of the lights and colours around it.

303

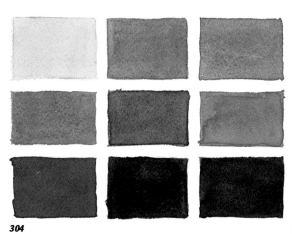

304

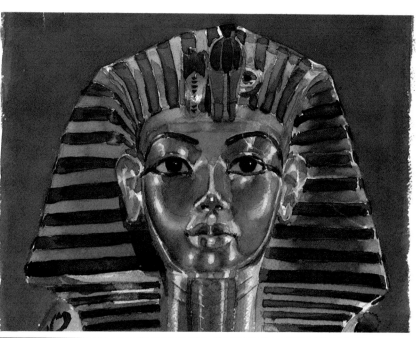

305

Fig. 304 Here is a basic range of colours for painting a gold object.

Fig. 305 With this range of colours I have painted the subject on the right. As you can see there is no gold colour, but there is a series of colours and shades which, viewed and copied precisely, allow us to represent a gold object.

Painting a watercolour with three colours

If you have painted the colour ranges as I proposed to you in the last few pages, you're now ready to use the same three colours to paint a still life that you can prepare yourself. This is a very profitable exercise for anyone who paints watercolours: it reminds us of the importance of the three primary colours, and affirms the idea that in order to paint it is not necessary to use a wide range of colours.

But let's do it. Let's paint.

Choose the objects that will compose our still life painting. Try to compose a motif, not a theme; thinking about an original image, place the objects on top of a table, in an apparently casual arrangement. But let this arrangement respond, insofar as possible, to a concrete scheme of composition. I have tried to follow this road: I have positioned the objects of the model in a triangular scheme. I have made up my mind, besides, to paint as a colourist, using a range of cold colours, factors that may be guessed from the photograph of the model (fig. 306).

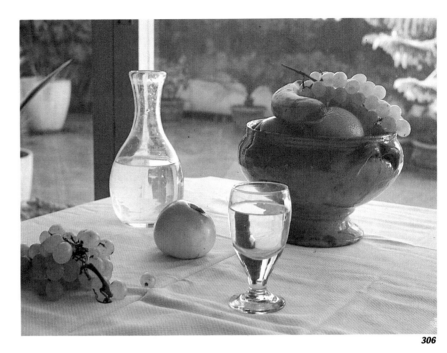

306

First stage: drawing and applying masking fluid (Fig. 307) First I do a test sketch, which I afterwards redraw with more precision; I draw without shading, using only lines made with a no. 2B pencil. Next, using synthetic hair brush no. 4, I cover and reserve some white areas with masking fluid. Pay attention to this point. There are two aspects that I want to underline: first, masking fluid is a means, not an end. Use it as a resource, but do not abuse it. As we will see shortly, it is much better to reserve whites by leaving out paint than using the masking fluid. Second, apply the masking fluid with a great deal of care, anticipating the *situation and exact dimension* of the white space. Masking fluid has a colour; it is visible, and is therefore easy to apply.

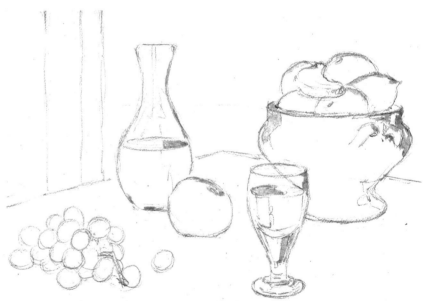

307

Second stage: general tinting in the background and large areas (Fig. 308) I begin by wiping the entire surface with a damp sponge filled with clean water, in order to eliminate any possible residues of grease left by my hand when I was drawing. Once it's dry, I again wet the background area behind the fruit bowl and water jar, using a brush made of marten hair, no. 12 (I paint with the drawing board slanted about 60 degrees on a desk easel). I mix a cold grey for the background. As I apply it, I mix in strokes of blue, carmine and yellow, mixing and varying the original grey on the paper. I continue with the light grey-blue-green of the tablecloth, making it

darker in the foreground, and attempting as well to enrich and diversify the colour (notice how I have bypassed the top edge of the wine glass and jar); and I end up tinting with washes some of the larger areas such as the apple and the fruit dish.

Fig. 309 (Right) Using masking fluid, I reserve only the objects made of glass and ceramic. Nevertheless, when the fluid is lifted off, the awful blanks constitute an unpleasant surprise, and throw doubt on the use of the liquid rubber.

Third stage: colour intensifying colour, modelling, removing the masking fluid (fig. 309) I now paint the bright colours of the fruit in flat tones without shadows, as well as the fruit dish, also as a colourist. I paint the lone apple. With cold greys I model the wine glass and the water jar. Next I remove the masking fluid by rubbing with my finger, at the same time rubbing out the residue of lead pencil. Observe the state of the watercolour in fig 309, and note the sharp contrast of the forms reserved with masking fluid. These will require retouching to smooth some edges and soften transitions with glazes.

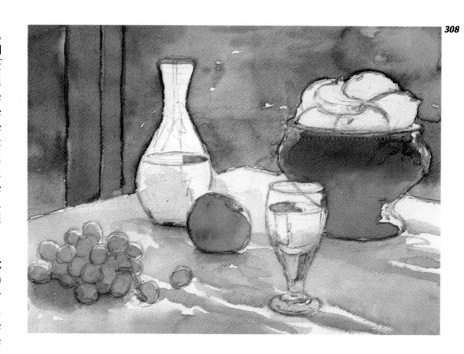

308

Fourth and last stage: general adjustment of colour and finishing touches (Fig. 310) I have begun by painting some glazes (very clear washes), harmonizing some of the harsh whites reserved by the masking fluid in the reflections in the jar and wine glass, in the luminous haloes of the fruit, the fruit dish, and

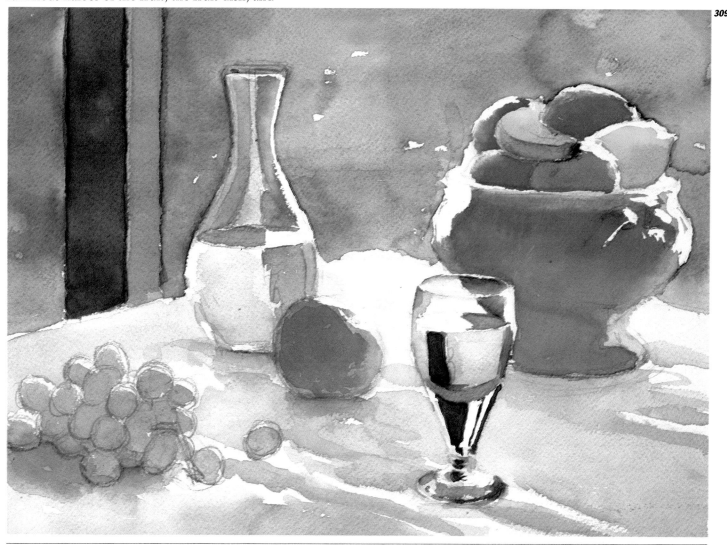

309

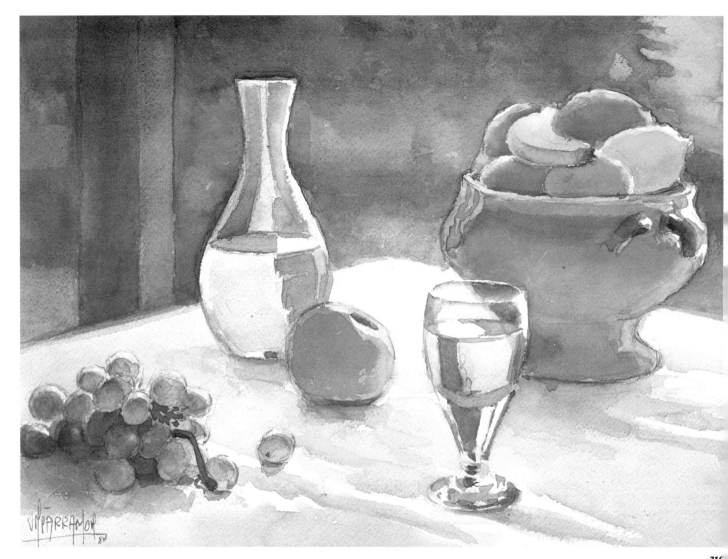

310

the apple. Next, I reinforce the colour of the fruit dish, adjusting some of the colours. I finish modelling the wine glass and jar. Be careful there! It would be fun to mix a general grey colour and to paint everything with the same colour. But on the contrary, we have to change and diversify the colours, accentuating the warm and cool tendencies offered by the model. Lastly, I finish the wrinkles of the tablecloth in the foreground. Before signing it,

I spend a day without looking at the painting. It is always true that the next day there is something one hadn't seen, something that could be improved. I have only painted with the three primary colours: cadmium yellow medium, Prussian blue, and alizarin crimson carmine. I have worked on 300 g paper, mounted on a block, and I have painted with moist watercolours in tubes and brushes of marten hair nos. 8, 12, and 14.

Fig. 310 If you have painted a watercolour like this, using your own model and composition, it will probably be difficult for your family and friends to believe that you painted with only three colours. You will have to prove to them that it is true and convince them that in fact, with only three colours, it is possible to paint all the colours that are found in nature.

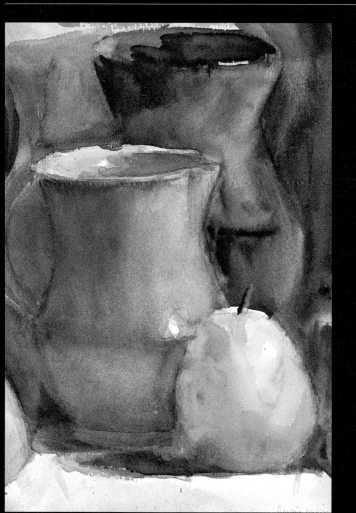

Technique

Dry watercolours, wet watercolours

Dry painting is basically painting with transparent paints, using the shine of the paper and defining the contours and limits of the objects where called for by the model. This does not mean eliminating the breakdown or diffusion of cylindrical or spherical objects, nor does it call for painting the background in absolutely clear-cut and defined terms, as the latter would mean doing away with atmospheric effects.

Of course, dry painting involves the risk of the watercolours separating (see fig. 312), because the wash may dry while painting.

Dry painting with watercolours must progress from less to more, painting the light sections first, which may be used to finish large areas, and then applying darker coats.

Well then, if you look closely you will agree that *dry watercolour painting is like classical watercolour painting*, with no particular special technique: in fact, when someone uses the term 'dry watercolour' they are differentiating it from 'wet watercolour' because the latter does indeed require special techniques.

The technique for wet watercolour painting consists basically of painting on damp paper,

so that the limits and contours of the objects appear diffused and not clearly defined. This lack of definition also appears in interior forms or profiles. The two paintings shown on the following page explain the technique of damp watercolour painting better than words. The degree of dampness is a basic factor; the greater the dampness, the more the colours will run and the greater the effect of 'bleeding' or lack of definition, and vice versa. Therefore, one must control the degree of dampness by moistening with the brush or by absorbing and decreasing the dampness with an absorbent paper towel. Remember, one must paint on damp, but not wet, paper. An artist friend of mine who is an expert in this technique told me: 'One must always be watching the paper from an angle that shows the reflections: if the surface shines, then there is too much water and one cannot paint. The surface is perfect when it has totally absorbed the water but is not yet dry.'

Damp watercolour painting is recommended for painting landscapes or seascapes on grey days, for urban scenes on rainy days, for fog, and so on.

312

Fig. 312 Here is a watercolour with a *break* in it; a consequence of having been painted without the necessary continuity.

Fig. 313 Guillem Fresquet, *Naturaleza muerta*, private collection. This is a classic watercolour or *dry* watercolour. As such, the boundaries and outlines of the objects are clearly delineated, but to create atmosphere the artist has toned down the shapes in the background.

313

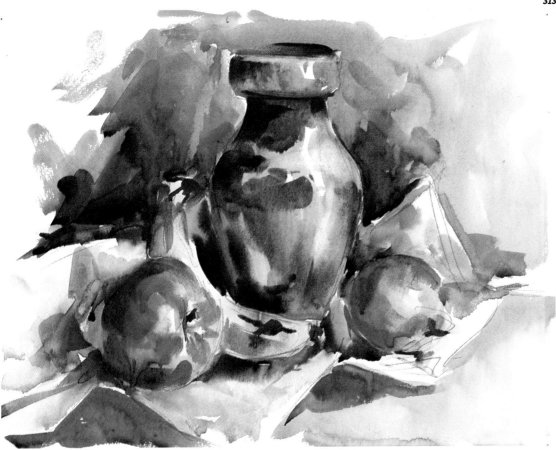

Wet watercolours

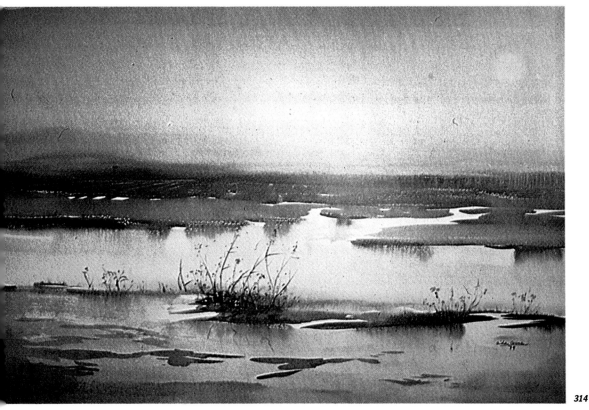

Fig. 314 Aida Corina, *Marsh* (First medal at the XLVII Autumn Exhibition, Madrid). Swamps and marshes on plains like this are an excellent subject for painting wet in watercolours, beautifully achieved in this picture which combines diffused shapes without boundaries with a number of concrete profiles, and some foreground shapes which are perfectly defined.

314

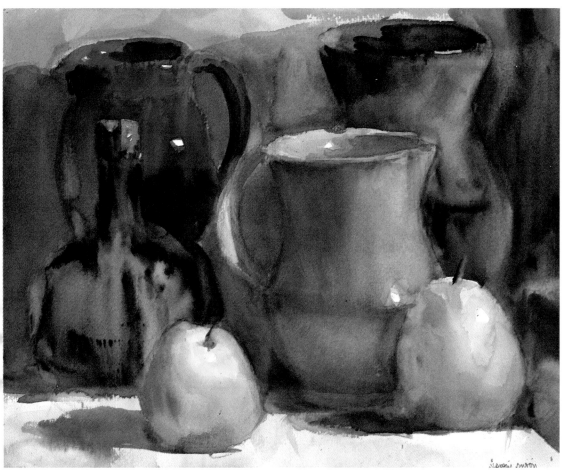

Fig. 315 J. Martin Anton, *Still Life*, private collection. The undeniable artistic quality of this watercolour stems in large part from the use of the wet-in-wet technique. The author, a teacher, painted this watercolour as a demonstration for a course organized by the Catalan Association of Watercolour Painters.

315

Synthesis

Giorgio Vasari, the renowned chronicler of the Renaissance, compared the styles of Donatello and Luca della Robbia this way when writing in 1550: 'The same feeling of beauty and vigour may frequently be observed in those rapid drawings which arise out of creative frenzy and are achieved with a minimum of lines, while an excess of industry and patience on the part of the artist who will not leave well enough alone robs the work of force and freshness.'

In all periods, but more so since the Renaissance, the great masters have felt the need to synthesize in their drawings and paintings, to summarize, to abbreviate. The famous 'shorthand' of Velázquez, who painted a rose with fewer brushstrokes than there were petals, was greatly admired, and served as a lesson to the great masters of Impressionism, such as Manet, who travelled to Madrid to see and copy it first-hand. And speaking of Manet, on 10 August 1907, the writer Georges Jeanniot explained in the French magazine *La Grande Revue* that he was with Manet when the latter painted *The Bar at the Folies-Bergère*. 'The model,' wrote Jeanniot, 'an attractive woman, posed behind a table filled with bottles and food. Watching Manet paint, I became aware of his masterful simplifications. Everything was abbreviated. Later Manet told me: "In art, synthesis is a necessity and a mark of elegance. The terse man makes us think; the loquacious one bores us."'

The watercolours of John Singer Sargent are a

1. Squinting the eyes when synthesizing

Sargent, a master of synthesis, at one time had a few students to whom he repeated the following lesson: 'Always cultivate your powers of observation. Learn to see the model through squinted eyes.'

Wherever you are, if you look around you with squinted eyes, you will automatically cut out details, seeing only the large volumes, the large masses of colour. Squinting is simply looking with the eyes almost closed, maintaining a certain tension in the eyelids (see the adjoining illustration) so that the objects lose definition and appear blurry, like a camera image out of focus. It is good to get into the habit while painting of occasionally looking at the model with squinted eyes. This will involve

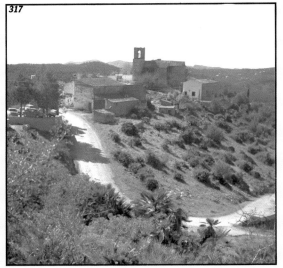
317

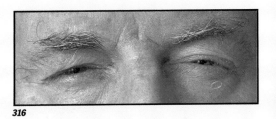
316

adopting an attitude which will undoubtedly develop your powers of observation and synthesis, essential for good watercolour painting.

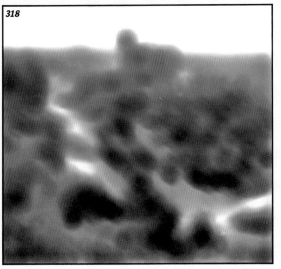
318

Fig. 317 In this photograph the landscape is viewed normally. The minute details of the windows and doors can be appreciated, as well as the leaves on the plants, and the trees and shrubs in the foreground.

Fig. 318 Here the same landscape is viewed as if the eyes were half closed. The merging of small forms, diffused shapes and elimination of small details makes it possible to appreciate the bodies in synthesis.

perfect example of synthesis. Sargent began studying drawing and painting at 14 years of age, first in Florence and later in Paris, where he learned from the painter Emile Carolus-Duran. Carolus-Duran taught his students to see and paint spontaneously, *au premier* coup as he put it. According to Sargent's biographers, Carolus-Duran would repeat over and over again to his students the following rule, which I want to emphasize:

'All that is not indispensable is prejudicial.'

Synthesis in drawing and painting is expression with fewer lines, fewer brushstrokes: 'corseting the details' as Ingres put it. Synthesis involves looking at the model with squinted eyes, painting with a wide brush.

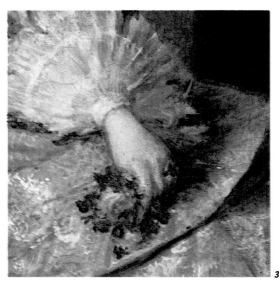

Fig. 319 Velázquez, *La Infanta Margarita* (detail), Prado, Madrid. I would risk asserting that Velázquez must have looked at the model with his eyes half closed to achieve this 'abbreviated manner', as his first master, Francesco Pacheco, called it.

319

2. Synthesizing using a large brush
This factor also has to do with your attitude, with a predisposition to summarize and interpret, difficult to obtain when painting with a fine brush, since the latter may lead you to feel an obligation to explain the small details, the intimate aspects of the shapes. Paint on rather large paper, don't paint small paintings, and paint with a large brush.

David Cox, the English watercolourist of the last century, wrote some books and treatises on watercolour painting. In one of them, according to his biographer Solly, he wrote: 'I like to work with a wide brush, very damp and as full as possible of paint.'

3. Synthesizing by painting rapidly
I have found, from my own experience, squinting and painting with a broad brush on a large surface, an attitude that favours creativity: looking at the model – rapidly turning the head to look at the painting – the typical gesture of leaning back and stretching out the arm – making a rapid stroke with the brush – again squinting at the model – returning to the painting and adding a new colour at great speed, etc. A procedure encouraging rapid painting – *al prima*, or *au premier coup* – and carrying within it the very idea of synthesis in painting.

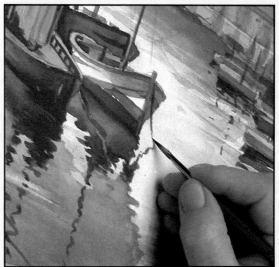

Fig. 320 If you work with small, fine brushes you will paint small, finely detailed things. A no. 3 or a no. 4 brush may be used for painting a super-realistic area, but I would venture my own opinion that super-realism is not appropriate for watercolour painting.

320

321

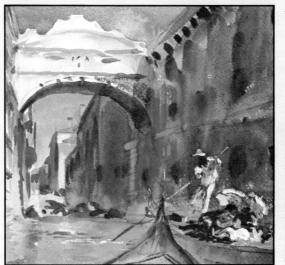

Fig. 321 John Singer Sargent, *The Bridge of Sighs*, Brooklyn Museum, New York. In an authentic watercolour it must be possible to see the transparency of the colours, the effect of the water and the action of the brush. The synthesis of forms and colours must be obvious, as well as the spontaneity and freshness of a premeditated but rapid resolution. This is what you see in Sargent's watercolours, where the immediacy of the brushstrokes is evident.

Synthesis and interpretation

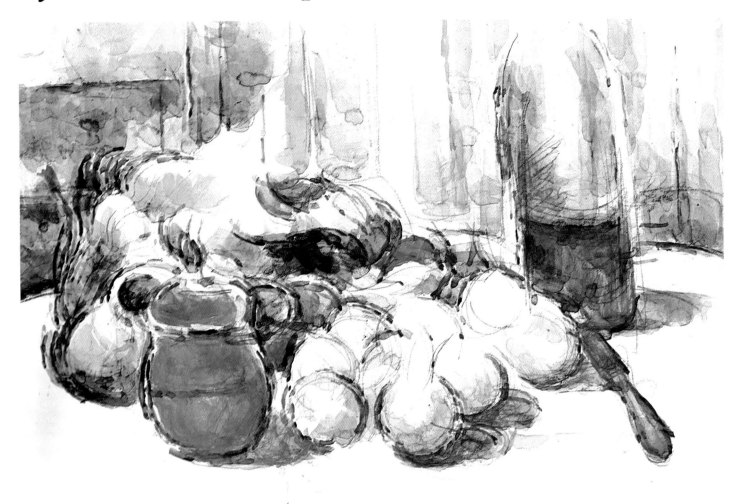

322

'In art there are two paths: one is architecture and allusion; the other realities as the world shows them.' This quote from the Spanish playwright Ramón M. del Valle Inclán expresses in a few words the two options an artist has: a) painting reality, limiting oneself to the imitation of nature and copying the forms and colours just as they appear in the model; or b) painting the architecture of nature and the construction of the model by seeing them and interpreting them in one's own way, even modifying reality. The choice between these two options leaves no room for doubt: artists have always tried to paint *their* paintings, making an effort to see the subject matter in their own way. In his 'Diary', Eugène Delacroix strongly defends the use of allusion during a discussion of the choice of subjects, saying: 'You are the subject, your impressions, your emotions when confronted with Nature. You must look and see within yourself, not around yourself.'

The idea of painting a painting as one sees it 'from within' has been predicated by many artists, from the primitives to contemporary artists. 'The primitives did not imitate Nature: Titian, Rubens and even Raphael, the classicist, interpreted much more than they copied,' said Bousset. 'We see Nature as something routine; the artist must see and paint it as something fantastic and fabulous,' said Chagall. 'The painter must set down on the canvas his internal impressions and visions,' said Picasso. To see the model in synthesis, to interpret, modify, change... that is what makes true art! In a word: we must bring the creative capacity into play.

But what is creativity? I would say it is a new attitude *towards something we wish to change*, and this attitude crystallizes, becomes effective through imagination and fantasy. Fischer analysed creative fantasy in his work *Art and Coexistence* and arrived at the conclusion that creativity depends on the capacity to represent

Fig. 322 Paul Cézanne, *Still Life with Blue Vase*, Norton Timon Collection, Los Angeles. At the beginning of the century, when Cézanne was already 60 years old (he died when he was 67), he painted by suggesting rather than constructing forms and colours. These pictures are fine examples of synthesis and personal interpretation. Their success is partly due to Cézanne's ability to continue painting his picture for hours (Cézanne was slow), without allowing himself to be influenced by the changing forms and colours of the model, as the hours passed.

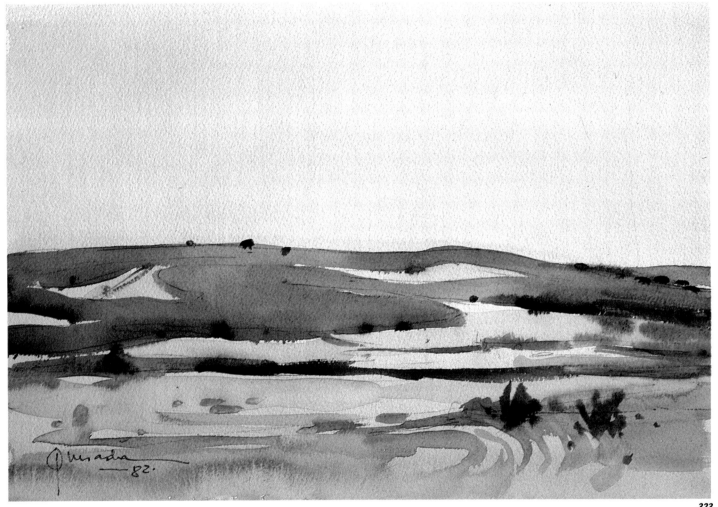

323

and the *capacity to combine*. In applying Fischer's theories to artistic interpretation we may say that: a) from the moment the artist analyses the artistic possibilities of the model he recalls representations of other images he has seen and recorded because of their impact, beauty, and a personal style; for instance the colours used by Van Gogh, Cézanne's forms, atmospheric effects seen in the past, chromatic harmonies recalled from a film, etc.

Recalling these images, the artist dreams, fantasizes, modifies, and changes. And we may also say that b) the capacity to represent an idea different from that offered by the reality of the model causes this reality to give way to the subject that the artist 'sees' with his inner eye. From there on, the artist combines what he is seeing with what he sees in it, discovering combinations of reality and memory, studying new possibilities... and believing.

All very abstract, perhaps, but here are three concrete techniques for interpreting:

Augment: *make real, exaggerate, intensify*
Reduce: *decolour, soften*
Suppress: *eliminate, cover, nullify*

Still, these and other theoretical and practical concepts are useless if, as Bonnard puts it: 'The initial idea for the painting tends to evaporate when the appearance of the real model, sadly, invades and dominates the mind of the painter.' Cézanne was one of the few artists who knew how to resist the seduction of the model's real appearance.

'I have a firm idea of what I plan to do with the subject matter, and I only accept from Nature what is in keeping with my ideas, my forms and my colours, according to my initial conception of the work.'

This isn't exactly a magic formula, but it is the only one I know, and a most useful one too, for synthesizing in painting and for interpreting the model *according to one's own personal conception*.

Fig. 323 Julio Quesada, *Tierras de Sigüenza*, private collection. The Spanish artist, Quesada, is known to be a master of synthesis and interpretation, but it is necessary to see his work to appreciate the intelligent abstraction of forms and colours achieved with just a few colours and brushstrokes. He represents figurative reality magnificently, and shows complete mastery of the watercolour technique.

Thumbnail sketches

Thumbnail sketches

Take an ordinary, medium-grain 20 × 15 cm (8" × 6") drawing pad and a 2B lead pencil, or black felt-tip pen, or ballpoint and go today, tomorrow, or as soon as possible, to a place where you can make thumbnail sketches of the people passing by, children playing, couples talking, sitting down, drinking a refreshment. If you've already done this, or are doing it, fine, skip the following paragraphs. But if you still haven't experienced thumbnail sketching, live from nature, don't delay, don't lose the opportunity. 'How wonderful,' said Picasso to his friend Genevieve, 'that a simple stroke can represent a living being, and not simply his appearance, but what he really is!' All professional artists make thumbnail sketches. A short while ago, I was in Lisbon and made a few rough drafts while wandering the streets of the neighbourhood of Alfama. Now I will be able to convert these drawings into paintings. 'What about the camera?' you might ask. 'Why not paint from photographs taken of the same model?' Well, it just isn't the same. I take photos to serve as documentation and to remember. But an artist's sketches are better than photographs, because you and I can synthesize. We can interpret, augment,

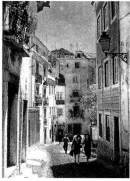

324A

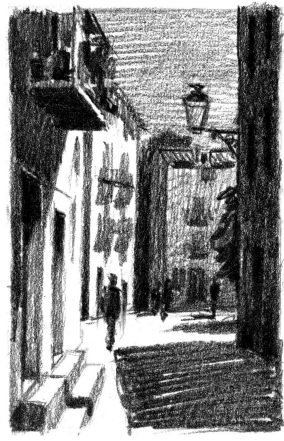

Figs. 324A and *B* On the right we see a rough lead pencil sketch of a street in the Alfama quarter, in Lisbon. Above is a photography of the same stree used as a background documentation for the sketch. Compare the two images, noting in the rough sketch the variations the artist has made interpreting the subject.

324B

Fig. 325 Eugène Delacroix, from *Album Sketches of Morocco*, Louvre, Paris. This is the famous 'Diary' in which Delacroix made watercolour sketches and entered written notes concerning places and people, during his trip to North Africa in 1832. This journey and the documentation recorded in the 'Diary' on Arab themes, is reflected in many of his fine paintings.

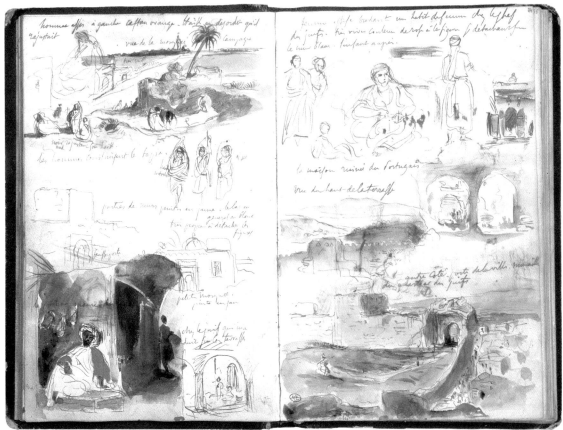

325

reduce, suppress, remember, and a camera cannot.

Making thumbnail sketches is useful in many ways. 'Making sketches is like sowing seeds in order to harvest paintings later on,' wrote Van Gogh to his brother Theo. In 1832, Delacroix travelled to North Africa carrying a diary in which he recorded, with brief notes and watercolour sketches, the architecture, native dress, sky colours, trees, and land of the places he visited. This was for him a tremendously rich resource of subject matter from which he drew a fantastic series of paintings about the daily lives of the Arab and Jewish communities.

I repeat: making thumbnail sketches is useful. There are drawing fairs everywhere, sometimes set up outside, where drawings and sketches are sold, and there are editors looking for sketches to publish in books of poetry, instructional books, and so on.

But most of all, sketching is useful because it constitutes a dynamic exercise which renews and affirms the capacity to draw. Furthermore, drawing is often imperative in watercolour

painting. When the subject is a cityscape, for example, and it is necessary to include some people in the work, one must always have the training and capabilities to draw and paint easily, and to be able to include figures which will add to the reality of the subject.

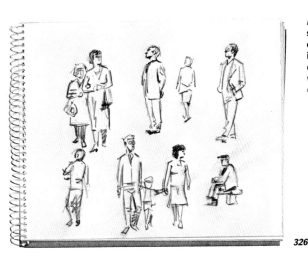

Fig. 326 Making rough sketches of people walking, chatting, relaxing, is essential in order to 'keep in form' and draw and paint human figures without difficulty, whenever you decide to do a watercolour.

326

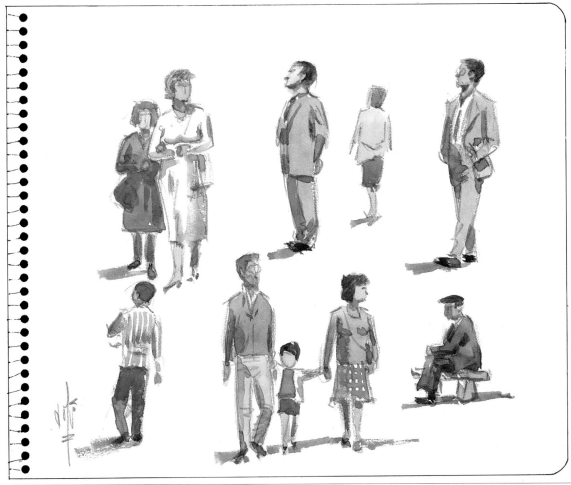

Fig. 327 In order to make my outdoor rough sketches more complete and serviceable, I paint in some of the figures when I get back to the studio, and then file them away as background for future paintings.

327

Thumbnail sketches

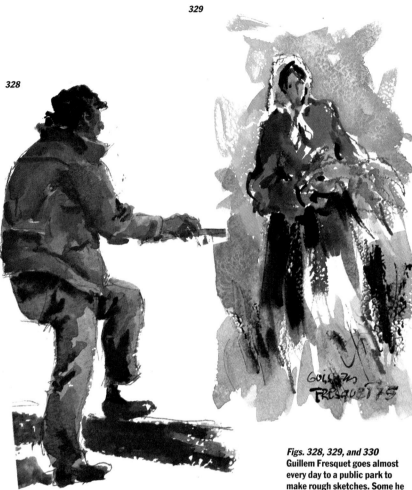

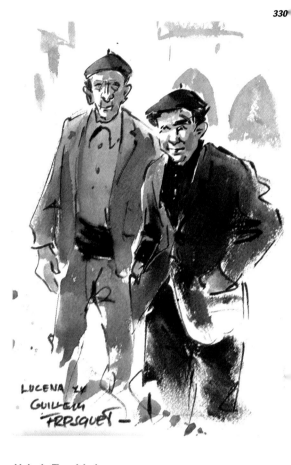

Figs. 328, 329, and 330
Guillem Fresquet goes almost
every day to a public park to
make rough sketches. Some he
paints on the spot, while others
he paints in the studio using
the rough pencil sketches as
his basis. The original
rough sketches measure
approximately half the size
of the reproductions, which is
why, in some cases, Fresquet
gives them to his dealer to sell
as small paintings.

Fig. 331 The late painter and
friend of mine, Federico
Lloveras, made many rough
sketches, exhibiting his
extraordinary skill, and
unbounded capacity for work.
A rough sketch such as this
took no more than twenty
minutes for Lloveras.

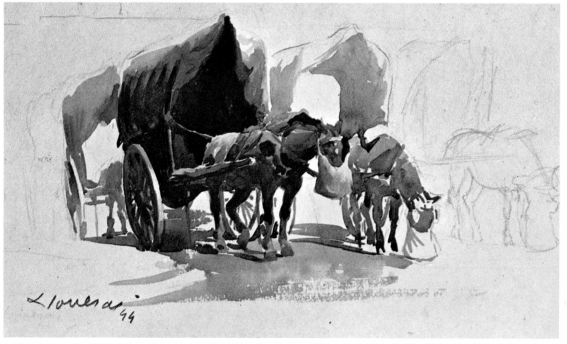

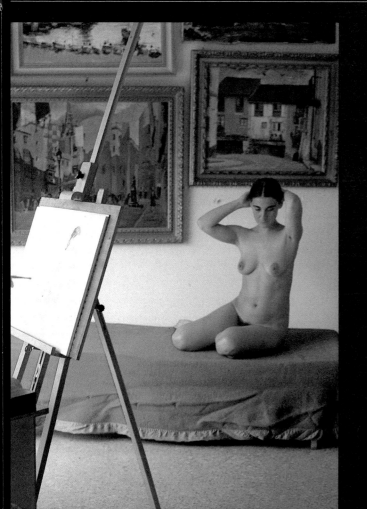

Watercolour

The human figure

To discuss drawing the human figure would require an entire book in itself (in fact, I have written such a book, entitled *How to Draw the Human Figure*). All the same, this book wouldn't be complete without a discussion of the human figure as painted in watercolours. So let us touch upon the principal points here. One of the major difficulties in drawing or painting the human figure is the problem of dimensions and proportions. Fortunately for us, the sculptors of ancient Greece, and more particularly Praxiteles, formulated an idea of beauty for men and women: a canon of eight heads high by two heads wide. See fig. 333 for the comparative canons of men and women. Observe the following differences in proportion between the two sexes:

a *Women have proportionally narrower shoulders*
b *Their breasts and nipples are somewhat lower*
c *Their waists are somewhat narrower*
d *Their navels are slightly lower*
e *Their hips are proportionally wider*
f *Seen from the side, the buttocks extend beyond the vertical plane drawn from the shoulder blades to the calves.*

In order to draw or paint the human figure, it is necessary to know artistic anatomy or, as Ingres put it: 'In order to express the surface of the human body, one must first understand the interior structure.' Structure and movement may be studied using a jointed wooden doll, and moulding may be understood by looking at the plaster casts of classical sculptures. But of course, neither these nor any other means of working will compare to the truth and quality of a human model, nude or dressed. Here the artist will find, as in no other subject matter, the opportunity to express his artistic capacities.

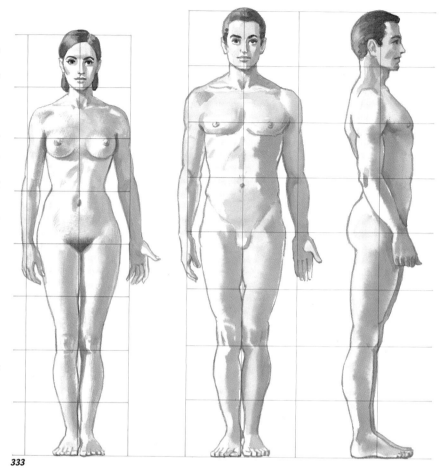

333

Fig. 333 This illustration shows the norm or ideal proportions for the human body, established as eight heads high by two wide. Apart from the fact that the woman is shorter, proportionally, compare the basic differences which distinguish the two sexes.

Fig. 334 The habitual study of the human body by drawing and painting from life – apart from the fact that it represents the greatest artistic merit – is essential in order, for example, to paint a human being when clothed. Leonardo da Vinci said in this respect: 'Clothing must not appear to be uninhabited. There must never be a heap of cloth or gown without support.'

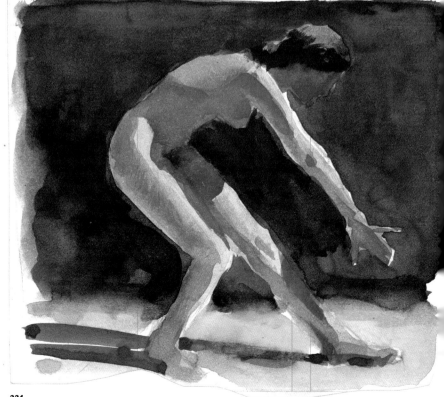

334

335

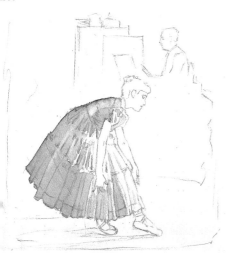

336

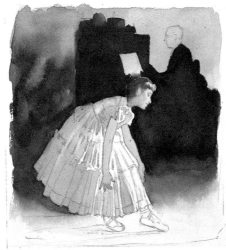

337

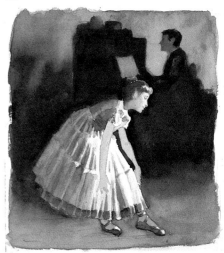

The clothed figure in watercolour

Fig. 335 I begin with a line drawing and then give a first coat to the dress, taking care to leave the folds blank, working the tonal variations from light to dark.

Fig. 336 I paint the face, arms, and feet with a flesh colour but do not put in the features yet. I give a first coat to the hair and then rapidly construct the background with a first coat of patchy ochre and a second darker coat made of Prussian blue, dark sienna, vermilion, carmine, and green.

Fig. 337 Now I can work with greater safety on the colouring of the dancing figure, her shoes, the floor...

Fig. 338 ...leaving for last the features of the face, the shadow cast on the ground and the final touches. For the darkest shadows in the dress I use Prussian blue, for the lightest, cobalt blue mixed with carmine, dark sienna and ochre. I have painted with medium-grain Arches paper in a block of a size almost twice this reproduction, using tube watercolour and sable brushes sizes 6, 12 and 14.

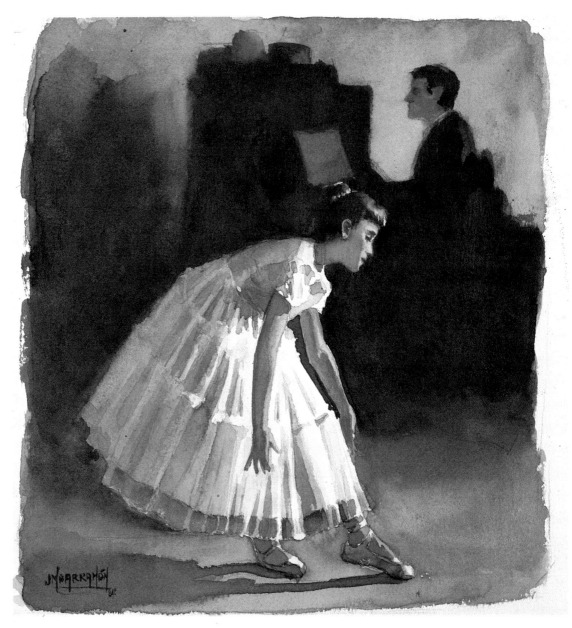

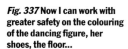

338

The human figure

Portraits

Painting the human head requires constant practice sketching and drawing. It is a speciality. But there is also a canon of ideal proportions which facilitates construction and drawing. See the adjoining study of this canon and notice its usefulness when you begin to draw a portrait. You will notice, for example, in all faces the distance between the eyes is equal to the width of another eye; the location and height of the top of the ears coincides with the eyebrows; the bottom of the ears lines up with the point of the nose, etc.

A good portrait should be an exact likeness but should also be a work of art unto itself. The resemblance depends on the features of the physiognomy and this, according to Ingres, 'always offers a caricature'. This same great painter offered the following practical advice to his students.

● The body should not follow the movement of the head.
● Before beginning, chat with the model so as to get to know him/her better.
● The eyes must be drawn as if they had no importance.
● Avoid an excess of reflections.

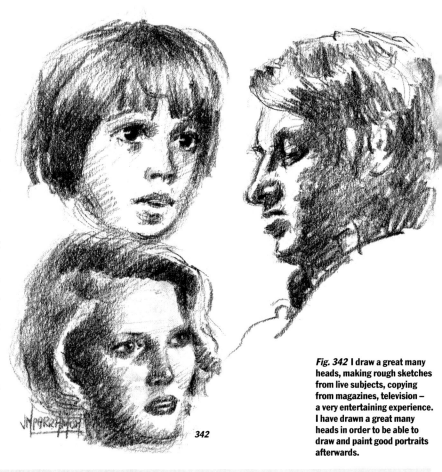

Fig. 342 I draw a great many heads, making rough sketches from live subjects, copying from magazines, television – a very entertaining experience. I have drawn a great many heads in order to be able to draw and paint good portraits afterwards.

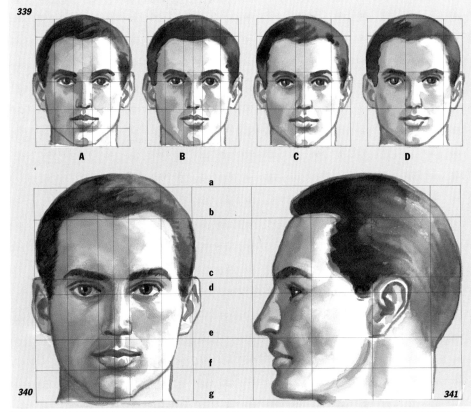

Canon for the human head

In figs. 340 and 341 you can see two male heads, one front view and one profile. Both are drawn according to the canon or ideal dimensions and proportions for the human head.

Fig. 339 shows the process to follow for drawing a front view of the human head according to the canon. Observe in A and B that the rectangle which encloses the human head is shown as three and a half units high, and two and a half units wide. Notice, finally, that in the front view shown in fig. 340, the eyes divide the height exactly in half and the nose symmetrically divides the width. In order to draw a human head or portrait, the basic lines which you should recall are letters a, b, c, d (centre), e, f, and g.

343

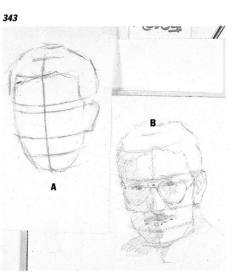

344

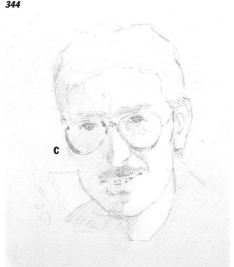

345

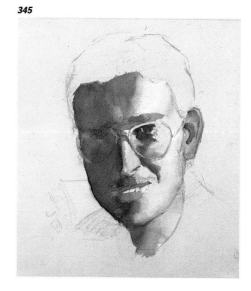

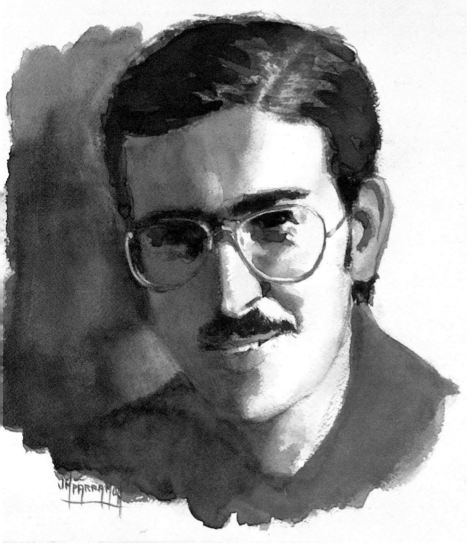

346

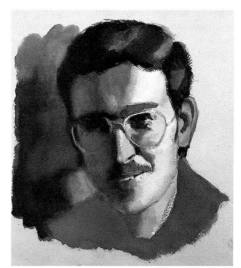

347

Painting a portrait in watercolour

Fig. 343 I draw the subject using the norm (A) as reference, after I make the golden gleam of the spectacles (C) by reserving this spot with masking fluid.

Fig. 344 First I paint a general cream-coloured wash, leaving blanks on the right-hand side.

Fig. 345 I paint the bright and dark colours of the face without going into detail. I tone down this dark colour with the brighter colours of the forehead, nose, and chin, using a flesh colour made of ochre, vermilion, just a touch of Prussian blue... carmine.

Fig. 346 While wet, I merge the dark colour of the face with the colour of the background. I give a first coat and some shaping to the hair, eyebrows and moustache. I sketch the mouth, and suggest the colours of the eyes. I finish by painting the shirt.

Fig. 347 Final work: to finish the hair, I remove the masking fluid and paint in the spectacles with siennas, ochres, and yellows. I paint the ears, the moustache, the mouth, and, while still wet, I draw the eyebrow and eye on the side of the face in shade... and leave it.

The human figure

The nude

A good watercolour reflects the unworried, spontaneous, creative freedom of the artist. These qualities are difficult to attain in a painting of a nude done in watercolours because usually when one is painting one worries, 'Should I leave it like this? Should I go on? Is this finish sufficient?' and this excess of fear and premeditation shows up in the painting. What can we do about this? Practise sketching; then approach the painting as if it were one more sketch – because a sketch is the maximum expression of artistic learning, a sort of miracle born of an unforeseen adventure, 'totally without worry; with spontaneity and absolute liberty'.

Always draw and paint your sketches using a model – a man or woman, friend or professional who will pose for a couple of hours. I would suggest using a professional, someone with a natural gift for posing. Read the art magazines and look into the possibility of getting together a group of two or three artists – no more – to work together and save money. Then plan each session, thinking up five- or ten- minute poses for rapid sketches and one-hour poses for more detailed studies.

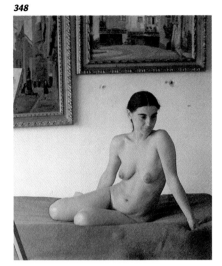

348

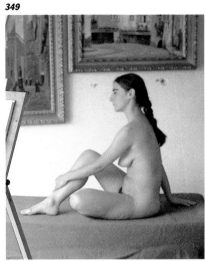

349

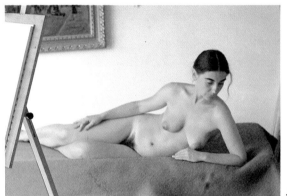

350

Figs. 348, 349, 350 While learning to draw and paint nudes, it is best to work with a professional model who has experience, knows the classical positions and can take up these positions naturally and with artistic knowledge. This professional model, posing in my studio, appears to be illuminated with daylight from the side, coming from a single opening, a broad glass window.

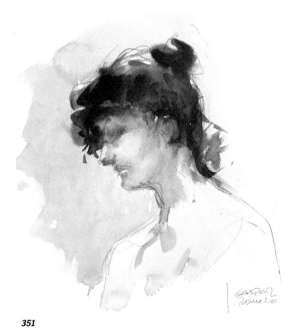

351

Figs. 351, 352 Every day Gaspar Romero goes to an art school where there is a nude session and draws and paints rough sketches like these. 'It is the best kind of practice to keep in form,' the artist assures me.

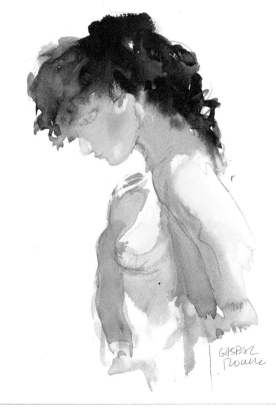

352

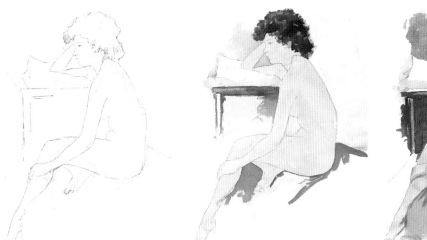

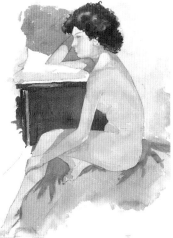

353

354

355

Gaspar Romero paints the nude in watercolour

Fig. 353 Romero first sketches the model with very light lines, making a sort of initial framework. From this, with increasingly more intense lines, he constructs the final drawing. He almost never uses a rubber.

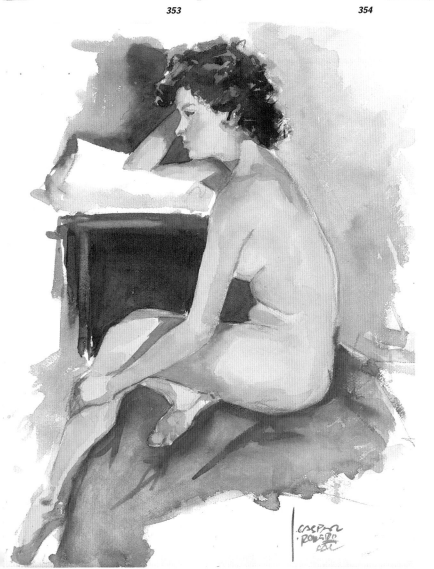

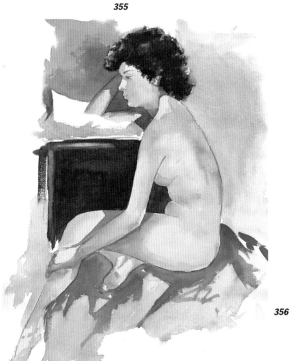

356

357

Fig. 354 The artist paints with a gouache of a light flesh colour that he extends all over the body. Next he applies a dry brush to absorb colour, 'open' spaces and work over the modelling. The artist also uses a piece of blotting paper that he keeps next to his left hand. He quickly paints the hair with ultramarine blue and sepia.

Fig. 355 He goes over the body with a stronger flesh colour containing a little cobalt blue. With this colour and a dry brush to absorb extra water now and then he works over the modelling. He uses Hooker's green to paint the background next to the head, burnt umber, Hooker's green and carmine for the piece of furniture and cobalt blue for the upholstered seat.

Figs. 356 and 357 Always using just a no. 12 brush, extending the flesh colour that now has slight traces of carmine and blue, and absorbing now and then either with a piece of blotting paper or a dry brush, Gaspar Romero reaches the final stage in deep concentration and feverish activity, modelling and finishing parts of the body, face features and so on. He stops only when he signs the painting. He has taken 40 minutes all in all.

Painting skies and clouds

In the English countryside, near Suffolk, at 9.00 a.m. on 15 September 1830, the sky was clear. At about 11.00 a.m. a strong wind came up out of the west which rapidly filled the sky with a partial covering of storm clouds.

John Constable was there, painting the sky and clouds in watercolours (fig. 358). On the back of this watercolour, Constable made a note of the place, day, and hour that these clouds appeared in the sky.

The sky has drawn the attention of many artists. Constable said: 'The sky is the source of Nature's light; it rules the entire landscape.' Alfred Sisley, the French-born Impressionist painter, considered the sky to be a very important part of a painting: 'I always begin with the sky; the sky is not a simple backwash, a shiny abyss. The sky is brother to the plain, and is composed of planes just like the earth. It forms a part of the general rhythm of the painting.'

Of course the sky is important and worth studying.

There are skies and skies: clear, smooth skies which may be easily finished with a simple wash, remembering only to *lighten the colour in the lowest part of the horizon*. There are clear skies with soft curlicues of clouds which look like cotton, also easily finished by absorbing paint and 'opening up' the white of the clouds with a clean damp brush and some absorbent paper tissues. In very wide skies in large watercolours, the white of these clouds may also be opened up with a sponge.

But then there are skies like those Constable painted, or skies with big, full-bodied cumulus clouds, with brilliant lights and soft shadows, sometimes combined with stormy, dark grey clouds... and these skies aren't so easy. All the same, they are perfectly possible. There are, in my opinion, three basic factors necessary to paint one of these skies:

1. *Construction.* A sky with concrete clouds cannot be improvised and shouldn't be painted without first preparing a well constructed line drawing which shows where and how each shape begins and ends: a calculated drawing, unhurried but without pauses.

2. V*olume and colour.* Carefully study the location of the sun and the direction of the light, observing that the sky-blue colour, whether dark or light, outlines the luminous white of the clouds and acts as a background. We should notice that often the grey colours of the shadows in the clouds are lighter than

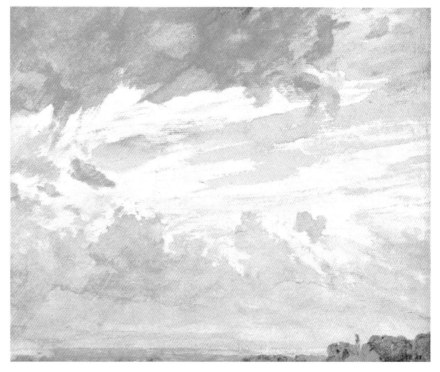

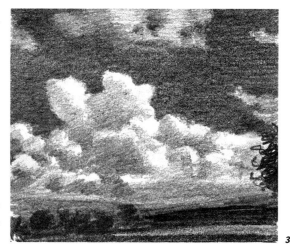

359

Fig. 358 John Constable, *Study of Clouds above a Broad Landscape Between 11 and 12 in the Morning – 15 September, 1830 – Wind from the West,* Victoria and Albert Museum, London. Constable painted various watercolours of clouds on the backs of which he recorded the type of wind and the date and time when they were painted. His consistent interest in, and study of nature was translated into painting the best English landscapes of his time.

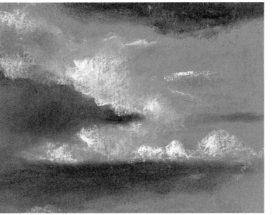

360

Figs. 359, 360 To begin, it is good to make rough sketches, life studies, and studies of skies and clouds, using a lead pencil on white paper. In addition, draw skies and clouds with a carbon pencil stump, and white chalk on coloured paper, studying the varying shades and volumes.

Fig. 363 I paint the top of the clouds with different shades of grey, basically ultramarine and dark sienna, but mixing in carmine, ochre, cobalt blue...

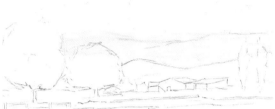

Fig. 364 I intensify some areas, particularly the bottom and darkest part of the clouds. I finish the clouds and outline the colour of the landscape; I moisten the sky at the horizon and working wet-in-wet, I paint the blue hill in the background and outline the two trees in bright green.

362

Watercolour study of sky with clouds

Fig. 361 A rapid but confident drawing – unfinished drawings, badly done, are of no use for our purposes.

Fig. 362 I begin with the blue of the sky – Prussian blue, ultramarine, and just a

suggestion of ochre – outlining the block of clouds and leaving a number of blank areas within. Then I fuse the cloud mass together with a general blue, creating only slight variations of tone and colour. On the fringe, where the sky joins the horizon, I lighten the blue with water and add just a touch of yellow.

Fig. 365 I continue with the landscape which suggests a dominant warm yellow-ochre, but including carmine, bright green, purples, and blues. To finish, I paint a very bright glaze of ochre and yellow on the clouds to give a warm tone, which blends with the dominant quality of the landscape.

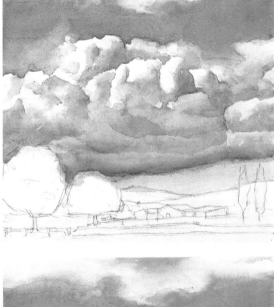

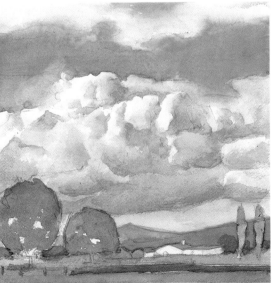

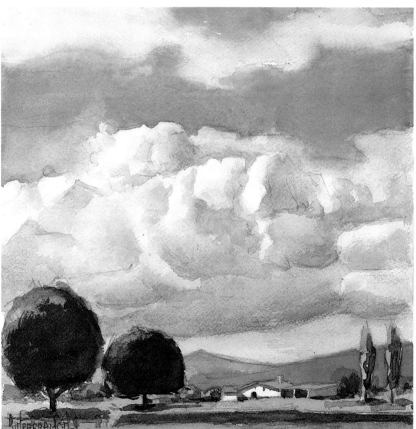

365

Painting skies and clouds

the blue sky of the background, and we must constantly compare the *values* of these greys and see the blue, pink, and golden tendencies of these shadow greys, so that the clouds will finally become real.

3. *Technique.* Finally, we should be aware of the watercolour techniques required in each instance, previously reserving whites, outlining illuminated parts, with the sky as the background, attaining the forms of the model, modelling with tones achieved with the brush and absorbent paper daubing here, adding there, working and painting with real drive – and with real urgency, because the clouds literally fly away! – without losing sight of the model, *without losing the white highlights* which define the basic characteristics of clouds.

'The sky comes first,' said Sisley, and all professional watercolour artists begin with the sky when painting landscapes. And they do it absolutely without worry, joyfully and with guile, as though making a bet with themselves: 'I'll bet I can! I can paint this cloudy sky with a few brushstrokes and a few dabs of absorbent paper.' And they do it! They succeed! It is a daily game: to start with the sky without thinking, without bother, without the fearful consciousness of an amateur. 'And, if it doesn't come out, I remarked to one of my students, leave it and start again.' Agreed?

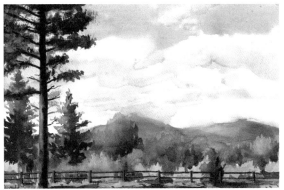

Fig. 366 In this high mountain landscape, I have painted a classic sky with clouds on a luminous day where the grey shadows of the clouds are brighter than the blue of the sky. The intensification of lights and shadows, without sliding into the latter, is very important.

366

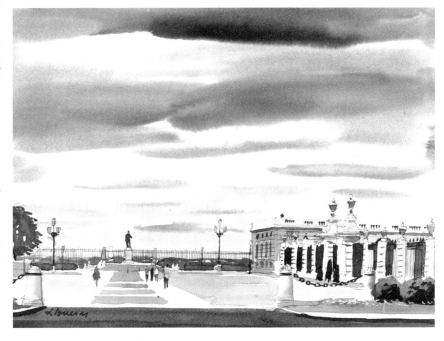

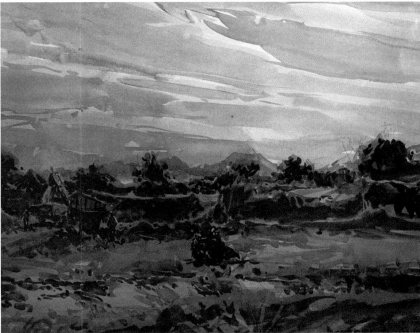

Fig. 367 Federico Lloveras, *Palacio Real (Madrid)*, private collection. Here, an overcast sky is painted wet-in-wet with applications of greys, perfectly controlled by the artist, which allow the sky to have a very important role, conditioning the colour of the urban landscape which he has resolved with a range of pale colour.

Fig. 368 Ceferino Olivé, *Arenales (Riudoms)*, private collection. Ceferino Olivé painted this dramatic landscape with a range of warm colours, working with coarse brushes in long and broad strokes, blending, absorbing, always 'straight off', giving it everything, staking everything.

Sky and clouds with a special range of colour

Fig. 369 Having finished the sketch, I lay on a uniform wash of ochre made to look dirty with just a whisper of blue and dark sienna, reserving white areas for the houses of the town, to be painted in later.

369

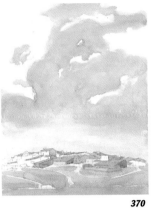

370

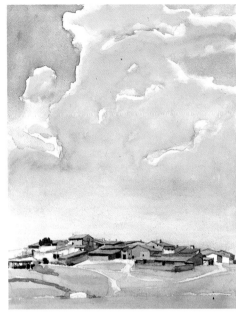

371

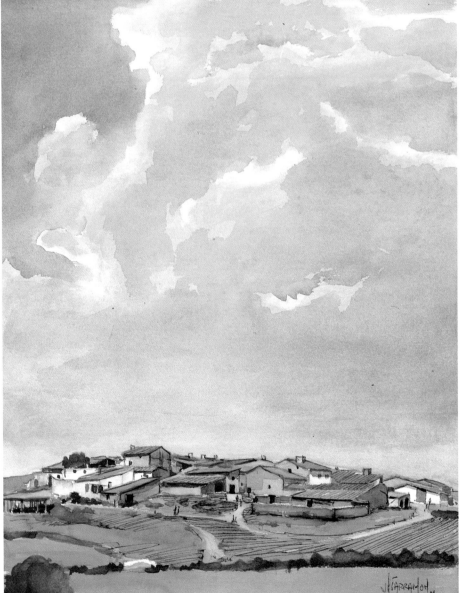

373

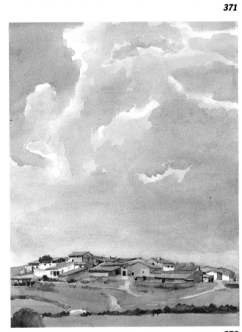

372

Fig. 370 Once the background is dry, I paint over it using the same colour, made darker with more sienna blending to bring out parts of the clouds. With different siennas I paint the houses and some areas of the ground.

Fig. 371 Now I paint the colour of the sky using ultramarine, carmine and ochre, brightening the colour on reaching the horizon. I continue with the houses, the shadows, and the roofs.

Fig. 372 I finish the sky with a last wet application in the bottom areas of the clouds and complete the plots of land and roads of the town.

Fig. 373 For the finishing touches I use a fine ballpoint pen with which I draw a number of the lines of the houses, the roofs, some furrows in the ground, some figures, etc.

Painting trees

The first thing to remember when painting trees is that they have a structure, a skeleton; they are trunks and branches with a covering of clothing made of leaves. The skeleton is important. If you draw or sketch trees without leaves in the winter, with only the scaffolding of the bare branches, not only will you have a great time but you will also rapidly learn to paint trees. And if you afterwards dedicate a good deal of time to drawing trees, bushes and thickets, as Van Gogh did continually, you will learn to paint trees placed far in the distance, or set up close in the foreground.

There are no tricks or secrets, only careful observation and understanding: branch groups extend from the trunk, leaves form clusters which determine the effects of light and shadow on the colours and forms of the tree. The combinations of trunks, branches and leaves are sometimes broken up, leaving spaces through which we see the light of the sky, illuminating their dark silhouettes. And we must paint them as they really are: with blues, yellows, and ochres (trees have a lot of green-ochre colour) in the top part, and with more green than yellow, more blue than ochre in the lower part, which is in shade, and reflects the colour and light of the earth. Tree trunks have the forms of small spheres or cylinders which are illuminated from above. When they appear alone or grouped together in the distance, they are always darker than the meadows and fields around them.

The next time you are in the country, look at them... and paint them.

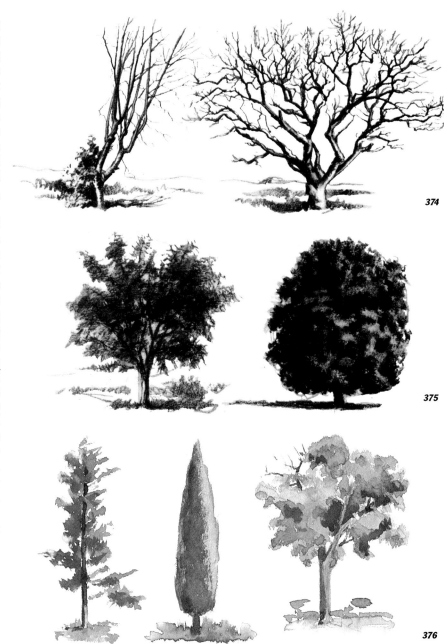

374

375

376

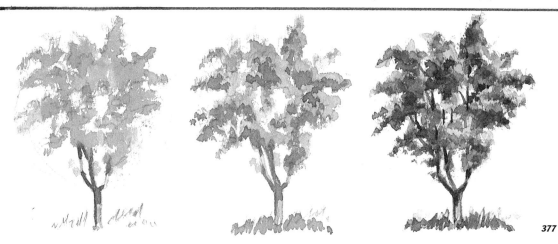

377

Figs. 374, 375 Making good sketches and drawings of trees without leaves is a good exercise for drawing them with greater familiarity.

Fig. 376 Here are several trees seen in the middle distance; thus their shapes and colours have been resolved using synthesis.

Fig. 377 A step-by-step demonstration of painting a tree seen in the middle distance, using only a few strokes to suggest form and colour.

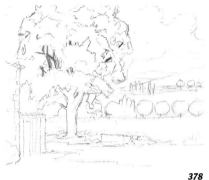

378

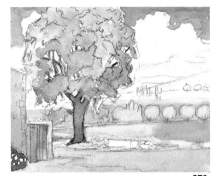

379

**Painting a landscape
with trees**

Fig. 378 Drawing trees in
the foreground, like drawing
clouds, is not something you
can half do, unless you have
extraordinary experience.

Fig. 379 First, applications
of uniform colour in diluted
washes, with certain shades
calculated to enrich the colour.

Fig. 380 I resolve the sky, the
clouds and the background of
grey and blue mountains using
the wet-in-wet technique.

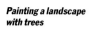

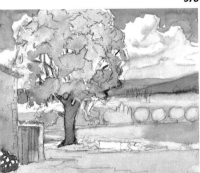

380

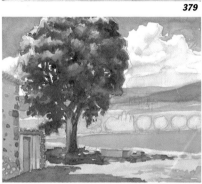

381

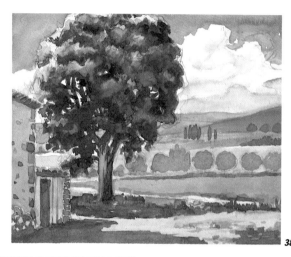

382

Fig. 381 I paint the tree in
the foreground, resolving
the shape and colour of the
groupings of leaves, painting at
the top with greens tending to
ochre and at the bottom with
greens which have a blue tint.
I paint the trunk and the
branches of the tree, as well as
the shade it casts, without
completing it. I complete the
fragment of a house which
appears on the left-hand side,
as well as the shade it casts.
I intensify the foreground
colours, and to the fields in the
middle distance I add a pink
and an ochre green.

Fig. 382 I finish the cast
shadow in the foreground
by the tree. I give a first
application, both drawing
and painting, to the trees and
bushes in the meadow in the
middle, and I paint a number
of dark highlights which enrich
the foreground.

Fig. 383 I finish the foreground
and background trees, intensify
a number of colours and add
some finishing touches.

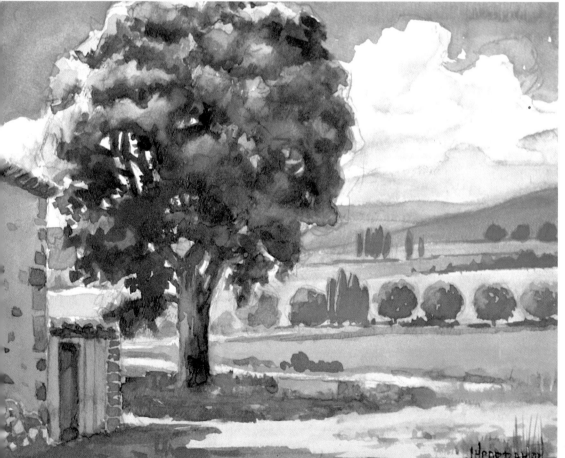

383

Painting a landscape in watercolours

In these pages we begin a series of exercises for watercolour painting in which, step by step, you will be able to study the resolution of several paintings painted by several artists.

The first of these watercolours was created by the renowned artist Ceferino Olivé, who has been awarded several national and international prizes for his watercolours, now found in museums and private collections in France, Britain, Germany, the United States, Japan, Italy and elsewhere.

Ceferino Olivé is a professional veteran, a partisan of pure watercolour without stains, without liquid glue or wax crayon. He doesn't wet the paper, nor does he mount it with glued paper strips (paper tape) in order to tighten it. He uses, exclusively, thick brushes made out of ox hair, of such high numbers as 12, 18, 24 and 30, each with a special handle as long as that of an oil brush (30 cm).

He paints with tube watercolour, using a metal palette, like the one reproduced on page 63, and works with a three-legged atelier easel. He paints with the paper in an almost vertical position.

A very personal technique

All watercolour professionals that I know of, including myself, use absorbent papers, raw cotton, a cotton rag, or a sponge, in order to discharge or absorb liquid, colour, or the water from the brush. Ceferino Olivé is different. Instead of a water jar he uses a water bucket like one used for mopping floors. He places the water bucket beside him, next to his chair. In order to wring moisture out of the brush, he shakes his arm with the brush in his

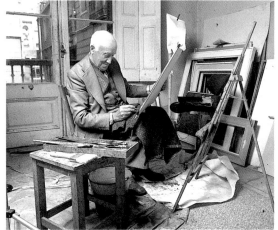

384

Fig. 384 Ceferino Olivé, a famous watercolour veteran with innumerable prizes and with works in museums and collections throughout the world, is an example of common sense, sobriety and simplicity, which is why a look at his studio is instructive for us. 'All my life I have painted in the open air,' he tells me, 'I have always done it with the same equipment: an easel to hold the board with the paper, a seat, and a case in which I carry the colours and utensils for painting. I never paint in the studio, and if sometimes I have to do it, then I prefer to work under exactly the same conditions as when I paint in the open air.' And so it is that in one of his studios, apart from a large table and a bookcase filled with books, there is no other equipment other than an easel set at a 45° angle, and a small low table. It is in this very place that we see him signing a painting.

385

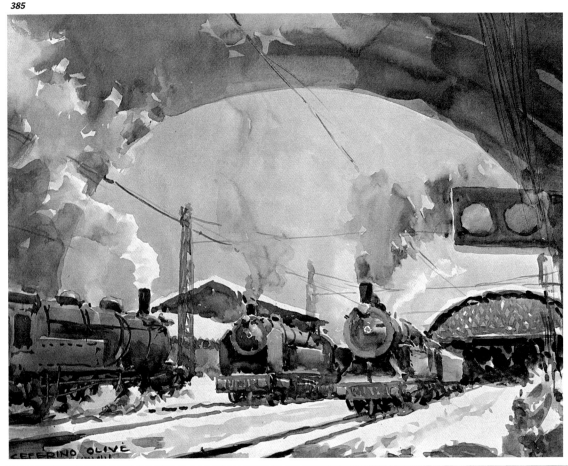

Fig. 385 Ceferino Olivé, *Smoky Tunnel*, private collection. Here is a good example of the style of Ceferino Olivé, in its composition, harmony of colour, technique, and drawing or construction, all of which are truly enviable.

hand, as if he were whipping it, as if sprin-kling, spattering water on the floor which he covers with wrapping paper to avoid wetting and dirtying it. It is to be noted, as well, the way in which he holds the brush very high up, with the end of the handle inside the palm.

As we shall see as we follow the development of his painting, Ceferino Olivé is everywhere when he paints, looking at everything at once, painting sometimes here, sometimes there, indeed everywhere at once, and in this way the painting advances progressively towards its final stage.

First stage: the drawing (Fig. 388)

Ceferino Olivé draws with a no. 2B regular pencil. He keeps at hand a very soft kneaded rubber which is a dark grey colour though he practically never uses it. He uses fine-grain paper which he secures to the drawing board with four metal clips. This watercolour is 70 × 50 cm. He draws with the pencil end inside his palm, rapidly, with very few lines, rapidly sketching the basic forms of the model with-out bothering with small details. What he does

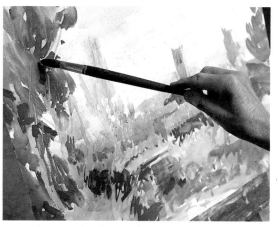

386

is to locate the basic forms: the tower in the background, the tiled roofs of the houses, the hardly indicated profiles of the trees, the thickest tree trunks.

'It's all done,' he says. 'There's nothing miss-ing.' And he gets the palette, fills it with colours and starts painting.

Second stage: trying out the colour (Fig. 389)

Watching Ceferino Olivé paint is a veritable

Fig. 386 Observe this special manner of holding the very end of the brush handle which, according to Olivé, obliges him to paint at a distance, free, without ever falling into the fatal pitfall of describing small details.

Fig. 387 Ceferino Olivé, *Reflections* (Castellón, private collection). Another example of the personal techniques of Ceferino Olivé, obvious proof of his extraordinary facility to construct and paint in a few strokes, explaining the subject with a language which is sober, correct, and at once different and brilliant.

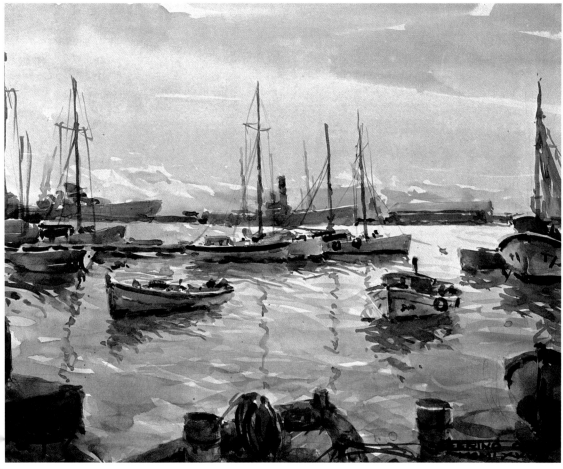

387

Painting a landscape in watercolours

spectacle. In the sky, for instance, he charges brush no. 24 with ultramarine blue. He dirties it with a bit of Payne's grey and paints with wide strokes from right to left, leaving white spaces, and with unexpected rapidity, I would dare say feverishly. He plunges the brush into the water bucket, rinses it, discharges the excess water, whipping and sprinkling, and within a fraction of a second he is back in the sky, diluting and degrading the blue with the white of the paper, in a technique that looks as if it were wet, because of the perfect blending of some watercolours with others. And he leaves it like this with the enviable certainty that he has 'resolved the blue colour of the sky.' Now, even faster – if that is possible – as if the success of the painting depended on it, he mixes an orange and applies it to the tower and to the houses in the background, modifying it as he goes along with some green, grey, blue and vermilion strokes, and in a few seconds he covers the white of the paper.

Third stage: determining the form (Fig. 390)

One should wait a few minutes for the previous stage to dry. In the meantime, Ceferino Olivé looks attentively at the sky, making faces while he holds the brush in his hand. 'The sky is the roof,' he says. He observes the towers, the houses...
Suddenly, he mixes a light grey using ultramarine blue, sienna, and a little grey, and dilutes it with water. With this light grey, he paints the whites that remain in the sky. He rinses, whips, sprinkles. He blends the greys, and... the clouds make their appearance! Now he lightens this grey with water, adds a bit more sienna, and resolves the colour of the sky at the horizon. The sky, 'the roof', is done. This is how the painting will remain.
Ceferino Olivé now mixes up a sienna-carmine-vermilion colour and, with varied but certain strokes, resolves the shadows of the houses, grass and bushes in the foreground. He then changes the colours and paints the mountains in the background, the green of a tree and the grass at the edge of the foreground. With this he has achieved the forms and their volume. It reminds me of the words of Edouard Manet who, in his letter to the young G. Heannot, said: 'It is in the forms that I look for the most intense light and the deepest shadow; everything else is given to me in the bargain.'

Fourth stage: the 'maestro's phase' (Fig. 391)

Ceferino Olivé calls this phase the 'master

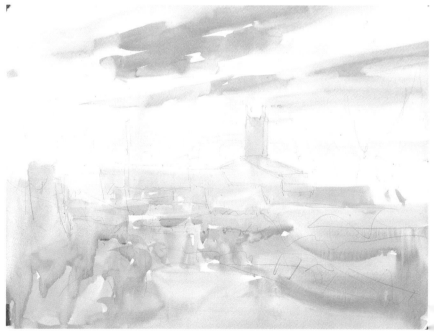

Fig. 388 A drawing, barely indicated with a no. 2B pencil, already places and proportions the forms and elements of the subject. A fact which will become more obvious in the following figures is that Olivé draws as he paints.

Fig. 389 Observe in this and the subsequent stages how Olivé does not paint isolated parts or areas of the picture, but paints, draws, and shapes 'everything all at once, pushing ahead with the whole picture at the same time', so that he could stop painting halfway through and he would already have done a painting.

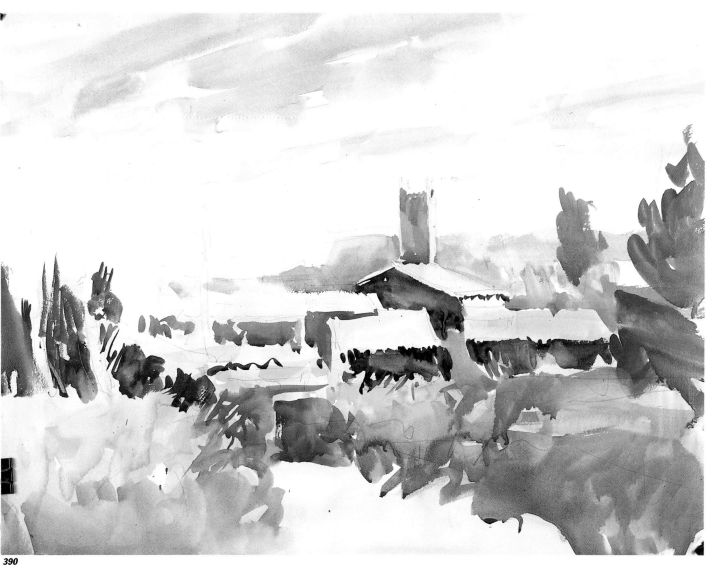

390

Fig. 390 Ceferino Olivé is a classicist. In a previous stage he coloured the paper. On reaching this, the second stage, he painted the most important shadows of the subject, as if he were following the advice of Corot who said: 'First the values; second the shadows.'

cloak'. 'After this phase,' he explains, 'it's only a question of embroidering, that is to say, of detailing, rectifying some forms, creating some contrasts, but the painting is finished for all practical purposes.' Ceferino Olivé washes the palette with water, using one of his thickest brushes. He then intensifies the colour of the tile roofs of the houses with a series of vertical or diagonal lines, many of which blend in a regular watercolour area. He now paints the thickest of the tree trunks on the left with a warm grey; he applies a dirty green to the fore-ground right and to the trees on the left, with wide and daring strokes, intensifying and clarifying as he goes along, opening up whites by scraping with the back of his thumbnail or the nail of his little finger, to expose strokes of light colour. To the green of the trees he adds a light red-ochre on the left-hand side, always with the formula of first applying the brush filled with colour, and next degrading the intense paint by means of diluting with water. At last, having made his additions and dilutions, he leaves the piece alone.

Painting a landscape in watercolours

Fig. 391 According to Ceferino Olivé this is 'the master stage or phase of the painting.' When this stage is finished the painting is already right regarding composition, form and colour. There remain only the possibilities of enriching the colour, of creating greater contrasts.

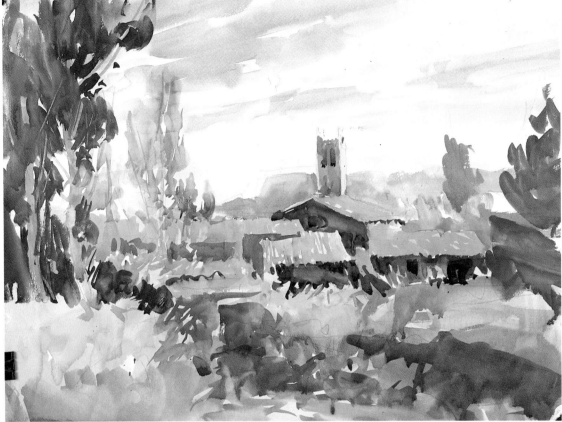

391

Fig. 392 In fact, between the painting of the previous illustration, fig 390, and these two more advances stages there has been a general enrichment both of forms and details, contrast, and colour. But the intellectual effort, the uncertainty and anguish of the painting which is taking shape, is already passed. What follows now is an *entertainment*, a true festival in which the artist feels himself carried away by the colour and the contrast.

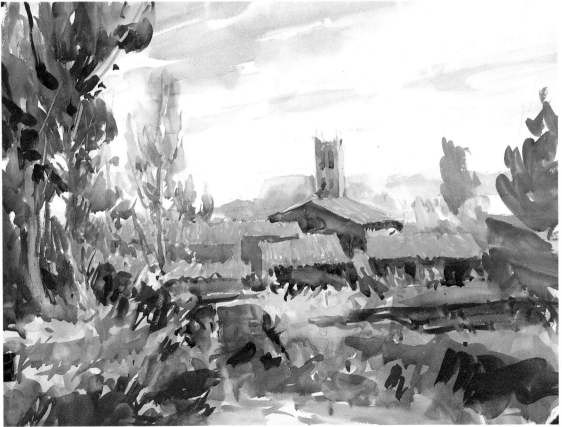

392

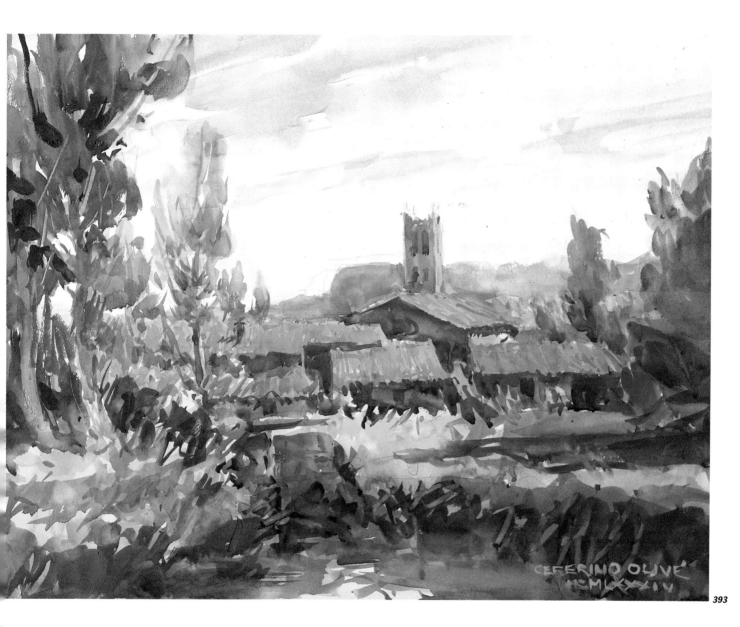

393

Fifth stage: almost finished (Fig. 392)

He cleans the palette again before he paints the vertical and diagonal strokes of the tile roofs, always with that loose air which, in the long run, promotes the feeling of lively, vibrant colour. He finally fills the brush with a dark, earthy colour with which he decidedly resolves the foreground contrasts, placing with capricious strokes the stains on the trees on the left, clarifying some contours, as his brush 'walks' around the painting, working here and there, everywhere – except in the sky.

Sixth and last phase: final touches (Fig. 393)

Little remains to be done. Almost everything is finished... but the artist, after a long pause, after having looked alternately from the painting to the model, after cleaning the palette and smoking a cigarette, begins making small last-minute changes. He finishes the trees on the left, reinforces the hills in the background, accentuates the tile roof of the house on the left, and clarifies the bushes in the right foreground, and the reflection of the small stream. After a long silence, during which he looks ecstatically at the painting, Ceferino Olivé says: 'It's done. let's leave it.'

Fig. 393 In this last stage Ceferino Olivé has done very little. He has spent a lot of time looking, observing... it is the moment of considering and reconsidering, and even of getting up and taking a walk, of having a cup of coffee, before returning with the mind cleared to either continue or to *leave it to time*. 'Yes, to leave it to time is important,' Olivé emphasizes.

Painting a sea port in watercolours

Guillermo Fresquet, the second guest artist who is going to paint a watercolour for us, chooses a theme on the sea port. His experience as a watercolour painter places him among the top artists of Spain. His paintings have been given awards in numerous contests and his extraordinary capacity as a draughtsman and painter allows him to paint for us in his studio, using some notes and sketches drawn in the open air as his model.

Fresquet has created this watercolour from some notes taken in Barcelona port, and has added the old carriages pulled by horses that used to meander around the freight piers of 20 or 30 years ago.

Fresquet uses medium-grain paper, about 350 g. He paints with tube watercolours and a white metal, enamelled palette, with compartments in the centre to hold the colour. He paints with round brushes of marten hair, generally nos. 9, 12, 14, 18, and 22. He also uses the flat brush, no. 16, for backgrounds and wide grey hues. Occasionally he uses a round brush no. 14 and another no. 6 to execute lines and thin strokes. He works with two plastic flasks of water: one for the water with which He paints, and the other to clean his brush. He paints on an ordinary table with a drawing board slanted about 30 degrees, in a small studio, as can be seen here.

First stage: the drawing (Fig. 394)
Fresquet draws with an HB pencil and rarely uses his rubber. He draws with an amazing certainty, defining the forms with a few strokes, eliminating shading, drawing figures, carriages, and animals from memory and knowledge.

Second stage: general background tones (Fig. 395)
Fresquet begins with the background. First the sky is painted using a flat no. 16 brush. He starts by painting in the light orange-yellow colour in the upper sections, and immediately following while the orange is still wet, he lays in the overall grey of the sky. The layers become mixed and diluted, producing the illusion of the sun on a half-misty morning. He continues with the grey on both sides and towards the lower part. He may first discharge a little of the grey by wringing the brush with a cotton rag. He adds a generous rose tone to the horizon, reserving a brief thin strip of white paper for the sea. With a warm colour he paints the reflection of the sky on the water and land, again reserving a few strips of white

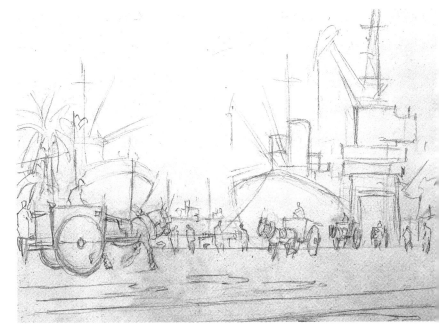

Fig. 394 As can be seen in this illustration, Guillermo Fresquet carries out the drawing of his watercolour with considerable detail and perfection.

Fig. 395 Note that the watercolour with which Fresquet paints the sky extends over the whole picture; only the strip of sea and the pools of water in the foreground have been reserved. While the sky was still wet, Fresquet used a fine brush to 'open up' the diffused white smoke of the boat in the foreground and the nebulous white in the left-hand background.

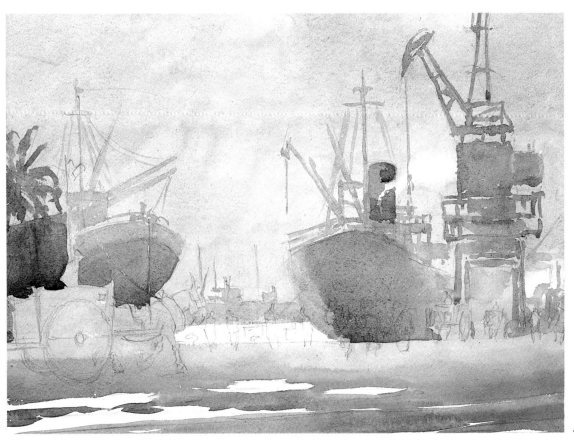

Fig. 396 In Fresquet's watercolours the first application is the one that counts; there is almost never a second or third application. Studying the development of the watercolour, in the phases described on the following pages, you will see that the forms and colours of this second stage are already definitive, and will appear as they are here in the finished picture.

396

paper that will later serve to represent water puddles. Before leaving the first stage Fresquet wets certain areas and absorbs some of the colour into his brush; he diffuses the intensity of the colour in the areas which correspond to the smoke billowing out of the ships.

Third stage: resolution of the basic forms (Fig. 396)

Fresquet works slowly but without pauses. His extraordinary experience as a watercolour artist, and his notable capacity as a draughtsman, allow him to resolve the painting step by step, thinking ahead which parts are definitely resolved, which forms are on hold, and what areas he will have to elaborate on later, in order to finish the painting. In this third phase he paints the middle ground, superimposed on the general tone of the sky, always maintaining a perfectly harmonized colour range. Observe the slight differences in contrast between foreground and background, especially to the right side of the painting where he begins to suggest atmosphere and depth.

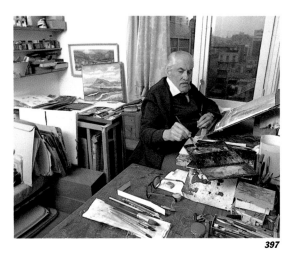

397

Fig. 397 The artist Guillermo Fresquet working in this studio. Observe that the board on which he paints in the studio appears to be very steeply inclined, some 20 to 25 degrees, and is supported in a very rudimentary manner. What is more, the studio is a very small room.

Painting a sea port in watercolours

Fig. 398 So far, Fresquet has painted this watercolour *in planes*, that is to say, resolving the background first (fig. 395), and now superimposing a nearer plane as with the house curtains of a stage.

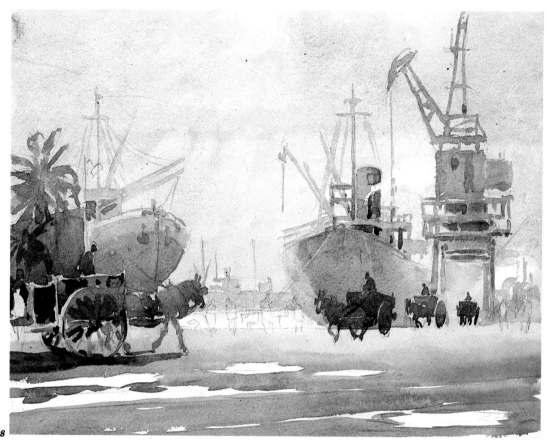

398

Fig. 399 Fresquet continues with the idea of working *in planes*, working in specific areas, contrasting and accentuating the carriges in the foreground to bring them nearer.

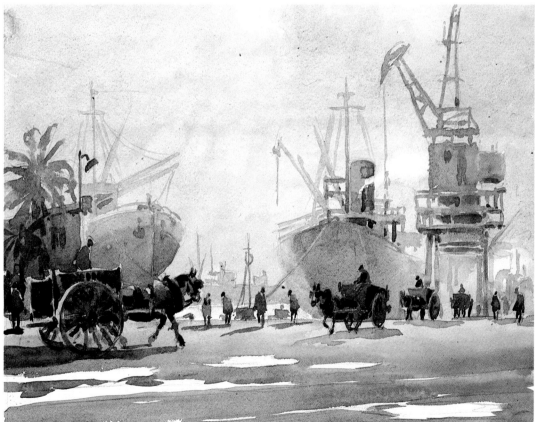

399

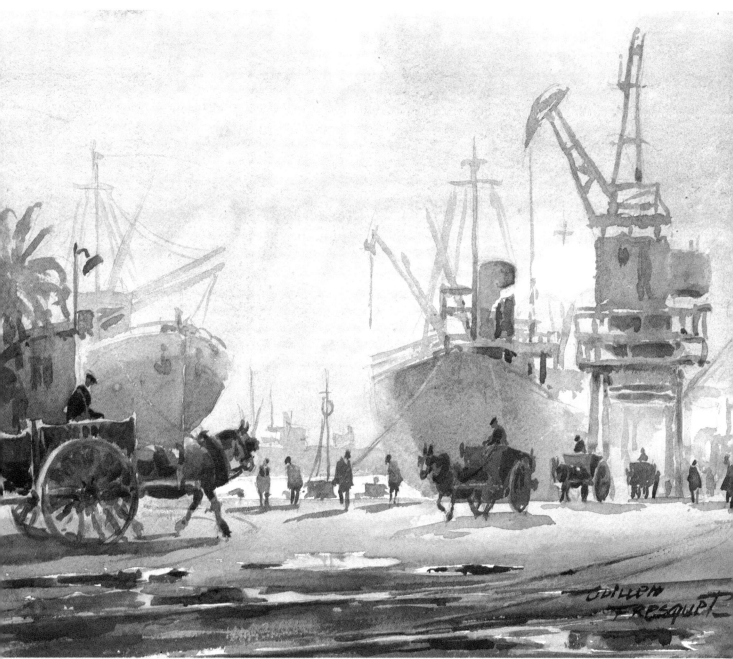

400

ig. 400 At this point compare ie various stages with the nished painting; study the ades used in the range of ie colours, the resolution of ie planes, creating the idea of graduated distance and tmosphere; note the contrast etween tones and how they re accentuated in the nearest rms. Notice the synthesis of rms and colours, particularly ovious in the figures and rriages; and, finally, enjoy esquet's easy and oontaneous way of painting a atercolour.

Fourth stage: emphasizing the depth (Fig. 398)

In this fourth stage Fresquet defines distances with colour. He intensifies some colours in the middle ground formed by the crane and the ship on the right, but leaves the more distant forms in light grey, and in the more sketchy drawing of the last stage. With more colour and detail he defines the horse and carriage in the foreground but leaves the activity in the distance, in a penumbra of shapes and colours. The colour range is kept to sepia, ultramarine blue, Payne's grey, green... painting loosely, with plenty of water.

Fifth and last stage: final touches (Figs. 399 and 400)

We have divided the final stage into two steps in order to understand the sequence of these last touches applied to resolve the painting. He begins by defining the carriages and animals in great detail, especially the figures in the foreground. He adds figures, shadows, some small shapes, the ground in the foreground, the reflections in the water puddles... and his signature.

Painting a seascape in watercolours

Gaspar Romero is the author of the luminous watercolour on page 169, painted in the dock of a sailing club.

Until a short while ago, Gaspar Romero was an excellent amateur, but he recently became a professional, and has for some years been the president of the Watercolourists' Congress of Catalonia, a group with more than three hundred associate members, including some of the best watercolour artists in Spain. Our guest artist has written and lectured on many occasions about watercolour painting, and is an expert in the field.

Gaspar Romero habitually paints on fine-grain paper, in this case on a tablet 62 × 146 cm, made by Fabriano. He uses three brands of paint interchangeably: tube watercolours by Grumbacher or Winsor and Newton, and the line of moist watercolour tablets by Schminke. His brushes are a special type featuring a mixture of synthetic and sable hairs recently introduced by Winsor and Newton, in size nos. 6, 8, 12 and 14. Explains Gaspar Romero: 'These brushes with mixed hairs work well. On the other hand, those with all synthetic hair fail to hold enough water, as

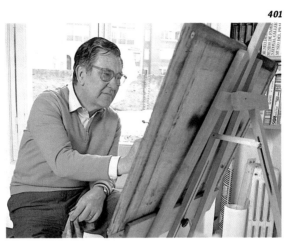

401

Fig. 401 Gaspar Romero paints with the board supported on an easel, almost vertical. 'You should emphasize,' he tells me, 'that it is perfectly possible to paint in watercolour with the board or support almost vertical.'

40

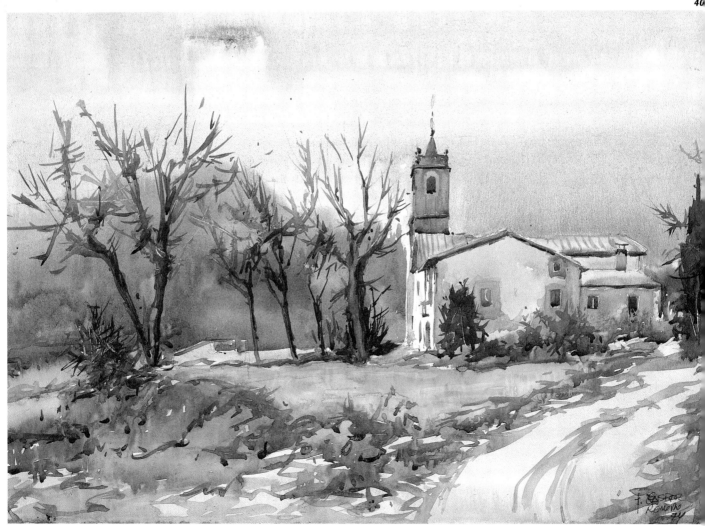

if they reject or spit out the watercolour liquids.'

Gaspar Romero uses the typical palette, with indentations in the middle and mixing trays on each side, made of metal and finished with white enamel. His studio easel is the classical workshop tripod, but when he paints outside he uses a tripod with three folding legs. 'It is perfectly possible to paint in watercolours with the support almost vertical, changing the idea that some amateurs have, that it is necessary to work with the support in an almost horizontal position.' Romero paints with only one small container of water (about one half litre) because, as he says: 'It is good to paint with the water a little bit dirty because this relative dirtiness helps to create atmosphere and to harmonize the colours.'

First stage: drawing (Fig. 404)

Gaspar Romero draws with an ordinary no. 2B pencil and a Pelikan G-20 plastic rubber, dark grey in colour and quite soft. He draws very carefully, considering every stroke, even using the ruler for those shapes that demand it. He draws only a few lines, with no shadows. 'I work slowly, paying a lot of attention to my drawing, partially because I want to avoid using the rubber which can alter the fibres of

403

Fig. 403 To draw a boat is relatively simple, so long as perspective is taken into consideration and is present in all the lines flowing toward the horizon.

404

Fig. 402 Gaspar Romero, *Landscape, Santa Maria de Besora*, artist's collection. A landscape of a small town in the Pyrenees, painted on a cold autumn morning, with the mist invading the background. Distance is emphasized with the paintbrush, painting the belfry and the church façade to contrast with the violet and cobalt blue background mist. Also to be noted is the interpretation of forms and colours in synthesis, particularly the white road and its environs.

Fig. 404 Gaspar Romero draws slowly and pays particular attention to construction of the theme, 'partly to avoid using the rubber', he explains, 'but also to paint afterwards with more certainty'.

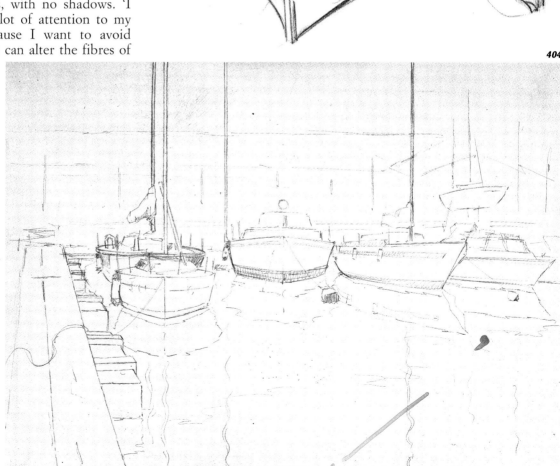

Painting a seascape in watercolours

the paper, but also so that I can paint with a surer hand afterwards.'

Second stage: the background 'from the top down' (Fig. 405)

'Yes, I'm going to paint this watercolour from the top down,' says Gaspar Romero, 'because the sky and the pier in the background, behind the boats, make a unit that must be finished first, and everything at the same time.' And that's just how he does it. Starting with the sky, using a no. 14 brush with a rounded tip, he paints large washes of weak colour, first a green mixed with sienna, then a cobalt blue. He paints everything very rapidly, directing the wash to one side and then the other. Suddenly he turns the support upside down and paints with the painting upside down, still controlling the wash, and slowly building up the colour in the upper part of the painting, where the sky will be later on. While he waits for this application to dry, he paints the sides of some of the boats with a very light wash, 'in order to be able to play with a reserve of whites later on'. He reinforces the blanks with a darker colour of ultramarine and sienna in the shed in the background and in the building on the right-hand side. Painting while it is

still damp, he reinforces the blue and dark sienna of the base, and then uses the bevelled handle of the paintbrush to rub forcefully, drawing white strokes which correspond to the masts and railings of the pier. Using sienna, he delineates the upper part of the roof of the pier with a horizontal stroke, and then moves to the right-hand side to begin the form of the reddish boat in the shipyard.

Third stage: the boats (Fig. 406)

There isn't much to explain: Gaspar Romero finishes the forms and colours of the boats, drawing and painting buffers, gangways, cabins, small details. Afterwards he darkens the base of the pier, and before it is totally dry he scratches with the nail of his index finger, opening the vertical lines at the base. Using a flat no. 8 brush of synthetic hair, he 'opens up' the white of the parallel masts of the boats on the left-hand side, in the following manner: first he dampens the masts with water, using the edge of the brush, going over it a few times, from top to bottom. Then he cleans the brush and returns, softening and diluting the blue colour. Finally, he drains the brush, absorbing the water and colour, allowing the white to appear on the paper.

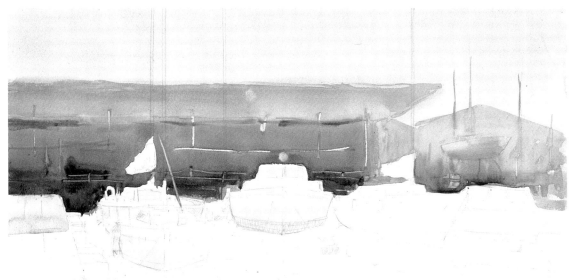

Fig. 405 At this second stage, Gaspar Romero paints wet-in-wet and tries out the effect of marking white lines with the brush handle ends. Some of these lines, the grey of the sky, the greys of the background, and some dark areas are already defined and will remain like this in the finished watercolour.

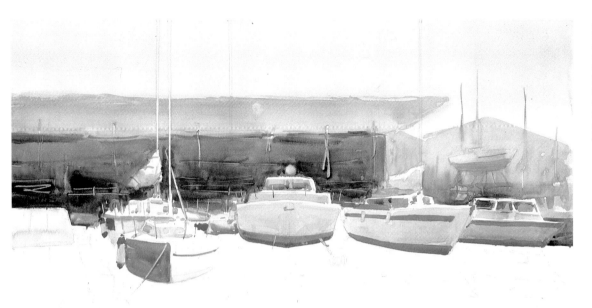

Fig. 406 Gaspar Romero has now created a major contrast obscuring the background where the boats are; he has 'opened out' some vertical lines in the background (with the end of the brush), and the whites corresponding to the boat masts, damping and absorbing colour with a synthetic hairbrush.

406

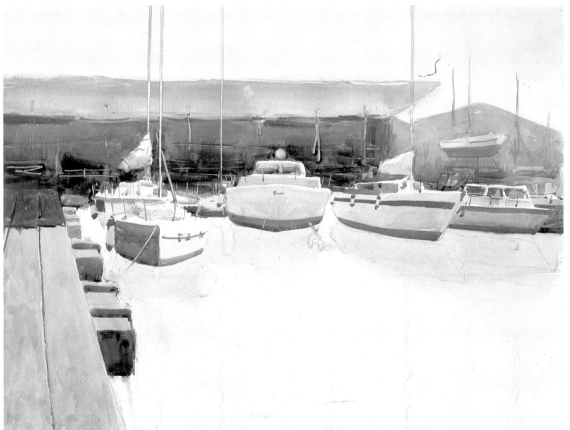

Fig. 407 The landing stage on the left side and also the hull appearing in the background to the right have been worked out, painted with some lack of definition so that they are situated further out. Note the care with which the artist has presented the luminous outlines of the boats and see how these colours, which were worked out in the preliminary drawing, are still defined in the painting.

407

Painting a seascape in watercolours

Fig. 408 This dark wash, the reflection of the boats on the sea, was painted quickly and decisively, clarifying the boundaries of the bottom part of the picture, while deliberately leaving a number of small white areas in the interior. Most important is that he painted wet-in-wet, diversified the colour with different shades, mixing on the paper itself with ultramarine, dark sienna, carmine...

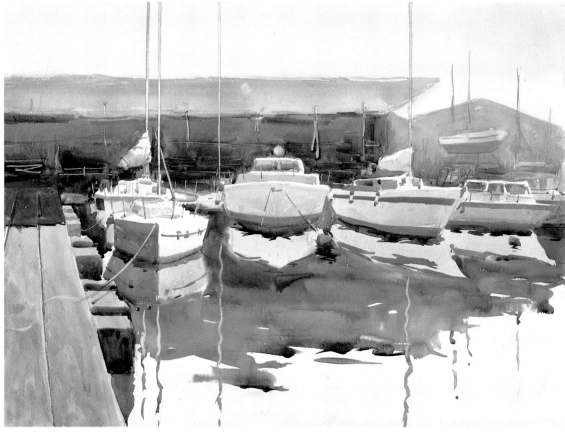

408

He uses the same brush and technique to 'open up' the white of the searchlight lamp on the top of the boat in the centre.

Fourth stage: a transitional phase (Fig. 407)

The decisive moment for the painting is drawing near. Soon Gaspar Romero will have to finish the reflections of the boats in the water with a few brushstrokes. If it comes out well, fine; but if it comes out wrong... For that reason he works more slowly now, looking at the water again and again, noticing unimportant shapes and details. He works on the right side a little bit, and then the dark base of the pier. He looks again at the water and finishes the ship in the shipyard, painting the dock in the left foreground... He stops.

Fifth stage: the big risk (Fig. 408)

'You'll risk it, right?' I ask him. 'Of course, but I have to *throw myself into the water* without fear,' he answers, smiling. And so Gaspar bravely 'jumps in'. Using a rounded no. 24 brush, with the slightly dirty water he has been using all along, he dampens the zone corresponding to the reflections, with the result

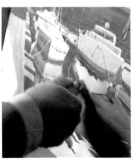

Fig. 409 At a specific moment, before this dark area has dried, Gaspar Romero finds his lighter, lights it, and brings it close to the painting to accelerate the drying, it is an original trick... which has its risk.

409

that since the dirty water is light grey, he can see and reserve the white forms corresponding to the actual reflections of the boats, while drawing the lower profile, the capricious shapes of the water in the foreground, etc. He follows with ultramarine blue, a little sienna and a touch of carmine, forming a blued grey that he applies to the zone he has already dampened, working rapidly, adding colour here, absorbing a little there, lightly varying the nuances.

'Nice job, Gaspar. You did it!' (Fig. 410)

Afterwards, with a flat no. 10 brush of synthetic hair, he 'opens up' the sinuous whites corresponding to the reflections of the light-

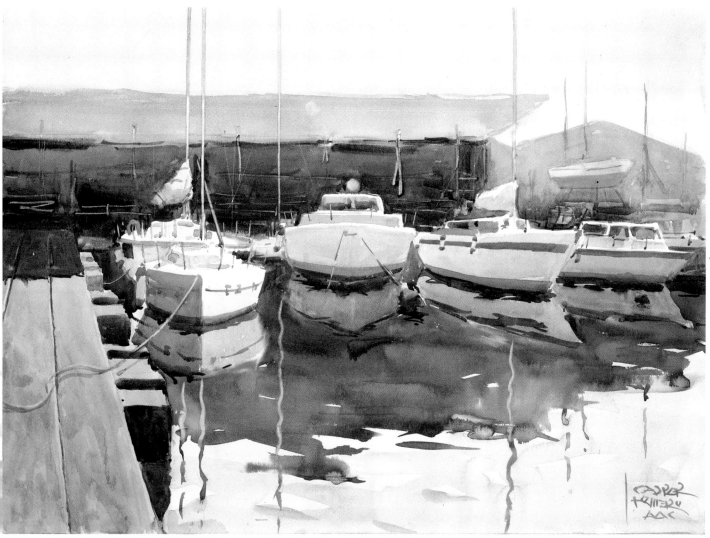

410

coloured masts, painting the reflections of the masts on the foreground white, darkening the reflection of the boat in the left foreground and... 'That's right, right?' I ask. 'Not yet,' says Gaspar, 'the reflections of the boats are too light, they look like holes, they must be darkened. Reflections are always darker than the actual colour of the reflected object.'

Sixth and last stage: finishing

And he does it. First he waits for the dark wash of the sea to dry (speeding up the drying process by holding a cigarette lighter flame up to the damp part). 'It's a little bit risky, but nothing will happen... if I do it right.' When it is dry he paints those nuances which conscientiously flee the uniform grey regularity. And still he paints, setting in the foreground light colour stains representing the movement of the water.

'Now it's done,' he says, and signs his name.

Fig. 410 This is the final stage of the painting – but watch what the artist does: he darkens the bright reflections of the boats on the sea ('the reflection is always darker than the colour of the form which is reflected') and with water straight out of the container (and somewhat dirty), he makes a number of brushstrokes which result in a very bright grey colour on the white paper in the foreground to represent the slight undulations of the sea.

Painting an illustration in watercolours

Maria Rius is a famous illustrator, with children's books published in many countries. She paints watercolours with liquid, transparent colours, using the white of the paper. Although her technique is not exactly that of the 'pure' watercolourist, her way of solving problems, her methods and procedures – including her tricks – I believe justify including her work in this book.

Mara Rius's palette of liquid watercolours covers the whole colour range – 18 colours in all – and all of a specific trademark. She prefers a line of colours called pastel paints which reflect the gentleness and bright luminosity of pastel colours. She uses high-quality fine paper, about 30 g. She paints with three brushes of marten hair: nos. 8 and 10 for the overall painting and a no. 3 for the small details. She uses two water containers, one for the first rinsing and the other with cleaner water for complete washing, absorbing colours, etc. Lastly, as is the case with all modern illustrators, Maria Rius uses the airbrush to fill in and resolve backdrops, blendings and gradating tones, and for large areas of uniform colour. The illustration created especially for this book does not correspond to a particular story or theme. I simply requested a *creative illustration*, and Maria Rius created a free image – for once without the conditions imposed by the editor! She has imagined an activity which everybody, children and adults, have dreamed of doing at least once: the act of flying. Congratulations Maria!

The technique

The classic watercolour demands cleanliness, will countenance only limited use of rubbing out, prohibits dirtiness, smudgy fingerprints, or muddying of the tones which might cause alterations in colour or stains. This type of care should be taken to a rigorous, antiseptic extreme for the art of illustration. The rubber is forbidden; the pencil foundation drawing must be very light to avoid showing through the applied watercolour. A small drop of water or saliva on a uniform background damages the illustration; one has to work with paper under the working hand so the palm will not dirty the work that has been done, or the white paper.

These precautions start as soon as the drawing begins. The professional illustrator never draws directly on the final piece of art. Rather, on a separate sheet of paper, she studies the composition, the pose, the attitudes and expressions of the figures and animals, all the

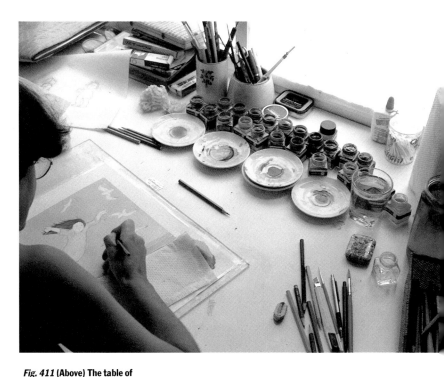

Fig. 411 (Above) The table of the illustrator Maria Rius with two water receptacles on the right-hand side, the bottles of liquid watercolour, and the porcelain dishes which the artist uses as a palette.

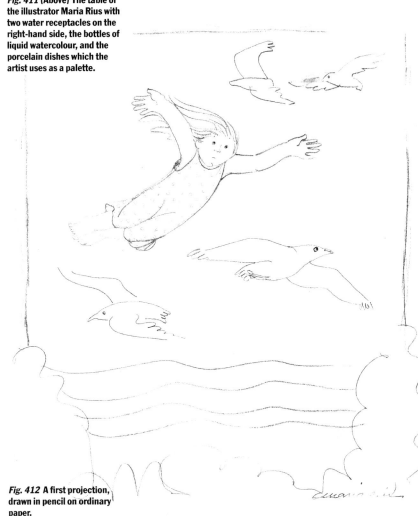

Fig. 412 A first projection, drawn in pencil on ordinary paper.

Painting watercolour with an airbrush

Generally an airbrush is not used for artistic watercolours, which does not mean that on certain occasions, in order to obtain certain effects such as smooth grading or blending, graded strokes, the effects of mist, etc., it might not be advisable to use it. Today in the field of illustration, the airbrush is undeniably an indispensable tool.

As a result of this requirement, and since under certain circumstances this knowledge may be useful to you, we thought it a good idea while, Maria Rius was producing her illustration, to explain briefly the function and technique of the airbrush.

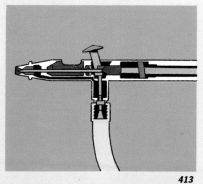

Fig. 413 Characteristics and mechanics of the airbrush for artists. The 'gun' is operated by an air compressor, which the artist controls with a pedal, leaving the hands free to control the extremely fine spray of paint forced out by the mechanism.

413

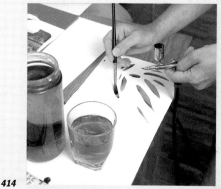

Fig. 414 Before beginning to spray the colour, the artist must check it on a separate piece of paper, having first prepared the necessary quantity of colour in a cup or small mug.

414

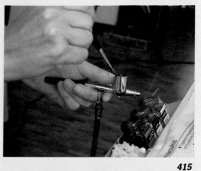

Fig. 415 With the colour already prepared, one should test the gun, loading it with water to prevent possible setbacks, such as the gun being dirty, blocked, etc. Having carried out this prior check, use a coarse brush to transfer the liquid paint from the cup in which it has been prepared to the small reservoir of the airbrush, filling it approximately halfway.

415

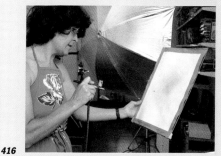

Fig. 416 Before finally painting, carry out a test on any piece of paper, making sure that there can be no splashing which on the paper and final drawing would mean an irreversible mishap.

416

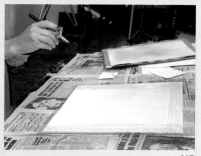

Fig. 417 Having taken all the necessary precautions, painting can begin with the airbrush, checking the intensity of the blend or the evenness of the grey, since, if it is very dark and requires more than one application, it is necessary to wait for it to dry in order to intensify it with new applications of spray. Notice how far away from the picture Maria works while she is holding the gun and painting.

417

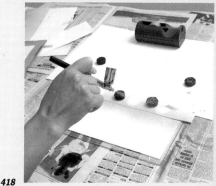

Fig. 418 Here Maria Rius is painting a change of shades or colours with a stencil. This remains fixed in place over the original drawing by some pieces of lead or small standard weights, typically used to make sure that the stencil is not moved by the movement of air from the airbrush. In order to better understand what Maria Rius is doing here, look at the blends and change of colours in the illustration shown in fig. 423.

418

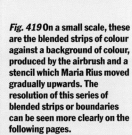

Fig. 419 On a small scale, these are the blended strips of colour against a background of colour, produced by the airbrush and a stencil which Maria Rius moved gradually upwards. The resolution of this series of blended strips or boundaries can be seen more clearly on the following pages.

419

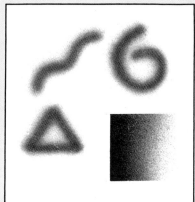

Fig. 420 The airbrush, with the outlet pipe suitably sealed, can draw fine shades and strokes of blended colours like those reproduced here.

420

Painting an illustration in watercolours

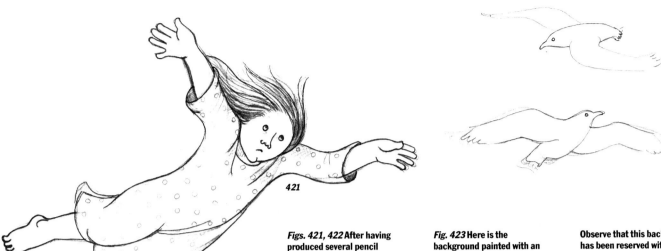

421

422

Figs. 421, 422 After having produced several pencil studies, Maria Rius drew these seagulls and this figure which could already be used for a finished illustration.

Fig. 423 Here is the background painted with an airbrush on which, if you look closely, it is possible to see the line drawing of the seagulls and the figure of the flying child.

Observe that this background has been reserved with adhesive tape in order to provide a frame or white margin around the illustration.

423

important elements. These studies are usually done in pencil, on visualizing or tracing paper, both of which are nearly transparent. In this way, if any one of these sketches turns out to be perfect, it may be transferred by tracing it onto the definitive drawing. The tracing is usually done by blackening the back of the tracing paper which has the selected drawing. This blackening, made with pencil, works as carbon paper. However, this can be messy and cause carbon to come off on the good paper. The best method of transferring is to use a light box with the tracing paper and drawing paper on top. Maria Rius drew several studies of seagulls and a little girl flying; she kept the drawing which is reproduced here. The sky in the background and the sea were executed with the airbrush, using the procedures I explain on page 171.

First stage: transferring the drawing, and painting with the airbrush (Fig. 423)

After the study of the girl and seagulls is traced onto the fine watercolour paper with a hard well-sharpened pencil, Maria frames the illustration with Scotch tape previously discharged of some of its glue by means of rubbing it on the edge of the table. Next, she paints the sky and sea with the airbrush. She first applies a blue-green background, creating the sky and nearly obliterating the pencil drawn figure. Using the same colour, Maria Rius paints a series of five undulating stripes through a template or stencil, applying paint as she moves the template down. Thus, beginning at the top, the second stripe is darker still, and so on. 'In the fourth stripe,' I tell

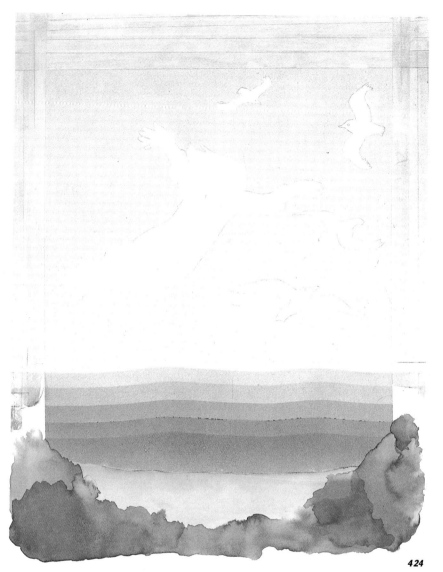

424

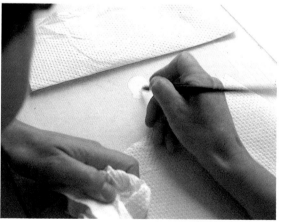

425

Fig. 424 Good illustrations are
actually the products of patient
and delicate work. Here, for
example, Maria Rius has had to
absorb the colour of the airbrush
at the bottom of the illustration
in order to paint the beach and
bushes in the foreground. She
has 'opened up' white areas for
the seagulls and girl but, not
satisfied with the absorption
effected by hand with the brush
and blotting paper, she has
patiently applied liquid bleach
diluted with water to achieve the
results she is after.

Fig. 425 Here Maria Rius is
'opening up' the blanks shown
in the previous figure, a job which
requires maximum precision so
as not to 'go too far'.

Maria, 'the template has dirtied the edge.'
'Have you noticed?' she replies in an amused
way, 'I've seen it; it wasn't planned. It's a
shame, but I thought that I could paint the
foam and win in the end.'

Second stage: painting the foreground and drawing the figures (Fig. 424)

Maria Rius carefully removes the transparent
Scotch tape covering the lower part of the
illustration, and paints this area, working with
a no. 8 brush and a light, yellow-green colour,
to represent the beach. Below this colour, as a
decorative border for the illustration, she now
paints some green shapes that remind us of
trees and bushes. The interesting point here is
that in order to paint the beach and bushes,
Maria Rius has had to wash this area which
was previously painted with green colour from
the airbrush. She must also dilute and wash off
the paint which covers the flying girl and seagulls. This is one of the tricks the watercolour
illustrator knows. This is a job that the illustrator will do quite often. The artist will rely on
the more malleable quality of liquid watercolours to help her. She first wets the shapes
with the brush and then absorbs the diluted
paint with a paper towel, repeating the procedure – always using clean water – as many
times as is necessary to leave the treated areas
free of colour. This is obviously harder to do if
the colour is very intense or if the pigment is
very permanent, as in the case of carmine,
Alizarin crimson, Prussian blue, emerald, and
several others.

Besides this procedure, the artist may also rely
on a trick which consists of washing the
whitened zone with lye diluted in water – this
leaves the paper absolutely white! (Beware:
while applying the diluted lye do not use a
brush with marten hair, but a brush with synthetic hair, the only material that will resist the
corrosive action of lye.)

Third stage: painting the figure (Fig. 425)

Once you know the system of washing and the
trick with lye, it's no secret how the sea foam
was 'painted', or how the seagulls acquired
their whiteness. But there is something left
that deserves a separate discussion.

Maria has removed the remaining Scotch tape
creating a bright clean rectangle around the
illustration, and has begun painting the flying
girl. She paints the colour of the flesh first,
next the rose colour of the dress, and finally
the reddish sienna hair. In each case, especially
in the skin and dress, Maria uses the same

Painting an illustration in watercolours

Fig. 426 There is a curious anecdote in connection with this picture. Maria Rius had not planned to paint the white foam on the peaks of the waves. Something unexpected happened: on finishing the last of these blends, Maria forgot to dry the edge of the stencil and when she lifted it, seeing these small stains as dots on the crest of the second wave (see them in fig. 424), she was desperate. 'The whole job was wasted,' she exclaimed aloud. But at that moment she found a solution and said, smiling happily, 'Good, I shall paint the foam of the sea waves. I remember the master Corot who said that when painting there is always, in addition, "the happy accident" which sometimes brings about a change, an idea which enriches the painting.'

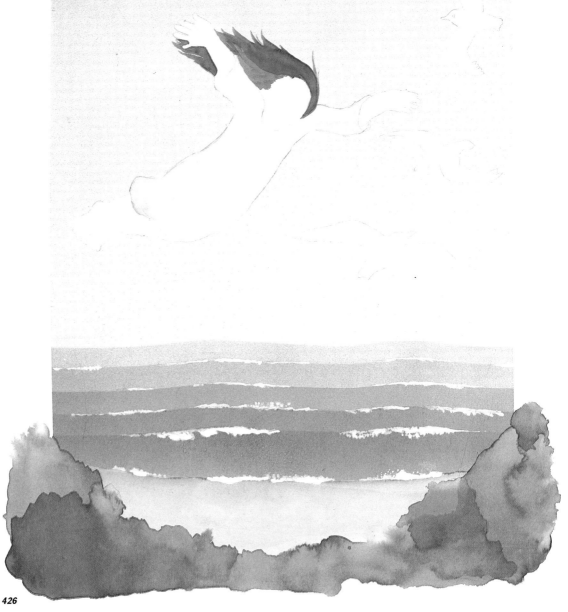

426

technique she will later apply to the seagulls, and earlier used to create the bushes and trees at the bottom of the painting. This is how it works: Maria applies a layer of watercolour. Almost immediately after, she partially removes the colour by blotting the area with absorbent paper. She applies a new coat and blots again, over and over, until she gets the desired intensity. At the same time she is mod-elling the figure, shaping the form with contrasts of light and shadow. This procedure reminds me of the method employed by the Old Masters of oil painting, the Flemish and Renaissance artists, who painted with fine transparent glazes, one layer on top of another, achieving a transparent, even finish.

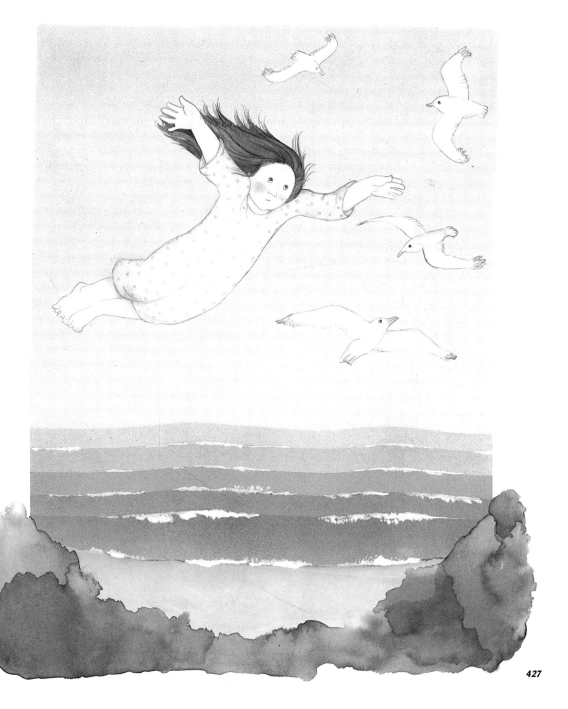

Figs. 427, 428 The final stage in illustration is finishing up, adjusting, profiling, touching up, completing. The technique of Mara Rius, and of many contemporary illustrators, involves applying liquid watercolour glazes, using coloured pencils (Caran d'Ache brand) to shape volume and heighten colour and using a hard 4H grading pencil to accentuate forms, greying and toning down areas with extremely fine twirls almost invisible to the naked eye.

427

Fourth stage: the finishing touches (Figs. 427 and 428)

In this figure and the next, we view the last stage, realized with a procedure that is truly unique: the intermingling of three mediums - watercolour, lead pencil, and colour pencils. With these tools the artist models the forms, and strengthens contours. Both the lead pencil - 4H, which happens to be a very hard pencil - and the colour pencils will create subtle grey ues, applied in minuscule strokes and dots, hardly noticeable at first glance, but which will give the illustration a warm, finely pebbled texture when it is reduced for reproduction in a book. With the lead pencil and colour pencils, Maria Rius models and completes the hair. She draws the features of the face, she models the delicate folds of the dress, and the girl's hands and feet, and goes on to give volume to the seagulls... All this of course is a difficult task, requiring technique, craftsmanship and creativity.

Painting an illustration in watercolours

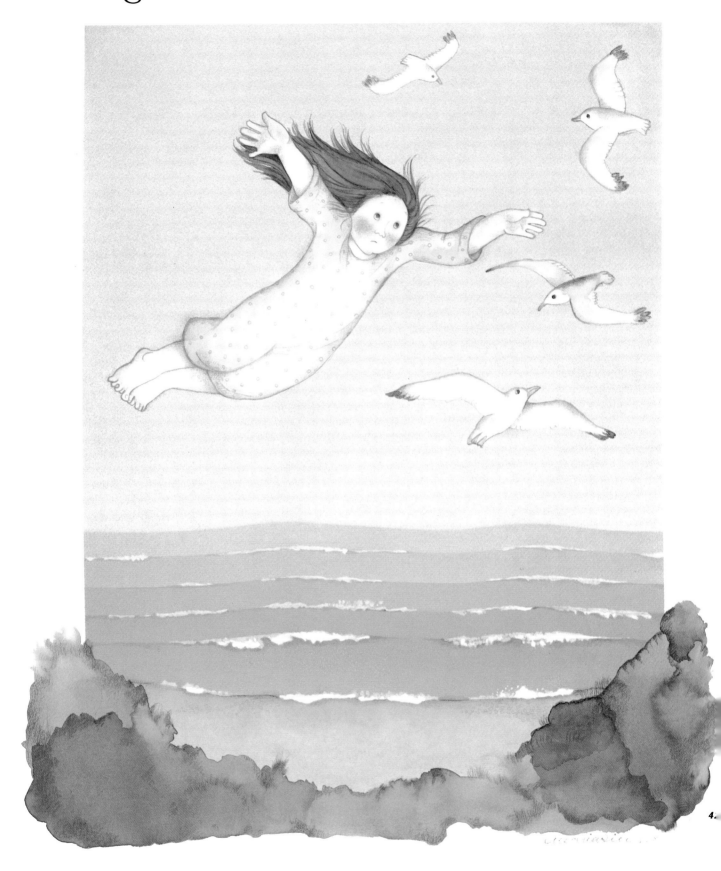

4.

Painting a snowy landscape in watercolours

I painted this same subject in watercolour in January of this year, and I will now paint it again, but this time in the studio, and explain the process in detail, not just showing the various stages of development in the painting of the work, but also the different processes and techniques.

This is the last of the step-by-step demonstrations presented in this book: a painting designed to be a final project, which I will paint for you myself, using many of the concepts, theories, and techniques that a professional uses when painting. I hope that this will be a complete lesson summarizing the things I have tried to teach you in the pages of this book.

To start with, look at figs. 429 and 430 which show the painting I did on the scene and a photo of the subject, and notice how useful it is to take the camera along when you go out to paint. With a photograph of the subject, you can compare the finished painting to the real image, and even rectify or finish some details later on, when the original scene in life is quite changed. Now then, starting with the photo and the painting I did, notice first that the scene offers a compositional scheme which I tried to accent, as you can see in the adjoining figures. Notice the differences between the paintings and the actual scene; these are changes I made during the process of interpreting: (1) suppressing those long trees beside the fence that surrounds the town, on the left-hand side, because they interfere with the view of the town; (2) interpreting the roofs as covered with snow, even though they actually were not; (3) suppressing three of the trees which appear in the ditch running diagonally across the landscape, and distributing them differently so that they will not interfere with our view of the town; (4) changing the diagonal ditch into a slight ridge, which lends variety to the composition, and allows the addition of the blue band of shadow thrown by the ridge, which aids the composition; (5) heightening the shadows of the trees on the ridge, adding variety to the scene; and (6) reducing the height of the grey band of the village and darkening the ochre colour in the railing in the foreground, in order to better emphasize the geometric zig-zag form which determines the composition of the painting.

Now let us look at the resolution of this watercolour painting, step by step. But first, allow me a brief commentary on the materials

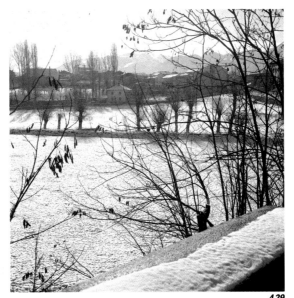

430

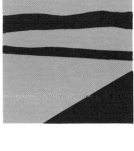

429

Fig. 429 (Above) Photograph of the snow-covered landscape which will be used as a subject for the watercolour of this last demonstration. The landscape of the photograph corresponds to this scheme of composition.

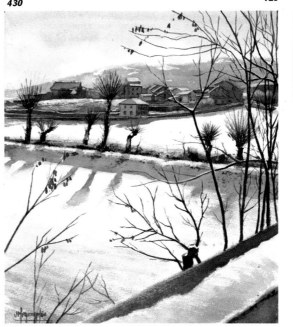

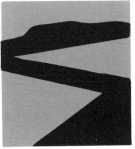

Fig. 430 (Left) A watercolour painting made a year ago of the landscape shown in the previous photograph (fig. 429). The interpretation of the subject using this scheme heightens the geometrical shape and improves the composition of the painting.

and tools I used, and about my work habits. When I paint outdoors, whether in the city or the country, I paint with a typical tripod of the box-case-tripod type. I have no objection to artists who paint with their paper almost vertical – a tablet or mounted on a board, as many artists do – but I am more comfortable with the tablet or board tilted at an angle of 35 or 40 degrees, as are many other artists. This preference means that in the studio, I always work with a tabletop easel in the form of a lectern, and an adjustable seat which can be raised somewhat higher than normal. I connect the table or sheet of paper with clips; that way

Painting a snowy landscape in watercolours

I never have to wet and dry the paper with it already mounted with tape (see fig. 431). I find it more practical to paint with the paper on the table, or with a sheet of paper thick enough that it can be adequately mounted with clips. I use tube paints and moist tablets of paint interchangeably. White paint recently squeezed from a tube facilitates rapid execution – you don't have to rub with a brush to pick up the colour – by the time it has been on the palette for two or three days, it has just about the same texture as moist tablets do. So, in the long run, both types are fine. I use pads of paper made by Fabriano, Arches or Canson, of medium or coarse grain, and brushes of sable hair in size nos. 6, 8, 12 and 14, and occasionally a no. 18 ox-hair brush and a Japanese stag-hair brush with flat bristles, the latter two for washes, and wide grey areas, as well as for dampening large areas with water. I also use a natural sponge for dampening, for example, before beginning a painting, and also, on occasion, to wash, wipe, reduce, draw, and lighten. I use H pencils, which smear the least, and an ordinary white plastic rubber (I don't like kneaded rubbers, which feel like modelling clay).

I use only one container of water, which I change every once in a great while – since I kind of like dirty water for painting. When I paint in the studio, I put the container on top of a rag, folded into four layers. This protects the table from water, and also serves as a means of removing water or paint from the brush. All I do is 'paint' the rag with the brush a little bit before I touch the paper. And as regards emptying the brush, I have waited until the end to mention the use of absorbent paper of the paper towel type sold in rolls for kitchen use. These towels are made of a spongy paper, which dries rapidly and easily absorbs the water and dampness of the watercolours. I use them constantly, having a folded or crumpled towel always available in my left hand, to clean the brush, reduce, absorb, blend or break down colour, pressing, more or

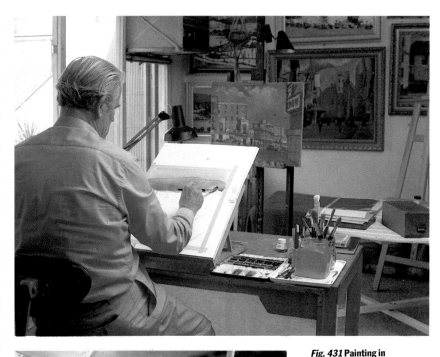

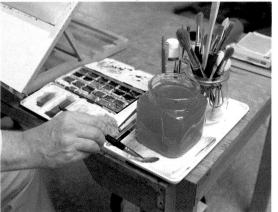

432

Fig. 431 Painting in watercolours, whether in the open air or in the studio, I feel better working with the board inclined at an angle of some 30 degrees to 45 degrees. In the studio this requires a tabletop easel in the form of a lectern (fig. 98) and an adjustable seat which can be raised somewhat higher than normal.

Fig. 432 A detail of no importance but which I believe is useful: under the water jar I place a piece of absorbent cloth folded several times, which, apart from protecting the table against drops and wetness, enables me to remove excess water from the brush by simply pressing, as if I were painting on the cloth.

less, on a recently painted area. Sometimes I even use it to draw, as sometimes happens with a uniform background of sky, when simply pressing with the paper towel can 'open up' a white spot which, if properly treated afterwards, can become a magnificent bank of cumulus clouds. And now let us return to the watercolour painting of the snowy landscape that I have chosen.

First stage: drawing and reserving whites (Fig. 434)

We begin, as always, with a precise, well defined line drawing, particularly in the area of the village houses, where the buildings and roofs must correspond to reality; the same is true of the ditch in the middle ground and the trees appearing there. But the trunks and delicate branches of the trees in the foreground may, on the other hand, be drawn with more liberty, representing, for the time being, the largest trunks.

Afterwards, I apply masking fluid with a no. 4 synthetic brush, covering the areas where I wish to reserve the white, these being: the roofs of the houses and the walls which surround the village, the small snowy areas of the mountains and their upper profiles, and the broadest trunks of the slender trees in the foreground. I also paint a little fluid in the right foreground to create some snowdrifts. It is very important to use masking fluid in the right quantity and not to overdo it; avoid reserving whites when normal watercolour techniques can be used.

Next I reserve a patch of white – using white wax – in the thin promontory on the left side of the village (indicated as A in the figure adjoining this first stage) and in the band of terrain in the centre (B). In zone A, I reinforce this reserve of white created with white wax by applying masking fluid, scrubbing and gradating it from the top down. (Masking fluid is cream or light blue in colour, which makes it easy to locate later on).

Second stage: painting the sky, the mountains, and the village houses (Fig. 440)

Before beginning to paint, let me mention that the scale of broken colours, and their cold feeling in this watercolour, are the product of a mixture of dark sepia and ultramarine blue,

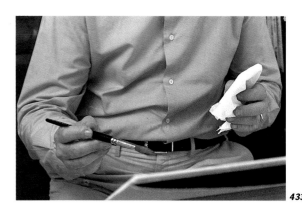

Fig. 433 Working, painting with the brush in the right hand; under the left hand is a piece of blotting paper folded twice or more, always ready to allow you to remove any excess paint from the brush, to blot the colour in a specific area, and to 'draw' by opening up white areas in a form or a colour which has been applied. The tissue paper or blotting paper, which mops up like paper towels used in the kitchen, is essential for watercolour painting.

433

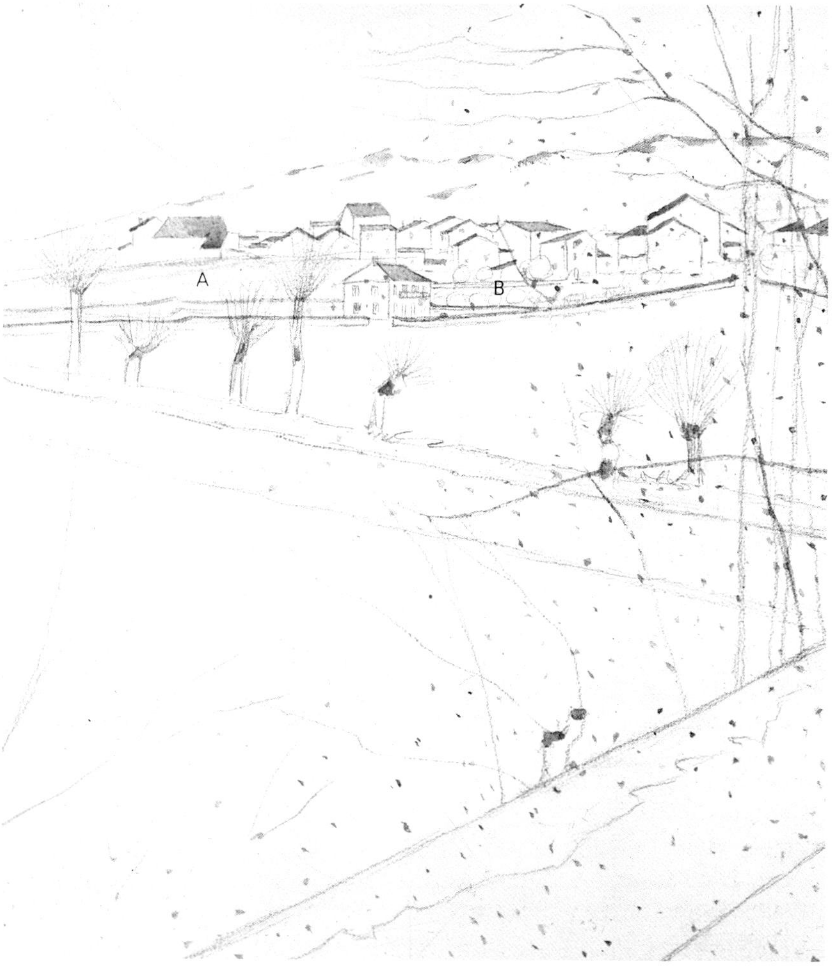

434

Fig. 434 Here is the finished drawing, with the masking fluid applied to reserve certain areas.

Fig. 435 Application of masking fluid to reserve certain areas with a synthetic no. 4 brush. The fluid which remains on the brush is diluted with water to wash it before it has dried, but some fluid always remains which has to be eliminated by squeezing the brush and pulling it through your fingers and nails.

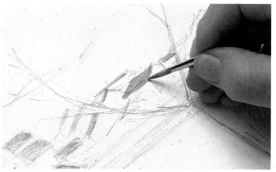

435

Painting a snowy landscape in watercolours

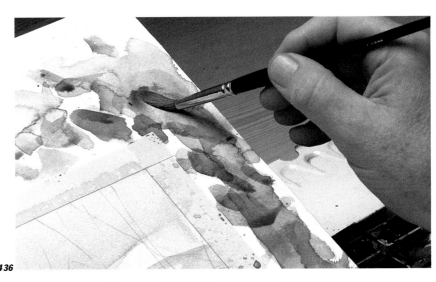

which gives a basic neutral grey that can be altered (as it has been) by mixing with carmine, ochre, emerald green, and Prussian blue, in order to obtain the different colours and nuances visible in my interpretation of the scene. For example, the sky was painted with the two basic colours mentioned above – ultramarine blue and dark sepia – by adding carmine a little bit at a time, using a lot of water, of course.

I customarily test colour mixtures on a separate piece of paper, or in the margins of the painting itself, as you will see I am doing in fig. 436.

I begin painting the skyline with the colour mentioned above, applying it to the group of houses, the mountains and the sky itself, paint-ing with the tablet of paper turned upside down (fig. 437) in order to achieve a wash that builds up colour in the higher part of the sky and leaves the horizon slightly lighter. While the wash is still damp, I 'draw' some white clouds with a paper towel by pressing on the area of the horizon and removing colour. Without waiting for the sky wash to dry completely, I rapidly paint the mountains with a darker grey-blue wash, consistent in colour but softened and diffused at the edges with a clean brush. This wash extends to the group of houses and to the village. On the edge of the house at the left-hand side of the village, I 'open up' a light spot like a cloud of smoke, using a small stick with a cotton swab on the end, the cotton absorbs the water, and with it, the colour: fig 439). Now I must wait until the second wash – for the mountains and houses – dries. I speed up the drying by using a hair dryer and then begin painting the houses, fences, and yards of the village, with different nuances and with similar but diverse colours.

436

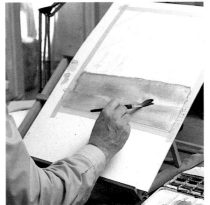

437

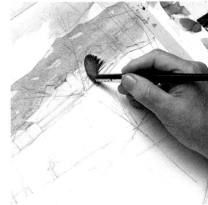

438

Fig. 436 I select from the samples of colours in the white enamelled palette, but before actually painting it I check the colour on a separate piece of paper or in the margin of the paper on which I am going to paint the watercolour, as you can see in this picture.

Fig. 437 To paint an even-coloured sky, one trick is to turn the board upside down.

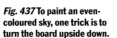

439

Fig. 439 Now with a small stick with a swab of cotton on the end, I absorb colour and open up bright areas like clouds of smoke on the top edge of the houses.

Fig. 438 When the grey of the sky has still not completely dried, I paint the darker grey of the hills with which I also cover the forms of the houses and the town.

I continue to use dark sepia mixed with ultramarine blue as the base, varying the amounts and proportions to obtain greys which are either bluer, darker, or more neutral, without forgetting the possibility – the necessity – of bringing into play the ochre, carmine, Prussian and cobalt blue tones. I paint the doors and windows of the houses without outlining, without too much fuss, and call this second stage over.

In a watercolour such as this one – but actually in all watercolours – which uses a scale of colours with a notable blue-grey tendency, the artist must always feel the need to enrich the colours, painting with different paints and different nuances, trying to attain a tonal unity within the variety of colours and nuances.

Third stage: resolving the uneven ridge in the centre (Fig. 441)

First I paint the trees, starting with the trunks, using dark sienna and a little blue, finishing the fan-like branches afterwards with a no. 6 sable brush and controlling the intensity with light, absorbent touches of the paper towel. Next, I turn my attention to the shadows in the gully and the grey-blue shadow on the ridge or uneven land next to the gully, where the long shadows of the trees also appear. I made this grey-blue colour by first mixing a base of sienna and ultramarine blue, and then adding cobalt blue and a pinch of carmine. I will paint the upper edges of these bands with the frottage or dry-brush technique.

The frottage or dry-brush technique – also called 'scumbling' – (figs. 245-7) demands constant tests, carried out on separate paper of the same quality and grain as the paper being used for the painting. Naturally this technique cannot be used on recently painted, damp surfaces.

I paint with this technique in the areas mentioned above (testing it on a separate piece of paper first, in order to know how much to dampen or dry the brush), controlling the dry brushstrokes with light and precise dabs of the paper towel, pressing and absorbing colour, blending more or less, etc. Then I use the grey-blue mixture to paint the shadows of the trees and the gradation of this same colour which appears on the right-hand side, as well as the shadow of the ridge, always using the dry-brush technique (fig. 441).

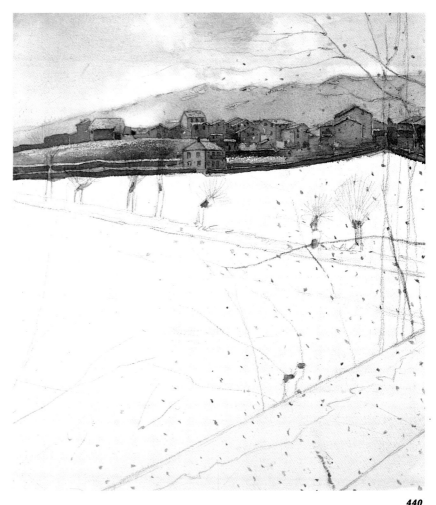

440

Fig. 440 In this second stage it is possible to see the need to diversify the colour, particularly on the fronts and roofs of the houses, on the land, and on the fences. This diversity, which is always a good idea, is particularly necessary when, as in this case, the subject suggests a marked grey tendency.

Painting a snowy landscape in watercolours

Fig. 441 It is important to paint *straight off*, without stressing anything, trying to achieve success with the first application and brushing without fear. This also involves the technique known as scumbling or dry brush, which makes it possible to blend with minuscule dots or spots caused by the rubbing of the half-dry brush on the grain of the paper. The success of this technique depends largely on trying the effect out on a separate piece of paper first, and on working carefully with the blotting paper to eliminate or remove colour if necessary.

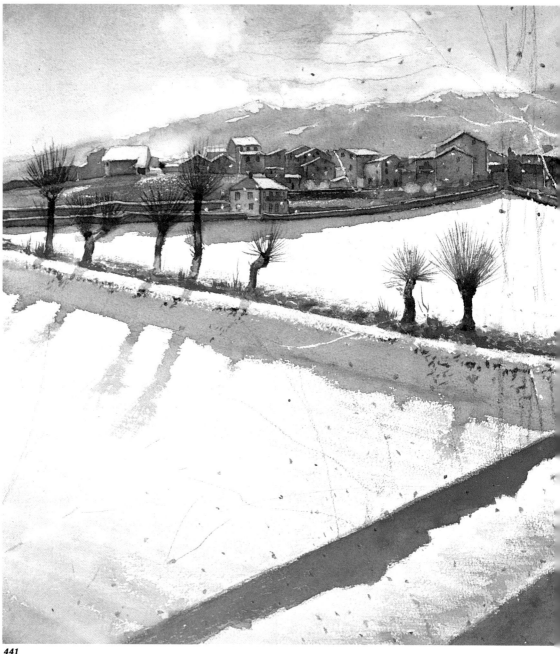

441

Fourth stage: finishing the gully and resolving the foreground (Fig. 447)

To finish off the middle ground of the gully, I paint in the interior with greys, siennas, and blues corresponding to the rocks and clods of earth not covered with snow, the bushes and clumps of grass, etc. This is a laborious task calling for a fine brush, but there is still room for interpretation and synthesis. But, hey! Wait a minute! The crest of the ridge, as the edge of the blue band, seems poorly explained and narrow.

It would be better if I could extend it, and I

will, using the sandpaper technique. First wrap the rubber end of a pencil with a piec of sandpaper, then I energetically rub the are just above and beyond the limit of the edge c the band mentioned above, in a movemen parallel to that area. This 'opens' and widen the white area. Afterwards I clean the are with my rubber (figs. 442, 443). Then I touc up this new, 'open' area and blend it in.

I begin now to paint the wall of the lowe right-hand side, as well as the snow on th land in the left foreground, resolving ther with the dry-brush technique. Attentio should be paid to the direction of the brush-strokes here, which should be diagonal for the snow, descending from left to right, parallel to the diagonal of the gully and ridge. For the stones of the wall, which is free of snow, the brushstrokes should also be diagonal, but in the opposite direction, descending from right to left (see fig. 445 for a better understanding). These are the wide 'frottage' sections, done with a wide brush, continuous and decided, and their success depends as much on the amount of paint and relative dampness of the brush – which I will, of course, test before-hand many times – as on the simultaneous control exercised by the absorbent paper towel. I will begin with the snow on the left-hand side, using thee colour nuances: first, a neutral light grey, which serves as a base, breaking down and becoming lighter in colour as it grows more distant from the foreground. As I have already mentioned, the frottage must be carried out with a broad brush and in a continuous and decided manner, therefore I have taken the precaution of covering the edge of the wall with a piece of cardboard, as you can see in fig. 446. In this way, I avoid the risk of 'running over the line', that is, running into the ochre of the wall at the end of those large, rapid strokes of the dry brush. Finally, to fin-ish this fourth stage, I paint the snow in the foreground of the wall applying two coats of two different greys, the first a light grey which serves as a foundation, the second, alternating with the dry-brush technique, drawing the forms the snow takes on in this area. As you can see, I also use small touches of siennas and blues to clarify these forms (fig. 447).

Fifth stage: peeling off the masking fluid and general touch-up (Fig. 448)

Energetically rubbing with an ordinary every-day rubber, I remove the masking fluid from the mountains, the roofs of the houses, the mound and walls that surround the town, and the trees and trunks in the foreground, leaving the snowdrifts for last.

Horrible, right? I want you to see this view, this moment (fig. 448), so that you can better understand the disagreeable surprise of these whites – so terribly white – that stand out by virtue of their excessive contrast, and that may lead us to believe that our trick with the mask-ing fluid was a mistake. You will see that it is a good trick in the following stages, but obvi-ously it should be used with caution.

Now I begin to retouch, to blend these whites into the rest of the nuances and colours, grey-

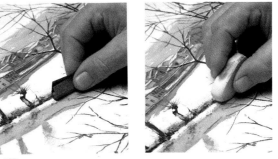

442

443

Figs. 442, 443 'Opening up' a white area with sandpaper, wound around the end of a pencil, and rubbing fairly energetically. When the rubbing is completed, the area must be cleaned with a rubber, then touched up as necessary.

444

Fig. 444 Here is an enlarged picture of the snow and the wall in the foreground, which I am resolving with the 'scumble' to more closely represent the texture of snow-covered surfaces.

445

Fig. 445 As you can see in this diagram, the direction of the brush differs depending on the place and the subject or element which is being painted.

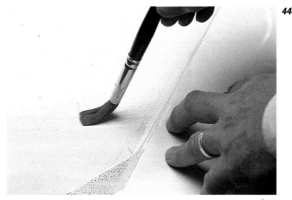

446

Fig. 446 To paint here with the 'scumble' (dry-brush) technique and with these broad and long brushstrokes and avoid 'going too far', I have covered the wall on the right-hand side with a piece of cardboard.

Painting a snowy landscape in watercolours

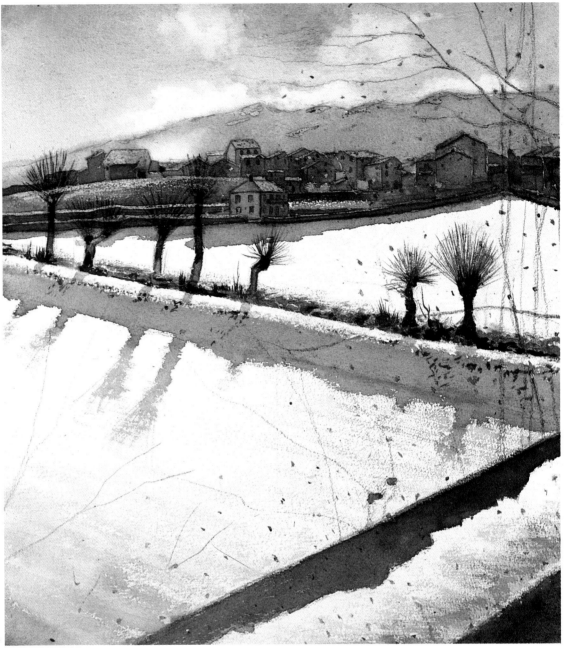

Fig. 447 The white at the top of the ridge or margin in the centre is now broader, after having been widened by rubbing with sandpaper, the irregularities and dark shapes of the ridge have already been reviewed and reconstructed. In the foreground I have resolved the texture of the snow by using 'scumble' or dry-brush technique. Everything is ready for the removal of the masking fluid.

447

ing them, dirtying and diffusing them, patiently working with the point of a damp brush where their edges are too hard, painting the 'holes' in the trees with blue-grey to represent the snow in the shade... and leaving it like that, as you can see in fig. 449.

Sixth stage: slender trees, snowdrifts and overall finishing (Fig. 450)
With a neutral black, made from dark sienna and a little blue, I paint, or perhaps I should say draw, the profiles of the slender trees in the foreground, retaining the white strokes made by the masking fluid. For this I take advantage of the fine point of the no. 6 sable brush, with which I also trace the fine branches – so fine that I wind up drawing some of

Fig. 448 This is the state of the watercolour once the masking fluid which reserved these blank areas has been removed – a result which is somewhat unpleasant due to the excessive contrast and the lack of balance caused by these white areas against the colour harmony of the watercolour in general. I hope that having seen this result, you will be aware of the fact that masking fluid to reserve certain areas is a good auxiliary for certain cases (to represent the flakes of snow, as we shall see further on, for example), but this technique should not be abused despite the good final result which I expect to achieve once these blanks have been harmonized.

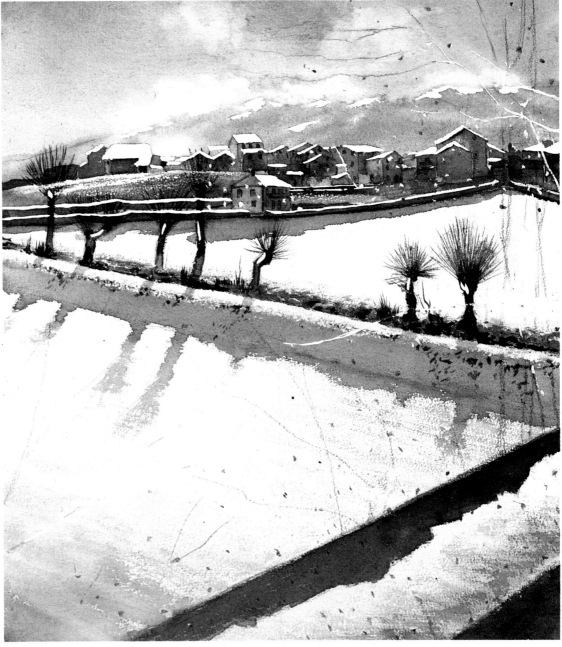

448

them with a black ballpoint pen. Afterwards, I paint the few dry leaves with ochre, a little carmine, and a pinch of blue. Then I remove the masking fluid from the snowdrifts and begin the final work of finishing. With the black ballpoint pen I draw some almost imperceptible contours, in the fan-shaped drifts in the trees of the gully, as well as some small branches. I outline the edges of some of the roofs and windows of the village houses.

Now I decide to open up some lighter, spherical-shaped areas on the left side of the village. I use the technique of opening whites with a synthetic brush, keeping in mind that these light areas correspond to sturdy village trees which animate and diversify the forms. I continue with the sharp point of a blade or mat knife, 'opening up' very fine points and lines, scraping and scratching the paper in the snowdrifts, in the trees, on the branches of the

Painting a snowy landscape in watercolours

Fig. 449 The excesses have been smoothed and harmonized with light glazes which cover the 'holes' which the masking fluid revealed. Just a few more touches to finish the painting.

Fig. 450 I paint the slim trees in the foreground with spontaneous, carefree strokes, using the dark liquid paint in such a way that the brush flows freely. There is no chance that with such a fine stroke I will end up with an excessively linear or too technical resolution. I give a few touches with a black ballpoint pen to the trees, the houses; I paint the eaves and remove the masking fluid over the snowflakes. I feel the cold air, the feeling of snow in the high mountain, and I am happy. I have finished.

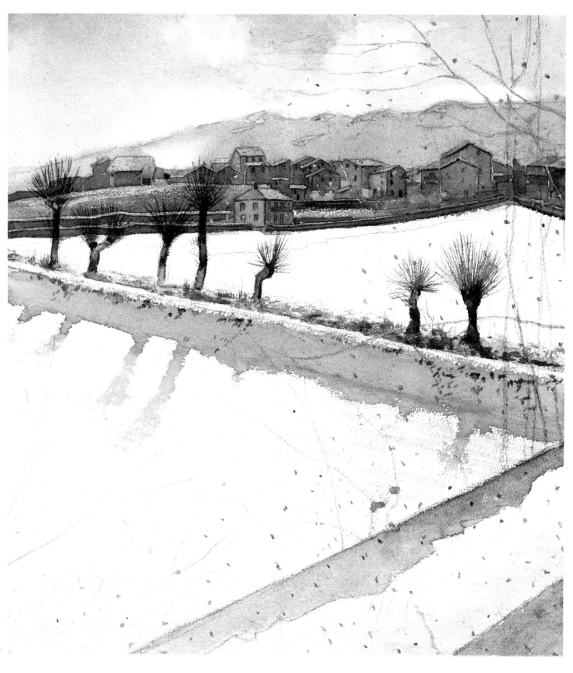

449

slender trunks in the foreground, adding snow effects... always correcting – just little things, almost nothing – the colour of a house, the colour of the village wall, the colour of the mound of earth...

Then I leave it alone, and sign it.
And now, I bid you adieu with the sincere wish that today, tomorrow, right now – partly by having read and looked at this book – you will feel the need to paint a watercolour.

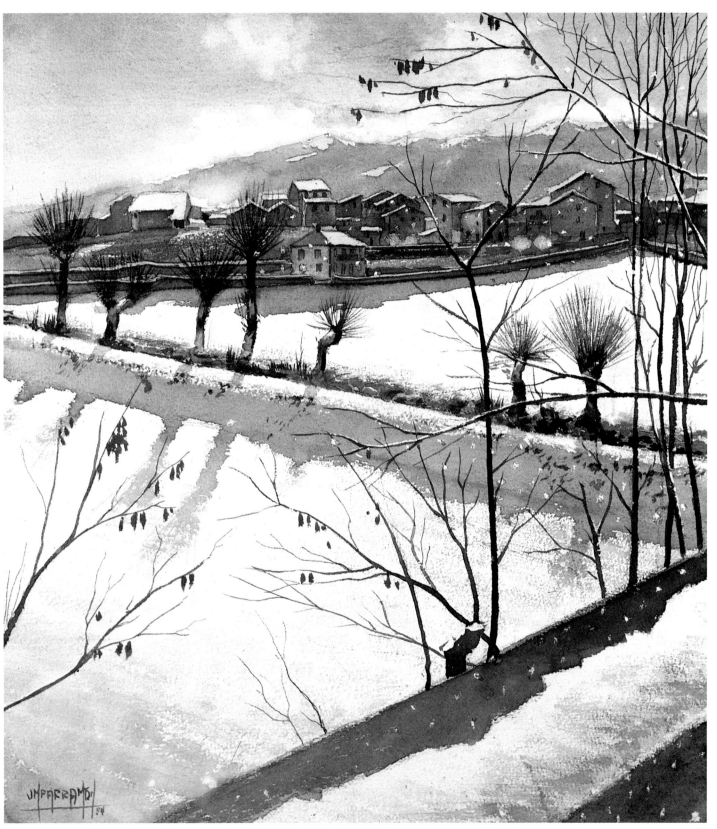

450

Glossary

A

Absorbent paper. A type of spongy paper which, by virtue of its absorbent properties, is used as a paper towel, most often in the kitchen. This type of paper is used in watercolour painting to absorb colour and to 'open up' white areas by removing white paint.

Agglutinate. Liquid products used to build up and bind powdered pigments or paints. In watercolour painting these products are water and gum arabic, and glycerine or honey combined with a preservative.

Airbrush. Process for painting with powdered or liquid colours. The principal tool is a *pistol* which is filled with a liquid paint. When connected to an air compressor, the paint can be shot in a jet of colour tones like a well-directed spray, allowing the artist to paint indistinct, gradated and diffused strokes. With the help of stencils made of thick paper or cardboard cut to shapes previously worked out, the airbrush also permits the painting of concrete shapes or forms.

Alla prima. Italian expression which translates as 'first time'. Refers to the technique of direct painting which completes the painting in one single session without any previous preparation.

Asymmetry. Free and intuitive distribution of the elements of a painting while still balancing the various parts with respect to each other.

Atmosphere. Term used in art which relates to the distance or air space between the foreground and the background. The interposed atmosphere is one of the factors used to represent the third dimension in a painting: it is a matter of decolouring and blurring the background with relation to the foreground.

B

Barb. Unequal edge or border of handmade drawing paper. It is a characteristic of good quality drawing paper.

Blocking in. Drawing the basic shape of a form using squares, rectangles, cubes, or rectangular prisms, which by analogy are called *boxes*.

Botanical painting. Painting which studies flowers, plants, trees, and fruits from a scientific and didactic point of view. This was an important subject in the 18th century.

Broken colours. Colours made from a mixture of two complementary colours mixed in unequal amounts with white. In watecolours, broken colours may be made up of only the two complementary colours, since the paper is white.

C

Cardboard. Thick sheets made with wood paste, usually grey in colour. Paper of a quality adequate for painting in watercolours is sometimes supplied with cardboard backing. If the finished watercolour painting is to be reproduced using photomechanical processes, this cardboard-backed paper will not permit reproduction by the *scanner* method, in which case it is preferable to paint on normal paper.

Cartoons. Small or reduced-scale drawing done on Bristol board or cardboard, used as projections or models for murals, mosaics, tapestries, etc. The cartoon, on cardboard, is transferred to canvas or to the wall through a graph or grid system with the contours drawn in, by means of a piece of cardboard enlarged to actual size.

'Cat's tongue'. Popular name for the filbert brush, flat with a rounded point.

Chalk. A small cylindrical or square bar which colours by rubbing. Chalk is made of powdered soil, milled with oils, water, and gummy substances. Chalk is similar to pastel, but more stable and with a harder line. There are chalks in white, black, light, sienna, dark sienna, cobalt blue, and aquamarine.

Chiaroscuro. Those parts or zones of the painting which, even when in intense shade, allow the forms of the object to show. It might be defined as the art of painting light within shadows. Rembrandt was one of the great masters of *chiaroscuro*.

Chromatic scale. The word 'scale' as applied to the system of musical notes (doh, ray, me, fah, soh, etc.), was invented in the year 1028 by Guido D'Arezzo to signify 'a succession of perfectly ordered sounds'. In painting, we refer to the succession of colours in the spectrum as the chromatic scale: 'any perfectly ordered succession of colours or tones'.

Colourists. Those artists who give more importance to colour than to tonal value, believing that forms and bodies may be differentiated and distinguished using only colour, lending the painting a certain effect. Contemporary painting is, in many aspects, colourist.

Complementary colours. Speaking in terms of *'light'* colours, complementary colours are secondary colours to which the addition of a primary colour will result in the recomposition of white light (or vice versa). Example: by adding dark blue to yellow – the latter being a combination of the *'light'* colours green and red – we recompose white light.

Contrasts. An optical effect by which a dark colour appears darker, the lighter the surrounding colours are, and vice versa.

Copper engraving. Sheet of copper covered with varnish, on which one draws with a metal point which cuts through the varnish, making incisions which reach down to the metal. Errors may be corrected by painting on new varnish. When the drawing is completed, the sheet is bathed in nitric acid, which corrodes and etches the exposed metal incisions. The nitric acid used to etch the copper lends this process the other name often used: *etching*.

Crayons, wax colours. Basically these are pigments or paints compounded with wax and grease and heat-fused at certain temperatures to form a homogeneous paste which, once dry, takes the shape of small cylindrical bars. They are stable colours, applied by rubbing and, to a certain point, cover, permitting the application of a light colour over a dark colour, reducing the latter by mixing with the former.

D

Dominant colour. The term dominant is used regularly in music to refer to the fifth note of a musical scale, or the most important note. By analogy, it may also be applied to painting in referring to a dominant colour. This may be a particular colour, or a set of *warm*, *cold*, or *broken colours*.

Draft. Projection of a painting drawn or painted as a study beforehand. The great masters made one or more drafts as projections before starting on the paintings themselves.

Dry-brush technique. The technique of watercolour painting in which a nearly dry brush, with very little paint, is rubbed against a textured paper so that the paint remains on the surface of the texture, leaving a granulated surface. Also called frottage.

Dry watercolours. Dry watercolours do not consist of any special technique, being the normal, classical watercolours. The adjective 'dry' is used to differentiate them from *wet watercolours*, given that the latter type involve some special techniques.

E

Etching. See Copper engraving.

F

Fauvism. French term derived from the word *fauve* (meaning 'wild' in English), first used by the critic Vauxcelles in referring to a 1905 exposition in the Salon d'Automne of Paris. The Fauvist style is distinguished by brilliant and strident colours, making for intense contrasts, sometimes related to the juxtaposition of complementary colours.

Ferrule. In a paintbrush, the shank, or metal part which surrounds and retains the hairs.

Filbert. Type of flat brush with a rounded point, commonly known as 'cat's tongue'.

Frottage. Term derived from the French verb *frotter* (to rub) which refers to the technique of painting in watercolours on a coarse-grained paper with an almost dry brush, holding very little paint. The brush is rubbed on the paper, allowing the texture of the paper to show in the paint. The frottage technique is also known as *dry-brush* technique.

G

Glaze. Transparent coat of paint, applied before or over another colour, which modifies the latter.

Golden Rule, Law of the. See *Golden Section*.

Golden Section, Law of the. Established by the Roman architect Vitruvius to determine the ideal placement of a line or point, aesthetically speaking, within a given space. The Golden Section states that: 'In order that a space divided into unequal parts be aesthetically pleasing, there must be a relationship between the smaller and larger parts such that the smaller is to the larger as the larger is to the total.' The mathematical expression of the Golden Section or Golden Rule is equal to 1.618.

Gouache. French term used throughout the world to refer to tempera paint, a medium similar to watercolour, made of the same ingredients but with a larger proportion of pigment or coloured earths, and with the addition of honey or gum arabic in order to obtain colours characterized by their opaqueness. Gouache (tempera) is a thick, covering medium, allowing the artist to paint with light colours over darker colours. It dries with a matt, pastel finish.

Grain. Structure or direction of the fibres in paper. The grain determines the roughness of the paper. Paper for watercolour painting is divided into fine-grain, medium-grain, and rough-grain, the latter having a rough texture apparent to the naked eye.

Gum arabic. Sap drawn from the African acacia tree which, when diluted with water, is used as an agglutinate, together with other products, for watercolours.

I

Images, Successive. Rule established by the physicist Chevruel, according to which 'viewing any colour creates, sympathetically, the appearance of the complementary colour'.

Induction of complements. This is explained by the statement: 'to modify a determined colour, one may simply change the background colours surrounding it'.

L

Lead pencil. Term used to refer to the ordinary pencil made of cedar wood with a 'lead' composed of graphite and clay.

Line drawing. Drawing made up only of lines, without shadows. This is the ideal way of drawing when painting in watercolours, since the colour values used to represent the volume of the objects painted must be resolved directly with the watercolours. By virtue of their transparency, watercolours appear dirty if one paints over a drawing containing shadows. The term 'line drawing' is also applied to industrial drawing.

Liquid watercolours. Watercolours are supplied in dry tablets, moist tablets, tubes and bottles of liquid. Liquid watercolour may also be diluted with water, is very transparent and gives an intense but luminous colour.

Local colour. This is the actual colour of bodies, in those parts where they suffer no alteration from the effects of light, shade, or reflected colours.

M

Masking fluid. Latex gum of light colour and in liquid form, utilized in watercolour painting to protect small forms, strokes, or to reserve white areas which may be painted over or around. Subsequently one rubs off the gum with the finger or with a rubber and the white spot reappears. Masking fluid may be applied with a narrow brush (no. 3 or 4), with synthetic hairs. It dilutes in water but if not applied very carefully, will leave residues which can cause the brush to deteriorate.

Mat knife (also x-acto knife). These are special knives with removable blades used for cutting paper. When cutting paper or cardboard with either, it is wise to use a metal ruler.

Medium. (1) Term used to describe a painting process. Example: watercolour is a painting medium, as are oils, etc.

Medium. (2) A mixing agent which may be mixed with or replace water. In watercolour painting it is used in order to eliminate any possible residues of grease from the paper. Watercolour medium increases the adherence and moisture of the paint and generally improves the chroma.

Monochrome. A painting is monochromatic when it has been painted in only one colour. 'Wash' drawing done with black or sepia watercolour, sienna, Venetian red, is monochromatic.

Motif. Is the modern word for 'subject' introduced by the Impressionists to designate a model without any apparent preparation, such as might be found in everyday life.

N

Neoclassical. A style of painting, sculpture and architecture dating from the end of the 18th century to the middle of the 19th century and inspired by the art and architecture of the Greek, Hellenic, and Graeco-Roman periods, imitating their formal content, and exhibiting romantic and academic influences from the same period.

O

Ox bile. Product made from the bile of oxen, used as a wetting agent by mixing a small portion of it with water when painting with watercolours. Sold in small containers.

Ox hair. The ox-hair brush made from hairs from the shoulders of this animal is a good addition to the pine-marten-hair brushes used for painting in watercolours. The higher number brushes are most often used, those numbered 18, 20, and 24, which serve for dampening and painting large areas.

P

Palette box. A metal box with a top or double top which contains the colours. When open, the top serves as a palette, with shallow indentations that allow mixing and making up of colours.

Papyrus. A fibrous plant harvested from the banks of the Nile by the Egyptians – *cyperus papirus.* The stem was formed into writing paper and was written upon using a *calamus*, a short stick bevelled on one end and hollowed out, like a quill.

Parchment. Animal skin, generally of a ram or goat, treated so that it may be written upon. It was prepared by treatment with limestone, then washed. The hair was cut off and then it was rubbed and smoothed with a pumice stone. For centuries, parchment was considered to be the best material for works of art, particularly for painting miniatures. Tradition has it that it was discovered in the city of Pergamum by King Eumedes II.

Pentimento. Term used when one modifies and reconstructs an important part of the painting, signifying that the artist regrets what he or she has already painted. The *pentimenti* of Velázquez are well known, and were discovered by infrared photography.

Perspective. The science of graphically representing the effects of distance on the appearance of size, form, and colour. We may distinguish between linear perspective, which represents the third dimension (depth) through lines and forms; and aerial perspective, which represents depth using colour, shade, and contrast.

Pigment. A pigment is any colour which, when diluted in a liquid, provides a colour for painting. Painting pigments are generally available as powders and may be of organic or inorganic origin.

Pre-Raphaelites. Artistic and literary movement active in England at the end of the 19th century, of notable importance to painting. The Pre-Raphaelites declared that they were followers of the artists of 15th-century Florence: Gozzoli, Botticelli, and other predecessors of Raphael – hence the name Pre-Raphaelites. They considered the art before Raphael to be more sincere and less artificial, and they opposed the academic rules fashionable in their own time in England which were inspired by Raphael, Reynolds, and so on, and by the sculptures of antiquity. The Pre-Raphaelites painted many watercolours and boasted such painters as Rossetti, Hunt, and Millais.

Primary. Basic colours of the solar spectrum. *Primary 'light'* colours are green, red, and dark blue; *Primary pigment* colours are cyan blue, purple, and yellow.

R

Reflected colours. This is a constant factor, given, on the one hand the surrounding colour, and on the other, the concrete reflection of one or more particular objects.

S

Sabeline hair. Sabeline hair brushes may also be used for painting in watercolours. Like sable hair it is of animal origin but slightly stiffer, as well as more economical.

Sable hair. Sable-hair brushes are undoubtedly the best for painting in watercolours. They hold water and paint better than any other kind of brush and have a tense but flexible hair which holds an excellent point at all times. These brushes are made from the tail hairs of a small rodent called kolinsky, or red sable, which lives in Russia and China; they are expensive but long lasting, and of high quality.

Secondary. Colours of the spectrum composed of a mixture, in pairs, of the primary colours. The secondary *'light'* colours are cyan blue, purple, and yellow. The *secondary pigment* colours are red, green, and deep blue.

Sketch. A free-hand drawing; the truly artistic drawing, done without the aid of rulers, compasses or other instruments.

Stag hair. Type of brush manufactured in Japan with the hair of this animal and a bamboo handle. Known as a *Japanese brush*, it is of equal or lesser quality than an ox-hair brush. The flat Japanese brush, in the wider sizes, is perfect for dampening or for painting washes on wide surfaces.

Sumi-e. Oriental watercolour painting technique, certain aspects of which are related to the eastern religious movement Zen. Painting is done with Chinese ink diluted in water and with a special brush, with a bamboo handle.

Support. Any surface on which a pictorial work may be realized. The specific support on which watercolours are painted is paper, either sheets or mounted on cardboard to make a compact support.

Symmetry. Relates to artistic composition and may be defined as: 'the repetition of the elements of a painting on each side of a central point or axis'.

Synthetic hair. Type of brush with synthetic hairs, offering greater tension than that of the sable-hair brushes but without the same capacity to hold water and paint. Some manufacturers call them 'amateur brushes'. They are quite resistant to corrosives such as bleach and are relatively economical.

T

Tertiary. A series of six *pigment colours* obtained by mixing primary and secondary colours in pairs. The *tertiary pigment* colours are: orange, carmine, violet, ultramarine, emerald green, and light green.

Texture. The visual and tactile appearance of a painted surface. This appearance or texture may be smooth, rough, broken into tiny squares, satiny, grainy, etc.

Tonal colour. This is a variant, more or less, of local colour, generally influenced by the reflection of other colours.

Topographers. English name from the 18th and 19th centuries, given to draughtsmen who reproduced buildings, monuments, gardens, private houses, or simply landscapes. Topographers were contracted to document or record voyages, scientific expeditions, etc.

Turpentine. Grease-free volatile oil used in watercolour painting for painting special effects. Turpentine, along with linseed oil, is the principal solvent for oil paints.

V

Value. Relationship existing between the different tones of the same image. Valuing is the same as comparing and resolving the effect of light and shadow by using different tones.

Value painters. Artists who paint the effects of light and shadow, valuing the tones and recreating the volume of the objects. The greatest proponent was Rembrandt; a modern example might be Dali.

Varnish, protective. Varnish may be applied to watercolours once they are dry, for their protection. It is sold in small containers and applied with a brush. It intensifies the colours of the paint and gives a perceptible gloss which increases with two or three coats. For this reason, some painters reject it. According to them, watercolour paintings should have a matt finish.

Veduta. Meaning 'view', was used to refer to drawings of countrysides with *views* of monuments from ancient Rome. Much in style during the 18th century all over Europe, but particularly in England where they contributed, indirectly, to a greater interest in watercolours.

W

Warping. Undulating form which drawing paper assumes as a result of soaking or dampening, particularly when the paper is thin and has not been mounted beforehand.

Wash. A limited-colour watercolour or drawing realized in Chinese ink or with one or two similar watercolours and water. The colours are usually black, sepia, or dark sepia with lighter sienna. The paper, the brushes and other tools, as well as the general techniques, are the same as in watercolour painting. Wash was practised by most artists of the Renaissance and Baroque periods. Cennino Cennini, the 14th-century Italian artist and educator, discussed the development of the wash in his writings.

Wet-in-wet. Special technique of painting in watercolours in which the artist paints an area previously dampened with water, or recently painted and still wet. This technique promotes the running of the water and colours, with a resultant diffusion of forms and contours. The English watercolour painter Turner utilized this technique.